MW00617011

THE GREAT GUIDE

THE GREAT GUIDE

What David Hume Can Teach Us about
Being Human and Living Well

JULIAN BAGGINI

PRINCETON UNIVERSITY PRESS

PRINCETON AND OXFORD

The Korean edition originally published in BOOK 21 Publishing Group
The English edition is published by arrangement with
Princeton University Press

Published by Princeton University Press
41 William Street, Princeton, New Jersey 08540
6 Oxford Street, Woodstock, Oxfordshire OX20 1TR

press.princeton.edu

ISBN 978-0-691-205434
ISBN (e-book) 978-0-691-211206

British Library Cataloging-in-Publication Data is available

Editorial: Matt Rohal
Production Editorial: Brigitte Pelner
Designer: Karl Spurzem
Jacket/Cover Design: Jason Anscomb
Production: Erin Suydam
Publicity: Maria Whelan (US), Amy Stewart (UK)

Jacket Art: Image of David Hume by Chronicle / Alamy Stock Photo

This book has been composed in Arno Pro

Printed on acid-free paper ∞

Printed in the United States of America

10 9 8 7 6 5 4 3 2 1

CONTENTS

THE GREAT GUIDE

INTRODUCTION

Scotland's Hidden Gem

Standing at the top of Calton Hill, close to the center of Edinburgh, is Scotland's National Monument, built to commemorate the Scottish soldiers and sailors who died in the Napoleonic Wars. Modeled on the Parthenon in Athens, it ended up resembling its inspiration more than its designers intended.[1] While the Parthenon is half destroyed, the National Monument is only half constructed, after work was abandoned in 1829 due to lack of funds.

The monument's evocation of classical Greece in modern Scotland might at first seem incongruous. When Plato and Aristotle were laying down the foundations of Western philosophy, Scotland, like the rest of Britain, was still a preliterate society. However, by the early eighteenth century, it could proudly claim to be the successor of Athens as the philosophical capital of the world. Edinburgh was leading the European Enlightenment, rivaled only by Paris as an intellectual center. In 1757, David Hume, the greatest philosopher the city, Britain, and arguably even the world had ever known, said with some justification that the Scottish "shou'd really be the People most distinguish'd for literature in Europe."[2]

FIGURE 1. Scotland's National Monument on Calton Hill, Edinburgh.

The city produced two of the greatest thinkers of the modern era. One, the economist Adam Smith, is widely known and esteemed. The other, Hume, remains relatively obscure outside academia. Among philosophers, however, he is often celebrated as the greatest among their ranks of all-time. When thousands of academic philosophers were recently asked which non-living predecessor they most identified with, Hume came a clear first, ahead of Aristotle, Kant, and Wittgenstein.[3] Hume has become the postmortem victim of a phenomenon he himself described: "Learning has been as great a Loser by being shut up in Colleges and Cells, and secluded from the World and good Company."[4] Hume is as adored in academe as he is unknown in the wider world.

Many scientists—not usually great fans of philosophy—also cite Hume as an influence. In a letter to Moritz Schlick, Einstein reports that he read Hume's *Treatise* "with eagerness and admiration shortly before finding relativity theory." He goes so far as to say that "it is very well possible that without these philosophical studies I would not have arrived at the solution."[5] Charles Darwin's notebooks also show he read several of Hume's works. Even the biologist Lewis Wolpert, who says philosophers are "very clever but have nothing useful to say whatsoever," makes an exception for Hume, admitting that at one stage he "fell in love" with him.[6]

Not even his academic fans, however, sufficiently appreciate Hume as a *practical* philosopher. He is most known for his ideas about cause and effect, perception, and his criticisms of religion. People don't tend to pick up Hume because they want to know how to live. This is a great loss. Hume did spend a lot of time writing and thinking about often arcane metaphysical questions, but only because they were important for understanding human nature and our place in the world. "The most abstract speculations concerning human nature, however cold and unentertaining, become subservient to practical morality; and may render this latter science more correct in its precepts, and more persuasive in its exhortations."[7] For instance, cause and effect was not an abstract metaphysical issue for him but something that touched every moment of our daily experience. He never allowed himself to take intellectual flights of fancy, always grounding his ideas in experience, which he called the "great guide of human life." Hume thus thought about everyday issues in the same way as he did about ultimate ones.

To see how Hume offers us a model of how to live, we need to look not only at his work but at his life. Everyone who knew Hume, with the exception of the paranoid and narcissistic

Jean-Jacques Rousseau, spoke highly of him. When he spent three years in Paris in later life he was known as "*le bon* David," his company sought out by all the *salonistes*. Baron d'Holbach described him as "a great man, whose friendship, at least, I know to value as it deserves."[8] Adam Smith described him as "approaching as nearly to the idea of a perfectly wise and virtuous man, as perhaps the nature of human frailty will permit."[9]

Hume didn't just write about how to live—he modeled the good life. He was modest in his philosophical pretensions, advocating human sympathy as much as, if not more than, human rationality. He avoided hysterical condemnations of religion and superstition as well as overly optimistic praise for the power of science and rationality. Most of all, he never allowed his pursuit of learning and knowledge to get in the way of the softening pleasures of food, drink, company, and play. Hume exemplified a way of life that is gentle, reasonable, amiable: all the things public life now so rarely is.

What Hume said and did form equal parts of a harmonious whole, a life of the mind and body that stands as an inspiration to us all. I want to approach David Hume as a synoptic whole, a person whose philosophy touches every aspect of how he lived and who he was. To do that, I need to approach his life and work together. I have followed in Hume's biographical and sometimes geographical footsteps to show why we would be wise to follow in his philosophical ones too.

When we look at his life and person, we also understand better why Hume has not "crossed over" from academic preeminence to public acclaim. In short, he lacks the usual characteristics that give an intellectual mystique and appeal. He is not a tragic, romantic figure who died young, misunderstood, and unknown or unpopular. He was a genial, cheerful man who died loved and renowned. His ideas are far too sensible to shock or not obviously radical enough to capture our attention. His distaste for "enthusiasts"—by which he meant fanatics of any kind—made him too moderate to inspire zealotry in his admirers. These same qualities that made him a rounded, wise figure prevented him from becoming a cult one.

If ever there were a time in recent history to turn to Hume, now is surely it. The enthusiasts are on the rise, in the form of strongman political populists who assert the will of the people as though it were absolute and absolutely infallible. In more settled times, we could perhaps use a Nietzsche to shake us out of our bourgeois complacency, or entertain Platonic dreams of perfect, immortal forms. Now such philosophical excesses are harmful indulgences. Good, uncommon sense is needed more than ever.

I'm going to use a lot of Hume's own words, simply because I find them so elegantly crafted that I can't see how paraphrasing improves them. I know that many people find Hume difficult to read, largely because of his eighteenth-century style, with its long sentences and archaic vocabulary. But within these seemingly meandering and long-winded texts there are so many gems. In particular, Hume knew the importance of beginnings and endings. Take the first paragraph of *An Enquiry concerning the Principles of Morals*:

> Disputes with men, pertinaciously obstinate in their principles, are, of all others, the most irksome; except, perhaps, those with persons, entirely disingenuous, who really do not believe the opinions they defend, but engage in the controversy, from affectation, from a spirit of opposition, or from a desire of showing wit and ingenuity, superior to the rest of mankind. The same blind adherence to their own arguments is to be expected in both; the same contempt of their

antagonists; and the same passionate vehemence, in inforcing sophistry and falsehood. And as reasoning is not the source, whence either disputant derives his tenets; it is in vain to expect, that any logic, which speaks not to the affections, will ever engage him to embrace sounder principles.[10]

If you can get beyond the use of words like "pertinaciously" (holding firmly to an opinion or a course of action), "whence," and "inforcing," you'll find a paragraph that is almost a mini-essay, capturing so much that is true of the nature of obstinacy and why it is objectionable. It also tells you that Hume intends to avoid the vice. Hume's inquiries are sincere, not attempts to justify his own preexisting beliefs. The reader should approach his work in the same spirit of openness.

I've extracted the essence of the lessons we can learn from him as Humean maxims and aphorisms. From the above passage, for instance, we can distill the principle: **When reason has nothing to do with why people hold their beliefs, reason is powerless to change them.** Usually these are in my words, sometimes they are in Hume's. They are gathered together in the book's appendix. On some occasions they are negative lessons: things we can learn from Hume's mistakes and failings. The self-detracting and humble Hume would surely have approved of this. He once wrote that one of the things that makes a human superior to other animals is that he "corrects his mistakes; and makes his very errors profitable."[11] After giving his verdict on the character of Sir Robert Walpole, he even noted that "the impartial Reader, if any such there be; or Posterity, if such a Trifle can reach them, will best be able to correct my Mistakes."[12]

All the maxims can be identified in the text by my use of a different font. A good one to start us on our guided journey comes directly from the pen of the man himself: *"There are*

*great Advantages, in travelling, & nothing serves more to re-
move Prejudices."*[13] Hume traveled a great deal during his lifetime. Two of the most significant trips were both to France.
They came at opposite ends of his career and had very different
characters. As a young man, he went to sleepy La Flèche in the
Loire valley to work in virtual solitude on his first major philosophical work, *A Treatise of Human Nature.* As an older man, his
oeuvre complete, he spent a little over two years in bustling
Paris, feted by the intelligentsia. These bookends, both sym-
metric and asymmetric at the same time, frame his life and
work in a way that helps us to better understand both. They
show that Hume speaks to us all, at every time of life, whether
solitary or sociable, well-known or obscure, successful or struggling, young or old. Hume and his philosophy are companions
for life.

CHAPTER ONE

The Foundations of a Thinker

There is a God within us, says Ovid, who breathes that divine fire, by which we are animated. Poets, in all ages, have advanced this claim to inspiration. There is not, however, any thing supernatural in the case. Their fire is not kindled from heaven. It only runs along the earth; is caught from one breast to another; and burns brightest, where the materials are best prepared, and most happily disposed.

Lothian Beginnings

Knowing more about the point of departure often helps us to understand the nature and meaning of the journey as a whole. Edinburgh was the very first and last point on Hume's journey through life. He was born there on April 26, 1711, the baptismal registry showing he was the son of "Mr Joseph Home of Ninewells, advocate, and Katherine Ffalconer, his lady."[1] His family was comfortable enough to employ servants, as was usual for the middle classes of the time, but it was not rich.

John Home kept an apartment in a tenement on the north side of the Lawnmarket in Edinburgh, near the Castle. Although Hume was born there, the main family home was

Ninewells in the south of Scotland, not far from the English border, near the village of Chirnside. This is where Hume spent most of his boyhood. The area is a low-lying plain known as the Merse. When I visited it was typically *dreich*, an essential Scots word for a dull, overcast, gloomy day. Even today Chirnside is quite isolated: in the eighteenth century it must have felt extremely remote. In later life Hume would often talk of his love of solitude and his dislike for large gatherings, preferring "the company of a few select companions, with whom I can, calmly and peaceably, enjoy the feast of reason, and try the justness of every reflection, whether gay or serious, that may occur to me."[2] Given how much solitude he would have experienced in his formative years, this is perhaps unsurprising.

Despite its isolation, the little corner in which Ninewells stood would have been an idyllic place for a child to grow up in freedom. The house and grounds sat near a bend in the White-adder Water, the second word being redundant, since "White-adder" means "white water." The sometimes rapid flow of the river through this section explains the name. Much of the land near the riverbank is wooded today, and given that over recent centuries the general trend in the United Kingdom has been toward deforestation, it is probable it was like this or more so in Hume's time. This was the place Hume was referring to when he wrote of how he would take "a solitary walk by a river-side" when he was "tired with amusement and company" so as to feel his "mind all collected within itself."[3] This would have been as wonderful a setting for a young boy to play as it was for a man to gather his thoughts.

The building Hume lived in was destroyed by fire in 1840, but the name on the stone gate post at the entrance to the grounds today still reads "Ninewells House," indicating that the more recent construction inherited the old name. The land is private

FIGURE 2. The "David Hume Walk"
from Ninewells, Chirnside.

but public footpaths run around it. One of these has been named the "David Hume Walk" by the Scottish Borders Council. It is one of five "Border Brains Walks" alongside trails commemorating James Hutton, James Small, Alexander Dow, and Duns Scotus. Hume's walk soon trails away from the grounds of Chirnside and for most of its length follows a disused railway line that obviously wasn't even there in his day. Mostly flat and through fields, it is hardly the most beautiful walk in Scotland, but with so little development in the area it must give a remarkably accurate sense of the land Hume grew up in: quiet and gentle but with an unassuming beauty.

The walk was only inaugurated in 2011, and up until several years ago there was almost nothing in the area to commemorate Hume. Recently, however, the village has woken up to its historic ties. A housing development inaugurated in 2006 included David Hume View, a street aptly named since it overlooks the Ninewells estate. To celebrate the tricentenary of Hume's birth in 2011, a local community group, the Chirnside Common Good Association, put up several information boards about his life and work. These no longer stand but a permanent plaque adorns the side of the community center, modeled after a famous medallion bust of Hume made by the Scottish artist James Tassie.

The village owes him at least this. In his will, Hume left £100 to rebuild the bridge over the Whiteadder. The three-arched stone structure still stands parallel to the more modern road bridge that now carries the public traffic. The old bridge is in the complex of a still functioning paper mill.

As part of the tricentenary celebrations, the Chirnsiders also put on a philosophy festival attended by delegates at the International Hume Society Conference at the University of Edinburgh. For these hundred scholars from fifteen countries, it was a very special day trip. In a local newspaper report on the visit, a journalist noted, "Many of the visitors commented on it being a fascinating eye-opener for them since they have spent years studying particular aspects of Hume's work but not necessarily the details about his life—how and where he lived."[4]

This observation reveals a lot about the limitations of Hume scholarship. Philosophy, especially in the English-speaking world, tends to treat ideas and arguments as though they were timeless and placeless. All you need to do, students are told, is attend to the validity and the soundness of the arguments. Who made them, when and where, is irrelevant. There are clichéd

FIGURE 3. The bridge in Chirnside rebuilt with £100 from Hume's will.

slogans that are routinely used to encourage this: "Follow the argument wherever it leads" and "Play the ball, not the man." (Presumably the same applies to "the woman," but since no one is paying attention to who is presenting the argument, philosophers have not noticed how much men have dominated philosophy and so many have not even stopped to wonder why.)

This makes sense if you think that philosophy is a set of discrete intellectual problems to be solved. It makes less sense, however, if you think philosophy is a synoptic discipline, in which all the parts link together to form a (hopefully) coherent whole. And it makes no sense at all if you think that this whole comprises both life and work, ideas and practice. I hope to convince you that attending to a philosopher's life helps make better sense of their work and that biography is a tool for the study of philosophy, not a distraction from doing it.

University Challenge

Hume's intellectual development would have started young, with private tutors. It began formally, however, when he went back to the city of his birth to study at Edinburgh University. The matriculation book showed him signing up to study under William Scot, the professor of Greek, on February 27, 1723.[5] This meant he was not yet twelve years old. This was not then an exceptionally young age to go to university, which was a very different kind of institution than what it is now. Hume was fortunate in his timing. Just one year before, three new chairs (professorships) were created, paid for by a two-pence duty (tax) on each pint of ale brewed and sold in the city and its adjacent parishes.[6] Beer has for a long time played an important role in the city. Whenever I visit, I am always struck by the malty smell from the breweries that blows across the city center. This scent has new meaning for me now, knowing the role it played in helping to educate Edinburgh's finest mind. However, the aroma may disappear in the not too distant future as the breweries move out farther from the expensive city center to its environs.

Hume's biographer E. C. Mossner called the Edinburgh of that age: "A paradoxical city of austerity and homeliness, of isolation and cosmopolitanism, of rusticity and urbanity, of the old world and the modern, a city imbedded in the past yet with aspirations for the future."[7] Sophistication and squalor, finesse and filth, existed side by side. Even the comfort of the affluent was relative. Consider how in France in late 1737, Hume wrote to the Rev. Hugh Blair when he found out the vicar had become his tenant: "It was perfectly clean of Vermine when I left it, and I hope you will find it so. I would advise you not to put a Bed in the little Closet near the Kitchen: It wou'd be stiffling to a Servant & woud certainly encourage Bugs."[8] Bugs, mice, and rats were irritants even the middle classes found it difficult to avoid.

But those were the least of the city's sanitary problems. Residents of homes on several different floors of the tall tenement buildings of the Old Town emptied their chamber pots full of feces and urine straight onto the streets. An account by one soldier who passed through the city tells us "it stinks intolerably, for which I believe, it exceeds all parts of the world." Walking the streets after ten o'clock in the evening meant risking a chamber pot being emptied over your head. After this time, city regulations stipulated that they should be taken down to the gutters to be emptied, but few busy housemaids complied. Hence the soldier reported that a common cry in the streets was *"Hoad yare Hoand"* (hold your hand), meaning, "Do not throw till I am past."[9]

Edinburgh today is mercifully free of such inconveniences, but like many major cities there is still a sense of the tension between affluence and poverty. The Old Town is filled with tourists, cafés, restaurants, and gift shops. But you don't have to look far to see the homeless struggling to survive, begging and sleeping in shop entrances. Get away from the tourist areas into some of the suburbs, and poverty is even more evident. *Trainspotting,* Irvine Walsh's novel about drug addicts in the late 1980s, turned into a film by Danny Boyle in 1996, was set in Leith, the port area of Edinburgh. A recent study that divided Scotland into seven thousand areas showed that four of the fifty most deprived were in Edinburgh.[10] It remains as much a city of contradictions and contrast as it did in Hume's time.

FIGURE 4. View of Edinburgh from Calton Hill.

Looking out across Edinburgh today from its most central vantage point, Calton Hill, it is possible to get a sense of Hume's city. Of course the city today is more densely built up than it was in the eighteenth century. But many of the landmark buildings were pretty much as they are now, and the topography of the undulating city remains unchanged. Straight in front of you is Edinburgh Castle, occupying the highest part of the Old Town. This is the area where Hume lived early in his adult life. The line of your sight to the castle passes over the southern edge of the New Town, built during Hume's lifetime. It was here that he bought a parcel of land on which he built the home where he lived during his last years. At the base of the hill you can see Old Calton Burial Ground, where a mausoleum holds Hume's

FIGURE 5. View from Calton Hill with Old Calton Burial Ground in the foreground. Hume's mausoleum can be seen blocking the view of the right-hand end of the bridge.

remains. And to the left of the castle, closer to the hill, lies Edinburgh University, where Hume began his formal studies.

Hume wasn't much impressed by the education he received at the university. "*There is nothing to be learnt from a Professor, which is not to be met with in Books,*" he wrote. "I see no reason why we shou'd either go to an University, more than to any other place, or ever trouble ourselves about the Learning Capacity of the Professor."[11] He left without taking a degree, as was common at the time. There was a simple economic explanation for this: only the Professor of Natural Philosophy was paid graduation fees so there was little incentive for anyone else to encourage their students to graduate.[12]

Hume was probably more intellectually stimulated by his membership in the Rankenian Club, the most important of the many societies of intellectuals formed in the time. The Rankenian was named after the tavern keeper in whose house they met.[13] This was Hume's first taste of the kind of society he preferred to keep: a select group of intelligent people, convivially gathering with food and drink.

Hume probably lost his religion in these times. Later in life, Boswell reported that Hume told him "he never had entertained any belief in Religion since he began to read Locke and Clarke," which he would have done in his university years.[14] Hume was particularly unpersuaded by the dominant ideals of religious virtue captured in a popular tract he would have read, *The Whole Duty of Man*. This counted "making pleasure, not health, the end of eating" and "wasting time or estate in good fellowship" as breaches of duty.[15] For Hume, such activities were exemplars of virtue, not vice. In his *Treatise*, he argued that virtues had to be either useful or agreeable, and that wasn't true of "celibacy, fasting, penance, mortification, self-denial, humility, silence, solitude, and the whole train of monkish virtues." These "serve to no manner of purpose; neither advance a man's fortune in the world, nor render him a more valuable member of society; neither qualify him for the entertainment of company, not encrease his power of self-enjoyment."[16] Elsewhere, he said, *"To imagine, that the gratifying of any sense, or the indulging of any delicacy in meat, drink, or apparel, is of itself a vice, can never enter into a head, that is not disordered by the frenzies of enthusiasm."* ("Enthusiasm" here means excessive zeal, of the kind found in religious extremists.) These indulgences are only vices when they are pursued to excess, preventing us from exercising other virtues such as liberality or charity or reducing us to poverty. "Where they entrench upon no virtue, but leave ample subject whence to provide for friends, family, and every proper object of generosity or compassion, they are entirely innocent, and have in every age been acknowledged such by almost all moralists."[17]

Although he entirely rejected Christian morality, Hume's letters suggest that he did not give up his faith easily. Looking back in 1751 he wrote that his propensity for the skeptical, for which he became famous, was not innate but "crept in upon me against my Will." He had been looking at an old manuscript book containing private writings from before he was twenty. It revealed "page after page" chronicling the gradual progress of his thoughts on religion. "It begun with an anxious Search after Arguments, to confirm the common Opinion: Doubts stole in, dissipated, returned, were again dissipated, returned again and it was a Perpetual struggle of a restless Imagination, against Inclination, perhaps against reason."[18] He lost his religion slowly and reluctantly. As Mossner put it, Hume "*reasoned* himself out of religion."[19]

The lack of lasting intellectual impact that university had on Hume's thought is mirrored by the lack of lasting architectural impact the university has had on the city itself. Although it was founded in 1582 and can claim to be the sixth oldest university in Britain, for two hundred years it occupied a hotchpotch of different buildings around this city and had no coherent base. The university Hume attended is therefore a merely ghostly presence today. It was not until 1789 that the foundation stone was laid at the site of Old College, the university's first purpose-built home. This is the oldest part of the university that can be visited today, on South Bridge. Surrounded by some of the city center's less fashionable shops and restaurants and coated in soot from years of traffic pollution, its potential grandeur is somewhat muted by its situation. One can imagine an

FIGURE 6. David Hume Tower, the University of Edinburgh.

eighteenth-century boy walking around its traditional courtyard "quad," but Hume never did.

There is no such period charm in the modern university,
the main campus of which is nearly half a mile south, around
George Square. There stands David Hume Tower, a building
so bland and functional it is almost an insult rather than an
honor to have Hume's name attached to it. It looks more like
an oversized social housing block than it does a place of
learning.

The contrast between the modern university and the one
Hume attended is of more than merely aesthetic interest. Hume
was an undergraduate at a time when very few people enjoyed
the privilege of higher education. Although we are often reminded in his own correspondence that Hume was not rich,
this is relative to his already privileged status. Hume belonged
to a small elite class, which meant that throughout his life he
would have known at least superficially every important intellectual in Edinburgh and many more from elsewhere in Britain.
To be a philosopher at that time was not to be a specialist working in an obscure corner of academe but to be part of a single,
relatively small community of scholars whose interests crossed
over what we now think of as clear disciplinary boundaries.
There was not even a clear category of scientist. What we now
call "science" was simply "natural philosophy" until well into
the nineteenth century.

It is therefore somewhat anachronistic to think of Hume as
essentially a philosopher. His education made him a man of
letters whose interests ranged through economics, science, psychology, history, and political theory. That is even more reason
to take seriously the synoptic nature of his life's work. His object of study was human nature and he used every intellectual
tool available to help him examine it. From this we can take the

maxim: *to understand how we should live—as individuals and as a society—learn from every source that offers something to teach you.*

Crisis and Epiphany

Hume's most intensive education only began in earnest after he left the university, probably in 1726.[20] He first tried to study law, knowing it was a reliable and respectable profession. But in a letter to a physician, he wrote that it "appear'd nauseous to me" and that the only way of "pushing my Fortune in the World" was as a "Scholar & Philosopher." So in spring 1729 he abandoned law and set about six months of intensive study. He was already formulating his own, original philosophy. "When I was about eighteen years of age," he recalled not long after, "there seemed to be opened up to me a new scene of thought."[21]

"I was infinitely happy in this Course of Life for some months," he wrote, but after six months, in September 1729, he found that "all my Ardour seem'd in a moment to be extinguisht, & I could no longer raise my Mind to that pitch, which formerly gave me such excessive Pleasure." Hume had fallen into a deep depression, what he called the "disease of the learned." The cure was to study less intensively, to exercise daily, and to make time for relaxation and social intercourse. He learned a lesson he would share in the *An Enquiry concerning Human Understanding* years later. *"The mind requires some relaxation, and cannot always support its bent to care and industry,"* he wrote. "It seems, then, that nature has pointed out a mixed kind of life as most suitable to human race, and secretly admonished them to allow none of these biasses to draw too much, so as to incapacitate them for other occupations and entertainments."[22]

From then on, he always maintained a balance between leisure, exercise, and work. In his last years, he counseled his eighteen-year-old nephew David that "every day, fair or foul, you ought to use some exercise," which is "absolutely necessary" for health, and bad health "is the greatest interrupter to study in the world." He summed up his message in an allegorical anecdote: "A man was riding, with great violence, and running his horse quite out of wind. He stopt a moment to ask when he might reach a particular place. In two hours, replied the countryman, if you will go slower; in four if you be in such a hurry." More haste, less speed is a warning for all areas of life, not just practical or urgent tasks.

His brief crisis is of much more than just autobiographical interest. The key lesson Hume learned from his depression became the cornerstone of his entire philosophical project: that philosophy must be rooted in an accurate understanding of human nature. *Philosophy succeeds when it addresses human beings as they are and fails when it treats them only as philosophers imagine them to be.* This is the point he leaves the reader with at the end of the *Treatise*, when he compares the world of a philosopher with the work of both an anatomist and a painter: "We must have an exact knowledge of the parts, their situation and connexion, before we can design with any elegance or correctness."[23]

His greatest lesson in how *not* to philosophize came from the ancient Greek and Roman Stoics, who believed that human beings could achieve a calmness of mind, *ataraxia*, by learning to detach themselves from worldly concerns and emotions. Their goal is to realize our rational nature as much as possible and let go of our more animal instincts.

Hume gave this a good try. He read many books by Cicero, Seneca, and Plutarch and, "smit with their beautiful representations of virtue and philosophy," undertook "the improvement of my temper and will, along with my reason and understanding. I was continually fortifying myself with reflections against death, and poverty, and shame, and pain, and all the other calamities of life."[24]

This is precisely what the Stoics advised: that we should be constantly reminding ourselves of how fragile wealth, health, and reputation are, and that death is inevitable. Epictetus, for instance, instructed his readers bluntly, "If you kiss your child, or your wife, remind yourself that you are kissing a mortal; then you will be able to bear it if either of them dies."[25] Epicurus reminds us, "Against all else it is possible to provide security, but as against death all of us mortals alike dwell in an unfortified city."[26] We should covet material wealth even less than we should life. Seneca wrote, "Money never made anyone rich: all it does is infect everyone who touches it with a lust for more of itself."[27] Musonius argued, "one man and one man only is truly wealthy—he who learns to want nothing in every circumstance."[28]

The key lesson the Stoics taught was to disregard as unimportant anything that is not within our control, which is everything apart from virtue. Epictetus summed this up well: "Apply the rule. Is this within or outside your choice? Outside it. Discard it. What have you seen? Someone mourning the death of a child. Apply the rule. Death is not within your choice. Discard it."[29]

Hume found that when he reminded himself of these harsh truths as one small part of an active life, they had some good effect. But when they become the focus of life, they "waste the spirits." While most of us are probably guilty of not thinking enough about our mortality, think about it too much and you'll simply become depressed. Similarly, we tend to overestimate the importance of wealth and health, but if we constantly tell ourselves they are fragile and worth nothing, we cannot enjoy either if we are lucky enough to have them. Too much such reflection, thought Hume, was part of the reason why he became so ill.[30] *It is admirable to refuse to look harsh reality in the eye, foolish and destructive never to avert our gaze from it.*

Even after he had rejected the Stoics as "too magnificent for human nature" he acknowledged that "they carry, however, a grandeur with them, which seizes the spectator, and strikes him with admiration." Socrates was not a Stoic, but Hume found him similarly admired by all for "his perpetual serenity and contentment, amidst the greatest poverty and domestic vexations; his resolute contempt of riches, and his magnanimous care of preserving liberty, while he refused all assistance from his friends and disciples, and avoided even the dependence of an obligation."[31]

Despite this residual respect, in some later writings, Hume attacks Stoicism very strongly. Most viciously, he protests that the "perpetual cant" of the Stoics "bred a disgust in mankind."[32] In his essay "The Sceptic" he offers some pithy replies to common Stoic injunctions. For example, the Stoic says, *"You should always have before your eyes death, disease, poverty, blindness, exile, calumny, and infamy, as ills which are incident to human nature. If any one of these ills falls to your lot, you will bear it the better, when you have reckoned upon it."* The Sceptic (in effect, Hume) replies, "If we confine ourselves to a general and distant reflection on the ills of human life, that can have no effect to prepare us for them. If by close and intense meditation we render them present and intimate to us, that is the true secret for poisoning all our pleasures, and rendering us perpetually miserable." More concise still, to the Stoic insistence that *"Your sorrow is fruitless, and will not change the course of destiny"* the blunt answer is "Very true: And for that very reason I am sorry."[33]

For Hume, the Stoics ask us to go too much against the grain of human nature. *"Philosophers have endeavoured to render happiness entirely independent of every thing external,"* he complained. *"That degree of perfection is impossible to be attained."* A more modest and realistic goal, pursued by every wise person, is to "endeavour to place his happiness on such objects chiefly as depend upon himself."[34]

This difference between making one's happiness rest *entirely* or *chiefly* on what is within one's control is very subtle but important. To make oneself entirely non-dependent on fortune is not only humanly impossible but undesirable. To do that you would have to cut yourself off from the kind of love that tears us to pieces when it comes to an end, by death or by a breakdown in a relationship. Any ambition that it is not completely under your control to fulfill would be deemed foolish, which is to kill any ambition other than the lukewarm one to "do the best you can."

Hume's more modest ambition could be summed up in the maxim: *do not depend on others or chance more than is necessary for attaining all the satisfaction that life has to offer.* This principle acknowledges that some lack of independence is necessary to live a full life, but asks us to constantly check whether or not we have made ourselves too dependent on what is outside of our control. You cannot be a good parent, for example, without making your welfare depend on that of your children. But if you make your role as a parent your sole and defining identity, you are making yourself too vulnerable should something happen to your child. If you are an athlete, it may be necessary to have the highest ambition in order to fulfill your potential, and that means you will inevitably feel disappointment if you fall short. But you do not have to believe that anything less than achieving your highest goal is a total catastrophe. If we never make ourselves vulnerable to failure or disappointment, we limit our ambitions and horizons. That does not mean we should be so foolish as to make our entire happiness depend on what we cannot control.

This firsthand experience of the violence of an abstract reasoning that denies human nature gave Hume a kind of intellectual epiphany that set the course of the rest of his life: "The moral philosophy transmitted to us by antiquity laboured under the same inconvenience that has been found in their natural philosophy, of being entirely hypothetical, and depending more upon invention than experience: every one consulted his fancy in erecting schemes of virtue and of happiness, without regarding human nature, upon which every moral conclusion must depend."[35] Voltaire passed on to us the Italian proverb *il meglio è l'inimico del bene*: the best is the enemy of the good. Hume's twist is that **inhuman perfection is the enemy of humanity's best.**

Hume came back to this idea repeatedly. In one of his later years he attacked "that grave philosophic Endeavour after Perfection, which, under Pretext of reforming Prejudices and Errors, strikes at all the most endearing Sentiments of the Heart." He gave as an example an ancient who disowned his brother on the basis that he was "too much a Philosopher" to believe that the mere fact of having sprung from the same womb ought to change their mutual opinions of each other.[36] Hume, in contrast, would make human nature the subject of his study and "the source from which I would derive every truth in criticism as well as morality."[37]

On leaving university, Hume then set about a self-guided course of study that would occupy the next five years of his life. By the end of it in 1734 he was able to confidently conclude that "there is nothing yet establisht" in philosophy and that its major works "contain little more than endless Disputes, even in the most fundamental Articles." This encouraged "a certain Boldness of Temper, growing in me, which was not enclin'd to submit to any Authority in these Subjects, but led me to seek out some new Medium, by which Truth might be establisht."[38]

A Failed Merchant

However, before Hume got on with the business of trying to set out his new philosophy, he felt obliged to try a more reliable way of earning a living. The result was a brief and unsuccessful "trial of an active life" working for a sugar merchant in Bristol.[39] The merchant was Mr. Michael Miller, who lived and traded at 15 Queen Square. Bristol has been my home for over fifteen years now, and I often walk through this large square with its tree-lined lawn crossed by diagonal paths. No eighteenth-century buildings remain today but the basic layout is the same. Half the buildings were destroyed over three days in 1831 when Queen Square was the focus of a riot that erupted in response to the Reform Bill, a (by modern standards) modest attempt to improve democratic representation. Bristolians like to think that the riot was an expression of the city's progressive character, but in truth it quickly degenerated into drunken looting and had little to do with principle.

The sweet thought that Hume passed through here too is somewhat tainted by the bitter fact that Miller was a sugar merchant and therefore inextricably involved in the slave trade. It is a reminder that for all his genius Hume was unable to transcend one of the most pernicious prejudices of his age. In a notorious footnote to his essay "Of National Characters" Hume wrote, "I am apt to suspect the negroes and in general all other species of men (for there are four or five different kinds) to be naturally inferior to the whites." His evidence for this was that "there never was a civilized nation of any other complexion than white, nor even any individual eminent either in action or speculation" and that "such a uniform and constant difference could not happen in so many countries and ages, if nature had not made an original distinction betwixt these breeds of men."[40]

Here it seems Hume was let down by a lack of experience and of imagination, uncharacteristic failings he lapsed into, blinded by the prejudices of his time. He should have known better because, as he remarked elsewhere, "in all questions, submitted to the understanding, *prejudice is destructive of sound judgment, and perverts all operations of the intellectual faculties.*"[41] He even saw how this applied to peoples, observing that prejudice often arises from the rash formation of bogus general rules such as "an Irishman cannot have wit, and a Frenchman cannot have solidity." Hume was smart enough to see that "human nature is very subject to errors of this kind; and perhaps this nation as much as any other," but did not always succeed in spotting this error in himself.[42]

Without in any way defending Hume's racist remarks, it needs pointing out that there is probably a good reason they were made in a footnote, qualified by the less than certain "I am apt to suspect." Hume made several other offensive remarks in his essay "On National Character," but this is the only one where he attributes differences to nature and biology rather than culture and geography. He seemed persuaded by the thesis we now sometimes call environmental determinism: that weather in particular shapes national characters. "There is some reason to think," he suggests, "that all the nations, which live beyond the polar circles or between the tropics, are inferior to the rest of the species, and are incapable of all the higher attainments of the human mind. The poverty and misery of the northern inhabitants of the globe, and the indolence of the southern, from their few necessities, may, perhaps, account for this remarkable difference, without our having recourse to physical causes."[43] That last phrase makes it clear that he does not think the explanation for the inferiority is down to any inherent physical defects.

This point is reinforced by his observation that "the manners of a people change very considerably from one age to another; either by great alterations in their government, by the mixtures of new people, or by that inconstancy, to which all human affairs are subject." People from the same bloodline can have very different characteristics, for better or for worse, depending on when in the history of the nation they were born. As an example, Hume claims that "the ingenuity, industry, and activity of the ancient Greeks have nothing in common with the stupidity and indolence of the present inhabitants of those regions."[44]

All of his racist remarks have to be seen in this light. So when he says "the Jews in Europe, and the Armenians in the east, have a peculiar character; and the former are as much noted for fraud, as the latter for probity," we can be fairly sure he thought the cause of this was culture, not biology.[45]

However, thanks to that dreadful footnote, we cannot be so sure that he thought the same about the supposed fact that "you may obtain any thing of the Negroes by offering them strong drink; and may easily prevail with them to sell, not only their children, but their wives and mistresses, for a cask of brandy."[46] According to philosopher John Immerwahr, Hume's choice of the phrase "other species of men" strongly suggests that Hume endorsed the theory of polygenesis: that different races were different species. This was often taken to imply that they were not all equally human.[47] Given his other remarks about climate and culture, it is perhaps more accurate to say that Hume did not have a coherent view on this at all. An essayist, like a newspaper columnist today, held forth on a wide range of views, not all of which they had given extensive, deep thought. Race was one such subject for Hume, and his comments betray a certain sloppiness of thinking.

For the last edition of his collected works, published posthumously, he did amend the footnote to at least lessen the suggestion of polygenesis and narrow his claim of inferiority only to black people. The revised note reads, "I am apt to suspect the negroes to be naturally inferior to the whites. There scarcely ever was a civilized nation of that complexion, nor even any individual eminent either in action or speculation." This is hardly a great improvement, and the fact that he revised rather than retracted the comments suggests his racism was "deliberate and considered," as Immerwahr charges.

For all his faults, it should be pointed out that Hume was no apologist for the various acts of violence and cruelty others did in the name of racial or cultural superiority. In his histories, he unambiguously condemned the Crusades "as the most signal and most durable monument of human folly, that has yet appeared in any age or nation."[48] And despite the fact that he briefly worked for a sugar merchant, he was highly critical of slavery, calling it "more cruel and oppressive than any civil subjection whatsoever." He is pleased that it had largely vanished from most of Europe, saying that "the little humanity, commonly observed in persons, accustomed, from their infancy, to exercise so great authority over their fellow-creatures, and to trample upon human nature, were sufficient alone to disgust us with that unbounded dominion."[49]

Yet even here it seems Hume turned a blind eye to the slavery that still existed in his age. A letter recently discovered by the historian Felix Waldmann shows that Hume went along with a request to encourage his patron, Lord Hertford, to buy a plantation in Grenada that he must have known was worked by slaves. The records show there were forty-two of them.[50] Hume knew slavery was wrong but seemed to act as though it was unreasonable to expect traders and investors to shun it.

By reading Hume carefully and seeing him as a product of his time, we can make his racism somewhat more understandable but we cannot deny or excuse it. The lesson is clear: *never slavishly follow even the greatest minds, for they too have prejudices, weaknesses, and blind spots*. In Hume's case, these blind spots were genuine failings and not merely an inevitable consequence of being an eighteenth-century European. In 1770, one of his contemporaries, James Beattie, wrote a scathing attack on Hume's philosophy. Although many of his criticisms missed the mark, his rejection of Hume's claims about the inferiority of black people was spot-on. Indeed, they employed precisely the kinds of good, empirical arguments that you would have expected from Hume. Beattie argued that "no man could have sufficient evidence, except from a personal acquaintance with all the negroes that now are, or ever were, on the face of the earth" to justify Hume's sweeping conclusion about them. Beattie also pointed out that there were many great non-white civilizations, such as those of Peru and Mexico. "The Africans and Americans are known to have many ingenious manufactures and arts among them, which even Europeans would find it no easy matter to imitate." Where societies were more "barbarous" it was not due to any inherent inferiority of their members.

"Had the Europeans been destitute of the arts of writing, and working in iron, they might have remained to this day as barbarous as the natives of Africa and America. Nor is the invention of these arts to be ascribed to our superior capacity."[51]

Hume should have been able to have seen this for himself or at the very least have accepted the arguments once they were made to him. Perhaps Hume gave them too little respect and attention because they came tucked away in more than five hundred pages of a vicious attack on the whole of Hume's system. Hume clearly had no time for Beattie, calling him "that bigotted silly Fellow."[52] Hume should have realized that *we should never completely dismiss even those who are almost always wrong, as they are almost always sometimes right too.*

In the light of these serious shortcomings, how should we judge Hume now?[53] There are increasingly many who argue that his comments on race disqualify him from honor. In 2020, a statue of the slave trader Edward Colston was torn down in Bristol, not far from where Hume worked, catalyzing calls to bring down monuments of other discredited historical figures. Hume soon joined the hit list. A petition was started to rename Edinburgh University's David Hume Tower and there were calls to remove his statue from the Royal Mile.

We can't just dismiss the unacceptable prejudices of the past as unimportant. But if we think that holding morally objectionable views disqualifies anyone from being considered a great thinker or a political leader, then there's hardly anyone from history left. A cautionary tale is that the first iteration of the petition to rename David Hume Tower proposed the name to be changed to honor Julius Nyerere, the Tanzanian anticolonialist politician—until it was drawn to the attention of the petitioner that "Nyerere was harmful in his own ways, both through his ties to dictatorship and through his homophobia."

However, the idea that racist, sexist, or otherwise bigoted views automatically disqualify a historical figure from admiration is misguided. Anyone who cannot bring themselves to admire such a historical figure betrays a profound lack of understanding about just how socially conditioned all our minds are, even the greatest. Because the prejudice seems so self-evidently wrong to us now, many of us just cannot imagine how anyone could fail to see this without being depraved.

Such outrage arrogantly supposes that we are so virtuous that we could never have been so immoral, even when everyone around us was blind to the injustice. We should know better. The most troubling lesson of the Third Reich is that it was supported largely by ordinary people who would have led blameless lives had they not by chance lived through particular toxic times. Any confidence we might have that we would not have done the same is without foundation. Going along with Nazism is unimaginable today because we need no imagination to understand just what the consequences were.

Why do so many find it impossible to believe that any so-called genius could fail to see that their prejudices were irrational and immoral? One reason is that our culture has its own deep-seated and mistaken assumption: that the individual is an autonomous human intellect independent from the social environment. Even a passing acquaintance with psychology, sociology, or anthropology should quash that comfortable illusion. The enlightenment ideal that we can and should all think *for ourselves* should not be confused with the hyper-enlightenment fantasy that we can think entirely *by ourselves*. Our thinking is shaped by our environment in profound ways that we often aren't even aware of. Hume's remarks on national character showed he understood this, even if the specific conclusions he drew were sometimes crude. Those who refuse to accept that they are as much shaped and limited by these forces as anyone else have delusions of intellectual grandeur.

The worry that taking a more understanding view of past prejudice would leave us unable to condemn what most needs condemnation is baseless. Misogyny and racism are no less repulsive because they are the products of societies as much as, if not more than, they are of individuals. To excuse Hume is not to excuse racism.

Accepting this does not mean glossing over the prejudices of the past. Becoming aware that even the likes of Hume were products of their times is a humbling reminder that the greatest minds can still be blind to mistakes and evils, if they are widespread enough. It should also prompt us to question whether the prejudices that rudely erupt to the surface in their most infamous remarks might also be lurking in the background elsewhere in their thinking. A lot of the feminist critique of Dead White Male philosophy is of this kind, arguing that the evident misogyny is just the tip of a much more insidious iceberg. Sometimes that might be true, but we cannot assume that it always is. *Many blind spots are remarkably local, leaving the general field of vision perfectly clear.*

The classicist Edith Hall's defense of Aristotle's misogyny is a paradigm of how to save a philosopher from his worst self. Rather than judge him by today's standards, she argues that a better test is to ask whether the fundamentals of his way of thinking would lead him to be prejudiced now.[54] Given Aristotle's openness to evidence and experience, there is no question that today he would easily be persuaded that women are men's equals. Hume likewise always deferred to experience, and so would not today be apt to suspect anything derogatory about dark-skinned peoples. In short, we don't need to look beyond the fundamentals of their philosophy to see what was wrong in how they applied them.

Had Hume persisted in the sugar trade he might have become more implicated in slavery and his racism would be even more problematic. As it turned out, within a few months he "found that scene totally unsuitable to me."[55] Business was not for him. His possibly half-hearted attempt at a commercial career stands as an example of the way in which he always combined the intellectual and practical. He had a lifelong desire to earn a living, which helped keep him grounded. At the same time he never allowed his pragmatic realism to dampen his spirit of intellectual adventure. *You can only follow your dreams if you're completely awake.*

His failure to make his new life in Bristol work was also in part due to his unwelcomed attempts to correct the grammar and style of his boss's correspondence. Miller told him that he had made £20,000 with his English and would not have it improved.[56] Hume was always a careful prose stylist, and it is fitting that what made him such a good writer helped ensure he did not end up becoming something else.

It was in Bristol that Hume changed the spelling of his name from "Home" because he realized that it was futile to expect the English to pronounce it properly and would continue to make it rhyme with "Rome," not "whom."

So Hume gave up on business and set out once again to try his fortune as the "man of letters" he had known for some years he really wanted to be. To do that, he removed himself from Britain and set out for France.

CHAPTER TWO

Natural Wisdom

Such is the nature of novelty, that, where any thing pleases, it
becomes doubly agreeable, if new; but if it displeases, it is
doubly displeasing, upon that very account.

FRANCE, LA FLÈCHE, 1734–37

A Traveling Mind

By 1734, the twenty-three-year-old Hume was ready to start
work on his magnum opus. To do this he decided on "prosecut-
ing my Studies in a Country Retreat." But why did he choose
one in France? First, it would no doubt have provided him with
fewer distractions than in his home country. Primarily, however, the choice seemed to be determined by economics. At that
time it was possible to live more cheaply in France than in Scotland, and Hume did not have a large amount of money. Hence
he wrote that "I resolved to make a very rigid Frugality supply
my Deficiency of Fortune, to maintain unimpaired my Inde-
pendency, and to regard every object as contemptible, except
the Improvement of my Talents in Literature."[1]

This simple statement reflects two important features of
Hume's life and career. One is Hume's lifelong desire for

independence, which depended on balancing his income and expenditure. This explains why his short memoir *My Own Life* mentions his financial success so much. Hume didn't value great luxury or excess but was delighted to have the kind of "modest fortune" that enabled him to pursue his work freely.

The second is his description of his chosen life as one concerned with "literature." This sounds odd to the modern reader, for whom "literature" means fiction, poetry, and theater. In Hume's day, it meant, as in Johnson's dictionary, "Learning; skill in letters," that is, learning of pretty much any kind. It's important to remember that Hume saw himself as a "man of letters" rather than a philosopher in the modern, narrow sense of the word. When he wrote about history and economics, he was not straying from his central concern but exploring different corners of his large field of interest.

Hume could have taken one of two sea routes to France. One was from Rye to Dieppe, the other Dover to Calais. He probably took the latter. I was born in Dover and grew up in the nearby town of Folkestone. From both it is possible to see the coast of France on a clear day. Even today, however, the cultural divide is much vaster than the nautical one. In Dover, only the boats give a clue that France is so close. In Hume's time the gulf must have been even wider. The world is vastly more interconnected than it was even a hundred years ago, and people travel with a speed and ease that would have seemed magical for almost all of human history. And yet in Hume's day there was a kind of non-geographical "Republic of Letters" that emerged in the late seventeenth century and through the eighteenth. Intellectuals across Europe and America exchanged letters and manuscripts in a kind of virtual university, thanks to a number of efficient courier systems, owned by private families such as the Taxis and the Thurns.

One of the most striking testaments to the efficacy of this network is the collection of objections and replies that was published as an appendix to Descartes's *Meditations* in 1647. These include objections from the Dutch theologian Johannes Caterus (Johan de Kater) and the English philosopher Thomas Hobbes, as well as those from thinkers around France. The first sentence is Gassendi writing, "Sir, Mersenne gave me great pleasure in letting me see your splendid book." The friar Marin Mersenne was a key facilitator of the Republic of Letters. In 1635 he set up the Académie Parisienne (*Academia Parisiensis*), an informal association of intellectuals that connected nearly 140 correspondents. Mersenne was a prolific copier of texts and letters, a skill that facilitated the exchange of ideas.

So before Hume had even set foot outside of the United Kingdom, he already had more of a connection with thinkers overseas than did the working people of Kent who could see the continent most days. Thanks to the Internet, it is now more true than ever that one can be an intellectual explorer without being a physical one and that *travel can only expand the mind if the mind is already expansive.*

The ferries that cross the channel at hourly intervals today are much quicker and more stable than the ones I took in my youth, which nauseatingly seemed to sway from side to side even on the calmest of days. It is difficult to imagine how Hume, who was prone to seasickness, would have felt during the several stomach-churning hours the sailing would have taken.

One aspect of the trip would have remained almost unchanged: the view of the White Cliffs of Dover slowly receding as he left his home nation behind. The White Cliffs have become a kind of symbol of Britain, paradoxically representing both the sense of familiarity and welcome they induce on first sight and also a kind of fortress wall, protecting the country from foreign invaders.

In Hume's day, this double-edged symbolism would also have been apt. During Hume's life, Britain was at war with France more often than it was at peace. It is some kind of miracle that Hume managed to schedule the defining journeys of his life into two brief intervals in these hostilities. I think that speaks to Hume's spirit of openness. For him, any scholar or thinker was a kindred spirit, a fellow traveler. Expanding our intellectual horizons by crossing physical ones was an opportunity not to be missed.

Arrival in La Flèche

Hume briefly stayed in Rheims before heading to La Flèche in Anjou, in the Loire valley. One imagines this a rural idyll, a charming French town on the banks of a river, surrounded by vineyards. When one arrives there today, such illusions are quickly quashed. La Flèche is an unexceptional small town. Wandering in search of *un express*, charming street-corner cafés with outside tables on cobbled squares are notable only by their absence. We ended up at a functional café off a major road with sports on the television, alone rather than surrounded by Gauloises-smoking locals. The dining options were no more promising, so we stopped at the supermarket and had *un picnic* at the bed and breakfast we had booked just outside the town, having been underwhelmed by the options in it. The Loir river, a tributary of the longer and better-known Loire, runs alongside the main road through the town, and although it is possible to walk along a few hundred yards of it, there is little enticing about the prospect.

Perhaps La Flèche had more character in Hume's time. But it still might have seemed an odd choice for someone who became known as "the great infidel," since at the time it was famous for one thing. As Hume wrote home, "besides the good company of the town" there was "a college of a hundred Jesuits, which is esteem't the most magnificent both for buildings & gardens of any belonging to that order in France or even in Europe."[2]

The Jesuits were not only Christians but Catholics and therefore steeped in the kinds of "superstitions" Hume so frequently criticized. Hume, however, was never a zealous atheist. All his life he remained friends with many members of the clergy, relationships that his correspondence showed involved plenty of good-natured teasing. He may have disagreed with the theology of the Jesuits, but the Society of Jesus, as they are also known, is also one of the most learned orders in the Catholic Church and Hume would have found plenty of intellectual stimulation in their company.

The college already had a number of eminent alumni. A plaque on the wall in the college today testifies that Marin Marenne was among them, attending between 1604 and 1612. Another plaque above this one remembers the college's most illustrious graduate, René Descartes, saying he had been a student from 1607 to 1615 (although Hume's most recent biographer dates Descartes's stay as from 1606 to 1614).[3] In 1638, Descartes described the fertile and rich intellectual environment the college provided: "The number of young people coming from everywhere in France, and due to their mutual conversation, produces a mix of humours that has almost the same learning effect as if they were travelling."[4]

According to Dario Perinetti, who has made a detailed study of the college's history at the time Hume was in La Flèche, in

1737 the college housed 90 Jesuits, 300 boarding students, 1,000 day pupils, and an unknown but significant number of non-registered students (*étudiants libres*). In addition, the college attracted a number of visitors.[5] In a letter, Hume remarked that it was "so much frequented by our Countreymen, that there was once 30 Englishmen boarded in this small Town."[6]

La Flèche seemed to be a particularly freethinking environment. According to Hume biographer James Harris, "The college seems to have been where Jesuits were sent who had become too interested in modern heterodoxies, especially the version of Descartes's philosophy developed by the Oratorian Nicolas Malebranche."[7] Malebranche is best known for his theory of "occasionalism," which says that objects have no causal powers, and that it is God who makes all effects follow from their usual causes. Hume certainly studied these philosophies while he was in La Flèche. In a letter of 1737 written there, Hume gave Michael Ramsay a list of recommended reading, which included Malebranche's *De La Recherche de la Verité* (The Search after Truth), Bayle's *Dictionary*, Descartes's *Meditationes*, and Berkeley's *Principles of Human Knowledge*.[8]

Of these, Descartes is most important to understanding Hume's project. Descartes was the epitome of the rationalist philosopher that Hume reacted strongly against. Descartes sought to establish secure foundations of human knowledge on the basis of pure reason alone. To do this, he engaged in a skeptical project of questioning everything, resolving only to hold on to what was certain and indubitable. Descartes explained this by analogy to someone who "had a basket full of apples and, being worried that some of the apples were rotten, wanted to take out the rotten ones to prevent the rot spreading." The only way to do this would be to tip the whole lot out, examine each fruit carefully, and only put back into the basket those which are unblemished. He proposed doing the same for our beliefs. We need to "separate the false beliefs from the others, so as to prevent their contaminating the rest and making the whole lot uncertain."[9]

The problem is that almost all the apples of belief turned out to be duds. Even the existence of the external world was not guaranteed: don't the mad see things that don't exist, and don't we all know what it is like to be dreaming, convinced that what we are experiencing is real? The whole world could be an illusion, a dream.

There was, however, one thing that could not be seriously doubted: the existence of the thinker doing the doubting. The very act of doubting your own existence undermines itself because in order for there to be a skeptical thought, there has to be a thinker. So although we cannot know we are material beings, sure that our bodies are not mirages, we cannot doubt that we think. Descartes concluded that meant we were essentially thinking things, *res cogitans*, not material things, *res extensa*.

From this seemingly secure foundation, Descartes attempted to rebuild the rest of human knowledge. He argued that a good God must exist, and that such a deity would not systematically deceive us. This allowed him to regain justified belief in the external world. Most philosophers since, however, believe that Descartes's project of reconstruction is less persuasive than his destruction. In short, he dug himself a skeptical hole that was too deep to get out of.

As we shall see, in his *Treatise*, largely composed in La Flèche, Hume rejected almost everything that Descartes stood for. This included his "method of doubt." Hume called this method "antecedent scepticism," a skepticism that you begin your inquiries with, rather than a skepticism your inquiries lead you to. This "universal doubt" is not only impossible to maintain but "would be entirely incurable; and no reasoning could ever bring us to a state of assurance and conviction upon any subject."[10]

But perhaps Descartes's more fundamental mistake was the same as that of the Stoics: he had grounded his philosophy in abstract principles rather than in human nature. "The science of man," Hume wrote, "is the only solid foundation for the other sciences," and the "only solid foundation we can give to this science itself must be laid on experience and observation." To put it another way, since human nature is a material reality, not an abstract concept, if we seek to understand it "we can only expect success, by following the experimental method, and deducing general maxims from a comparison of particular instances." Hume was thus bringing the experimental method of natural science into the domain of philosophy. This approach has come to be known as empiricism. Descartes's method, which started from pure reason, came to be called rationalism. Hume believed that this method "may be more perfect in itself, but suits less the imperfection of human nature, and is a common source of illusion and mistake in this as well as in other subjects."[11]

It is worth noting, however, that in one very important way Hume's approach was identical to that of Descartes. Both philosophers were looking for the secure foundations of knowledge. Descartes wrote that his intention was "start again right from the foundations, if I wanted to establish anything at all in the sciences that washable and likely to last."[12] Hume used very similar language, writing, "In pretending therefore to explain the principles of human nature, we in effect propose a compleat system of the sciences, built on a foundation almost entirely new, and the only one upon which they can stand with any security."[13]

Hume was right to argue that observation, the "science of man," is better than pure reason, but was then faced with the problem that even this was a shaky foundation. In this respect Hume did not perhaps go far enough in his rejection of Cartesian skepticism. He in effect accepted the demand for a secure foundation for knowledge that no one is able to provide. A. J. Ayer captured the problem this method creates well when he argued, "Not that the sceptic's argument is fallacious; as usual his logic is impeccable. But his victory is empty. He robs us of certainty only by so defining it as to make it certain that it cannot be obtained."[14]

A better way to defeat skepticism is not to sing its song in the first place but to argue that the demand for certain foundations of knowledge is unreasonable. Later empiricist philosophers have argued that knowledge has no foundations at all from which we can "build up." Rather, what justifies our claims to knowledge is simply the ways in which different truths cohere. As Wittgenstein put it, "I have arrived at the rock bottom of my convictions. And one might almost say that these foundation-walls are carried by the whole house."[15]

Although Hume advocated for empirical rather than rationalist foundations of knowledge, the irony is that in many respects, Descartes was more of a scientist than Hume. This is evident from the original 1664 edition of Descartes's *L'Homme* (*Man*), which can still be found in the library at La Flèche today. This remarkable book contains dozens of detailed anatomical drawings of the human body that display an extremely advanced understanding of how sense perception works. One contains a drawing of a man holding his hand over a flame, illustrating how nerves in the body transmit signals from the hand to the brain, leading to the sensation of heat. Another shows the lenses of the eye, correctly indicating that images on the retina are inverted and that therefore the brain has to correct for this so that we do not see the world upside down.

Hume never made such detailed scientific investigations of the natural world. His "experiments" were no more than careful observations of ordinary experience. There is a section of the *Treatise*, for example, devoted entirely to "experiments" designed to test his theories.[16] But these are no more than *thought experiments*, in which readers are invited to "test" one of his theories by introspection and imagination alone. This lack of any genuine experimentation was perhaps a weakness, as is the solitary way in which they are conducted. Annette Baier, for example, suggests that "to know our own minds, we need observant companions, so that our minds can be understood by them." So in seeking the solitude of La Flèche, Hume made the kind of objective observation his method required more difficult.[17]

Despite this, it was the experimenter Descartes who insisted that our essential nature as thinking beings was revealed not by scientific study but by reason and introspection. As the first line of *L'Homme* attests, Descartes believed human beings to be made of both a soul and a body. It seems that as a reader Hume saw the implications of Descartes's scientific approach to the human body more clearly than the author did himself. This is worth remembering today, when people are often quick to distinguish between those who take a scientific approach and those who don't. Hume and Descartes show this is not so straightforward. One can be a scientist but blind to the evidence by prior ideological or philosophical commitments. One can also be a nonscientist but better able to understand the implications of science than a scientist.

Both of these principles are often missed in an age when scientific credibility carries much weight. For example, there is a sizable minority of scientists who hold fairly orthodox religious views, and their co-believers often use this as evidence that science supports their worldview. On the other hand, the fact that the majority of scientists do not believe in God is not decisive the other way either, since the existence of God is simply not their area of expertise. Similarly, we should not assume that when scientists assert that free will or the self is an illusion, as many do, that they are speaking with authority. Any general, evidence-based worldview draws on more facts and observations than any one expert has at their disposal. We could then form another Humean maxim: *The ability to form an accurate view of reality and human nature requires a willingness to attend to all of experience and how it fits together, not specialized scientific knowledge.*

The fact that Descartes studied at La Flèche seems to be too good a narrative coincidence to be true. By Hume's time, however, his philosophy had been officially condemned by the Roman Catholic Church. In 1663, Descartes's complete works were put on the *Index Librorum Prohibitorum*, a list of books Catholics were banned from reading. The Jesuits, however, did not seem to take this too seriously. Perinetti told me that although "it would be wrong to say that the college was a center of Cartesianism or, as others have suggested, of Malebranchians," it is "most likely that Descartes's works were in the library." The 1776 catalogue definitely has an entry on Descartes, and editions of his work from that time are still in the collection today.

The library would have been extremely impressive and was surely one of the main reasons why Hume settled in La Flèche. Hume would have needed no special privileges to access it since, as Perinetti reports, "in eighteenth-century France, civil, Royal, ecclesiastical, and academic libraries were open to the

FIGURE 7. Bust of Descartes in the library of the former Jesuit college in
La Flèche, now the Prytanée national militaire.

public."[18] The original library rooms have been modernized beyond recognition, but it is still possible to get a flavor of what
they would have been like in the current library, where a large
bust of a now rehabilitated Descartes takes pride of place, his
severe expression perhaps expressing dissatisfaction at his years
of rejection by his alma mater.

The library is small, mainly compromising one long wooden
bookshelf-lined room, with some overflow space in a more
functional metal-shelved adjacent room. The collection is a bib-
liophile's dream, with dozens of books that were almost certainly in the library when Hume used it, perhaps even read by
him. Perinetti's research suggests that the present-day collection
contains at least 964 volumes from the original Jesuit library.[19]

Among those are Descartes's *Principia Philosophæ* (The Principles of Philosophy) and *Meditationum de Primâ Philosophia* (Meditations on First Philosophy), which the library card shows are editions from 1692 and 1698, respectively.

The books from this era are all beautifully printed, illuminated with woodcut prints of illustrations and initial drop capital letters. La Flèche itself had a tradition of book printing, but many volumes came from elsewhere, especially Paris and Amsterdam. This is another reminder that there was a healthy flow of intellectual debate in Europe at this time. This is also reflected in the copious contemporary secondary literature, such as the wonderfully titled *Voyage du monde du descartes* (*A Journey in the World of Descartes*) by Gabriel Daniel, now long forgotten.

A browse through any shelf reveals volume after volume of historic texts. Here is Malebranche's *Traité de morale* (Treatise on Ethics), another work Hume would have read. Next one of the most important works on Descartes, *Recueil de quelques pieces curieuses concernant la philosophie de monsieur Descartes* (*A Collection of Some Curious Pieces Concerning the Philosophy of M. Descartes*), by Pierre Bayle, another author Hume studied in France. A volume of the works of Tacitus would surely have been on Hume's reading list, as he was a big fan of the Roman, one of the first genuine historians, rather than a myth-chronicler or propagandist. Then there are the many obscure works such as *Les Lacunes de la Philosophie* (*Philosophy's Gaps*) by Francois L. D'Escherny. Written in 1783, this volume postdates Hume but it is possible its Swiss author met Hume after he moved to Paris in 1760, in time for the Scot's sojourn in the capital. The collection represents a historical philosophical discussion over time and space.

How did the library come to have such a marvelous collection? It was from the very start well-endowed. It was created in 1603 by Henry IV, who gave his castle in La Flèche to the Jesuit fathers "to instruct the youth and make them love science, honour and virtue, to be able to serve the public." Henry also gave them 10,000 ecus, including 1,000 to buy books. An annual allowance of 300 ecus plus gifts from private individuals over the years helped the collection to grow. We don't know how many books were there in Hume's day, but we do know that by 1776 it housed at least 4,869 books, a large collection for its time.[20]

The entire college would have been a very conducive place to think and work. It sits in thirteen hectares of land, enclosed in 1630. Two hectares of this is given over to gardens. The layout today, however, is in the formal French style, with wide perpendicular gravel pathways. The original would have been Renaissance style, with more elaborate geometrical landscaping. You can nonetheless appreciate the tranquility the gardens would have provided: an ideal place for Hume to wander and think over whatever he had been reading or writing about.

Today it is a Prytanée, a school for military families. Founded in 1764, the Prytanée was transferred to the site in 1808 by Napoleon. In 1870 it became the Prytanée national militaire, which it has been until this day. It is unlikely that Hume would have spent much time in the high-vaulted white stone chapel, built on the plan of a Latin cross, with five chapels on either side of the main area. The light simplicity of the nave grates with the darker baroque altarpiece and the organ gallery, again decorated in baroque style with angels, masks, foliage, and horns. This contrast unintentionally dramatizes the perennial conflict in organized Christianity between ideals of poverty and grandeur, temporal weakness and worldly power.

FIGURE 8. The Prytanée national militaire in La Flèche.

Hume would not, however, have allowed his religious skepticism to have prejudiced his opinion of the building or its cultural significance. Around 1767 he was taken to see St. Paul's Cathedral in London. His host informed him that very few attended the services there, remarking "how foolish it was to lay out a million . . . on a thing so useless." Hume unexpectedly disagreed. "St. Paul's, as a monument of the religious feeling and sentiment of the country, does it honour, and will endure," he said. "We have wasted millions on a single campaign in Flanders, without any good resulting from it."[21]

It was in any case evident enough from the start that the church in La Flèche was as much a testament to the glory of humans as to that of God. The transept contains the heart

FIGURE 9. The chapel in the Prytanée national militaire in La Flèche.

mausoleums of both Henry IV and Mary de' Medici, his second wife, making it plain that the building serves as a monument to his reign. Human ingenuity is also celebrated in the architecture and its decoration, the work of human, not divine, hands. Take away the invisible God whose house the church is supposed to be, and everything remains to be admired.

This is a good reminder of Hume's lifelong dislike of factionalism of any kind. As he wrote in an essay, *"When men act in a faction, they are apt, without shame or remorse, to neglect all the ties of honour and morality, in order to serve their party."*[22] In another, he adds, "Factions subvert government, render laws impotent, and beget the fiercest animosities among men of the same nation, who ought to give mutual assistance and protection to each other."[23] He would have despaired at the way in which many of our societies have polarized, with people showing contempt for those they disagree with while at the same time claiming to speak for "the people." *"Public Spirit, methinks, shou'd engage us to love the Public, and to bear an equal Affection to all our Country-Men; not to hate one Half of them, under Colour of loving the Whole."*[24]

The fact the Hume chose to spend three years living and working among people whose religious views he entirely disagreed with shows that he meant what he wrote. It suggests another Humean maxim: *A skeptical, open mind has nothing to fear and much to gain from seeking the company and opinions of those it seriously disagrees with.*

Of Miracles

We know that at least one of Hume's most important ideas came to him while at the college. He recalled later, "I was walking in the cloisters of the Jesuits' College of La Fleche (France), a town in which I passed two years of my youth, and engaged in a conversation with a Jesuit, of some parts and learning, who was relating to me, and urging some nonsensical miracle performed lately in their convent, when I was tempted to dispute against him; and as my head was full of the topics of my *A Treatise of Human Nature*, which I was at that time composing, this argument immediately occurred to me, and I thought it very much gravelled my companion."[25]

"This argument" was the one Hume articulated in "Of Miracles." It is entirely believable that the argument came to him almost completely in an instant, because its central principle is beautifully simple: "a weaker evidence can never destroy a stronger."[26] Since the evidence that a miracle has actually

FIGURE 10. The gardens of the Prytanée national militaire in La Flèche.

occurred will always be weaker than the evidence that it has not, there can never be any grounds for believing that a miracle has actually taken place.

But why can't the evidence for a miracle ever be strong enough to lend it credence? The nub of the argument is that "a miracle is a violation of the laws of nature." A merely unlikely event is not miraculous. If someone falls from an airplane and lands safely on the ground thanks to a combination of freak gusts of wind to arrest their fall and an exceptionally soft surface to cushion it, that is amazingly fortunate but not a miracle. Should someone fall from a plane and find themselves able to fly, however, that would be miraculous.

Hume argues that since the entirety of human experience stands as evidence that the laws of nature hold without exception, the evidence against any claim that they have not held and that a miracle has occurred "is as entire as any argument from experience can possibly be imagined." The uniformity of experience testifies to the fact that gravity is always at work, heat always melts ice, the dead do not come back to life, and so on. There is always "a uniform experience against every miraculous event, otherwise the event would not merit that appellation." Such a uniform experience is as good as a proof against the existence of any miracle.[27] Even inexplicably extraordinary events would not be sufficient evidence against the sovereignty of natural laws. In a letter, Hume said that even if the sun were to disappear for forty-eight hours "reasonable men would only conclude from this fact, that the machine of the globe was disordered during this time."[28]

In theory, it is possible to imagine a miracle so inexplicable and so widely observed and verified that we would have to accept its veracity. In practice, no supposed miracle has come even close to meeting this standard. Evidence that a miracle has occurred is never strong enough because it always ends up resting on the testimony of one person or a handful of individuals, and none are reliable enough to shake our assumption in the uniformity of nature. Sometimes the incentives to be too credulous or simply to lie are also stronger than those to tell the truth, since being the witness to extraordinary events makes us special. The key passage here is:

> There is not to be found, in all history, any miracle attested by a sufficient number of men, of such unquestioned good-sense, education, and learning, as to secure us against all delusion in themselves; of such undoubted integrity, as to place them beyond all suspicion of any design to deceive others; of such credit and reputation in the eyes of mankind, as to

have a great deal to lose in case of their being detected in any falsehood; and at the same time, attesting facts, performed in such a public manner, and in so celebrated a part of the world, as to render the detection unavoidable: All which circumstances are requisite to give us a full assurance in the testimony of men.[29]

La Flèche was not only the source of Hume's argument against miracles; it also provided a lot of the examples he used to illustrate it. At the time of his stay, there was an ongoing theological dispute between the Jesuits and the Jansenists. The Jansenists were a dissenting Catholic movement inspired by the posthumously published work of the early seventeenth-century Dutch theologian Cornelius Jansen. They placed great emphasis on original sin and the innate depravity of humankind, teaching that our predestined salvation depended solely on God's arbitrary grace. One of their most heated though philosophically insignificant disagreements concerned miracles allegedly performed in the tomb of the Jansenist Abbé Pâris. Hume used this dispute in "Of Miracles." "There surely never was a greater number of miracles ascribed to one person, than those, which were lately said to have been wrought in France upon the tomb of Abbé Paris, the famous Jansenist, with whose sanctity the people were so long deluded," he wrote. "The curing of the sick, giving hearing to the deaf, and sight to the blind, were every where talked of as the usual effects of that holy sepulchre."[30]

Hume offers this as an example of a miracle that seems to be well supported by the evidence of witnesses. "Many of the miracles were immediately proved upon the spot, before judges of unquestioned integrity, attested by witnesses of credit and distinction, in a learned age, and on the most eminent theatre that is now in the world." Not even the Jesuits, "though a learned body, supported by the civil magistrate, and determined enemies to those opinions," were "ever able distinctly to refute or detect them."

But not even this should be enough to persuade a rational person that a genuine miracle has been performed. *"A wise man . . . proportions his belief to the evidence."*[31] The wise, warns Hume, give little credence to any report that suits the reporter, "whether it magnifies his country, his family, or himself, or in any other way strikes in with his natural inclinations and propensities. But what greater temptation than to appear a missionary, a prophet, an ambassador from heaven?" We have to be on our guard against "the known and natural principles of credulity and delusion" which he believed to be widespread.[32] "The passion of surprize and wonder" is "an agreeable emotion" that tends people toward belief in stories of miracles. As evidence for this, he asks rhetorically, "With what greediness are the miraculous accounts of travellers received, their descriptions of sea and land monsters, their relations of wonderful adventures, strange men, and uncouth manners?"[33]

Ever the diplomat, Hume made it clear that his argument did not mean that the miracles reported in the Bible never happened. They simply show that we can never have good *reason* to believe they happened; we can only believe them by *faith*. And as he is happy to point out, "Our most holy religion is founded on *Faith*, not on reason; and it is a sure method of exposing it to put it to such a trial as it is, by no means, fitted to endure."[34] By acknowledging this, Hume could speak with a forked tongue. Those who have no faith, or who regard it as too weak a justification for belief, can conclude—as Hume himself surely did—that all reports of miracles are false. They will be encouraged to draw that conclusion from Hume's observation that reports of supernatural events "are observed chiefly to abound among ignorant and barbarous nations."[35] And when he says "the *Christian Religion* not only was at first attended with miracles, but even at this day cannot be believed by any reasonable person without one," one might easily conclude that it therefore cannot be believed.[36] But for those who have religious belief and who see faith as being central to it, belief in miracles becomes more special than ordinary belief. After all, anyone can believe what the evidence shows us to be the case: only those who have put their trust in their God and religion can believe on faith alone.

Against this, however, Hume includes an argument that strikes against Christianity as hard as it does against any other religion. Miracles are always invoked as evidence in support of a *particular* religion. But *all* religions claim miracles. Further, they are all in disagreement with each other, and none is believed by a majority of humankind. Therefore everyone who testifies for the truth of their own religion's miracles is offering evidence against the miracles of others. So "all the prodigies of different religions are to be regarded as contrary facts, and the evidences of these prodigies, whether weak or strong, as opposite to each other."[37]

Hume's argument has proven to be extremely resilient. Critics tend to say that Hume fails to demonstrate the impossibility of miracles, but that was never his intention. Given that nothing can be proved or disproved by reason alone, anything is possible, including miracles. But while miracles are not impossible, it is not reasonable to believe that any have actually occurred. Hume's argument concerns the impossibility of rational belief in miracles, not the impossibility of any such miracles occurring.

It could be argued that this is still too strong. Perhaps there could be a miracle that had so many witnesses, in conditions that made it almost impossible to doubt it really happened. But this purely hypothetical possibility can be ignored. Hume had no time for speculations about what might be true in some conceivable world if that world is nothing like the one we live in. This principle merits being included as a Humean maxim: *Do not waste time thinking about what may or may not happen in a possible world when you have no reason to believe it happens in the actual world.* If we accept this maxim, Hume's argument is very powerful against all the miracles that have been said to have occurred, for it is certainly the case that none of those are as based in reliable evidence as the belief that the laws of nature hold without exception.

Hume originally intended to include this argument in his *Treatise* but left it out, for fear that it would cause too much controversy and lend the whole work a notoriety that would prevent it from being taken seriously. Back in London, he would describe this act of excision as "castrating my Work, that is, cutting off its noble Parts, that is, endeavouring it shall give as little Offence as possible." Hume was clearly troubled by this, describing it as "a piece of Cowardice, for which I blame myself; tho I believe none of my Friends will blame me." Nevertheless, he went through with the self-censorship because he "was resolved not to be an Enthusiast, in Philosophy, while I was blaming other Enthusiasts."[38] The world would have to wait until the publication of his *Philosophical Essays concerning Human Understanding* in 1748 (renamed *An Enquiry concerning Human Understanding* ten years later) for Hume to make the argument public.

Hume himself enjoyed the irony of conceiving such an antireligious argument in the grounds of a Jesuit college. In 1762 he wrote that "the freedom at least of this reasoning makes it somewhat extraordinary to have been the produce of a convent of Jesuits." He was also able to mock himself, adding that "you may think the sophistry of it savours plainly the place of its birth."[39]

Yvandeau

Although Hume frequently made use of the library at the college, he lodged elsewhere. Biographers and locals agree that this was at the house Yvandeau, sitting on a hill overlooking the town around three kilometers from the college.[40] Yvandeau is today a private residence and there is no way to book a visit. So when I visited La Flèche I simply drove up the gateway of the extensive lands it sat on and rang the intercom. A woman replied and my wife explained in her imperfect—but better than my—French who we were and whether it would be possible to take a look. She asked if we would mind coming back in the afternoon, but we were due to leave and asked if we could at least see the house from the outside. To our delight she agreed.

Walking up the winding driveway to the house it was clear that Hume had chosen his lodgings well. With its views across the valley, there could not be a more idyllic spot in La Flèche.

Yvandeau exuded faded grandeur. It is a large house, although all the rooms are of modest size. Many of the features, such as the wooden stair rail, are if not originals then very old. It is a building that has clearly been lived in by several generations. Set out over two floors, it is L-shaped, each end and the corner having a four-pointed roof that creates the impression of three towers.

The owner showed us the room that they believed Hume occupied on the first floor, on the corner of the L, with one

FIGURE 11. Yvandeau, Hume's home in La Flèche.

window looking out over La Flèche and the other over the garden in the house. It is not an especially large room, but it does have a fantastic view and a gray marble fireplace. His desk is said to have been in front of the window with the best view. We cannot know that this is true but it is certainly the most obvious place to work.

Hume seemed happy in France and liked the people, whom he found to be "civil, & sociable."[41] In 1741 he wrote admiringly that "the French are the only people, except the Greeks, who have been at once philosophers, poets, orators, historians, painters, architects, sculptors, and musicians. With regard to the stage, they have excelled even the Greeks, who far excelled the English. And, in common life, they have, in a great measure, perfected that art, the most useful and agreeable of any, *l'Art de Vivre*, the art of society and conversation."[42]

The current occupant of Yvandeau conforms to this image of the French. Not only did she offer us an impromptu private tour, she gifted us a bottle of wine from the vineyard next door. "It's not a *grand vin*," she said, apologetically, merely a "*petit vin*." We discovered she was correct when we opened the bottle of Clos d'Yvandeau with philosopher friends. Despite being closed with a champagne cork the wine was a red and only slightly sparkling. At 12 percent ABV it was light and fruity, almost like a dry grape juice, as though not all the fruit sugars had fermented into alcohol. It is the kind of pleasant, easy-drinking rustic wine that is produced all over continental Europe and is probably closer to the style of wine that Hume would have drunk than the modern, stronger varieties. We were especially privileged to try it because the label revealed that it is not for commercial production and is *réservée aux members et adhérents de l'association Vignobles des Coteaux Fléchois*: reserved for members of the association of winemakers of the Fléchois hills.

Hume was impressed not only by French hospitality. Vices that were common elsewhere, he found absent in France. In Rheims he wrote, "I have not yet seen one Quarrel in France." He also claimed that you "scarce ever meet with a Clown, or an ill bred man in France." His explanation for this was that it was down to "the little niceties of the French Behaviour" that "serve to polish the ordinary Kind of People & prevent Rudeness & Brutality." Just as soldiers become braver by repeatedly practicing military maneuvers until they become instinctive, and the religious become more devout by repeatedly partaking in rituals, so people become more civil by practicing small daily acts of politeness, which although mere "trifles" allow "an easy Transition to something more material."[43]

This observation reflects a feature of Hume's moral philosophy. Hume believed that habit was the key to virtuous behavior: *practice doing the right thing in every situation, trivial or important, and you will build the kind of character that tends to act well in all situations.* Good moral thinking "by proper representations of the deformity of vice and beauty of virtue, beget correspondent habits, and engage us to avoid the one, and embrace the other." This idea is close to that of Confucius, which we have no reason to suppose Hume knew. However, we would have expected him to have known that it is also a key idea in Aristotle's moral philosophy, which he surely would have read. The library at La Flèche contained a volume of Aristotle's *Varia Opeucula* (various works) as well as the *Metaphysics* and the *Nicomachean Ethics*. Strangely, however, Hume barely mentions Aristotle in any of his writings. In fact, he only mentions the great philosopher a handful of times, usually to take issue with his metaphysics, once to cite his list of "manly virtues," and once to correct him on a point of human psychology, insisting that "men have, in general, a much greater propensity to over-value than under-value themselves; notwithstanding the opinion of Aristotle."[44]

The only small concealed acknowledgment of his debt to Aristotle is his mark that "a due medium, say the Peripatetics, is the characteristic of virtue."[45] The "Peripatetics" were a school of philosophers who were followers of Aristotle, and in Hume's day the word was used to refer primarily to the philosophy of the master himself. The "due medium" is the doctrine of the mean. This asserts that virtue is not the opposite of a single vice but lies somewhere between two extremes of vice: one of excess and one of deficiency. Generosity is the mean between the deficiency of meanness and the excess of profligacy; courage the mean between cowardice and rashness; flexibility the mean between rigidity and spinelessness. Hume himself uses the example of frugality with avarice as its deficiency and prodigality as its excess.[46] Hence Hume's claim that *"no quality, it is allowed, is absolutely either blameable or praise-worthy. It is all according to its degree."* Confucius developed almost the exact same concept, completely independently.

Hume's moral philosophy has another feature in common with those of Aristotle and Confucius. For all three, matters of morality, politeness, and etiquette are aspects of ethics. Ethics concerns how agreeable or useful our actions are to ourselves and others, and that means it concerns matters small and large. As Hume put it, "A blemish, a fault, a vice, a crime; these expressions seem to denote different degrees of censure and disapprobation; which are, however, all of them, at the bottom, pretty nearly all the same kind of species."[47]

It also means ethics concerns all our behavior, whether intentional or not. In this he was in agreement with the ancient Greeks, for whom "the distinction of voluntary or involuntary was little regarded." Nonetheless, "they justly considered, that cowardice, meanness, levity, anxiety, impatience, folly, and many other qualities of the mind, might appear ridiculous and deformed, contemptible and odious, though independent of the will."[48] Hume believed that this was closer to common sense than moral theories that sought to make only voluntary actions subject to moral appraisal. "I wou'd have any one give me a reason, why virtue and vice may not be involuntary, as well as beauty and deformity." Actions are virtuous or vicious to the extent that they are agreeable and/or useful. This definition says nothing about whether they are voluntary or not. In reality, many moral virtues "are equally involuntary and necessary," including "constancy, fortitude, magnanimity; and, in short, all the qualities which form the great man."[49] He also notes that

English is not "very precise in marking the boundaries between virtues and talents, vices and defects," suggesting that this is because "there is so little distinction made in our internal estimation of them."[50] So when Hume admired certain aspects of French customary behavior, he was taking them to be morally praiseworthy. Societal norms can be right or wrong even though societies are not agents acting intentionally.

Hume was evidently very productive in La Flèche, and the *Treatise* was largely composed there. He later claimed that he conceived the book before he left college, planned it before he was twenty-one, and composed it before he was twenty-five. This would date its completion in 1736. He also wrote in his autobiography that "during my retreat in France, first at Reims, but chiefly at La Fleche, in Anjou, I composed my *A Treatise of Human Nature*." But scholars agree that the book was not completely finished when he left France in 1737. Mossner believes that Books I and II of the *Treatise* were at least polished when he was back in Scotland while the third was completed there.[51]

Nonetheless, the bulk of the work was clearly done in La Flèche, and there is no reason to doubt Hume's claim that he had the general shape and argument of the work in mind before he sat down to write it there.

The *Treatise*

Hume captures the overall spirit of the *Treatise* in a short abstract he wrote three years after its first publication. "The reader will easily perceive," he wrote, "that the philosophy contain'd in this book is very sceptical, and tends to give us a notion of the imperfections and narrow limits of human understanding."[52] If we were to sum up the purpose of the *Treatise* in one sentence, it would be to end the hope of establishing anything about the real world that is certain and beyond doubt, and to reconcile philosophy to a more modest task of reaching only tentative conclusions that are grounded in experience. This would cut philosophy down to size. If we "enquire seriously into the nature of human understanding" we will find that "it is by no means fitted for such remote and abstruse subjects. We must submit to this fatigue, in order to live at ease ever after: And must cultivate true metaphysics with some care, in order to destroy the false and adulterate."[53]

A critical distinction Hume made in the *Treatise* was between reasoning that concerned the relations of ideas and reasoning about matters of fact. When we reason concerning the relation of ideas we do nothing more than analyze the logical relationship between concepts. Mathematics is therefore concerned with the relation of ideas. We know that $1 + 1 = 2$ simply because, given the meaning of every term in this sum, that is what it *must* mean. Similarly, "every unmarried man is a bachelor" is true purely by definition. Such truths can be known with absolute certainty.

Matters of fact, however, are different. "The contrary of every matter of fact is still possible; because it can never imply a contradiction."[54] There is no logical contradiction in a claim such as "The sun will not rise tomorrow." That defies experience, not logic. Logic alone can tell you nothing about how the world behaves. We cannot deduce by pure logic what happens when you take one of something and put it together with another. You might end up with two, but they might breed, explode, or become one. Nor can you deduce by pure logic whether a man is unmarried and therefore a bachelor. You have to gather information about his life.

For Hume, all reasoning is of these two kinds, concerning the relations of ideas or matters of fact. This principle is known as "Hume's fork." He ends his *An Enquiry concerning Human Understanding*, a later rewrite of Part I of the *Treatise*, with a bold and memorable assertion of the fundamental nature of this distinction:

> When we run over libraries, persuaded of these principles, what havoc must we make? If we take in our hand any volume; of divinity or school metaphysics, for instance; let us ask, *Does it contain any abstract reasoning concerning quantity or number?* No. *Does it contain any experimental reasoning concerning matter of fact and existence?* No. Commit it then to the flames: For it can contain nothing but sophistry and illusion.[55]

The most important ramification of the fork is that there can be no absolute certainty in matters of fact. In the abstract to the *Treatise*, Hume explains that "the common systems of logic" are all very well for "the forming of demonstrations"—that is, logical proofs—but they are not equipped to deal with probabilities and the assessment of evidence, "on which life and action entirely depend."[56] The most important problems of philosophy are not like those of mathematics, which are subject to strict proof, but are grounded instead on reasoning from experience, and so admit of no certainty.

The reason for this is fundamental. "All probable arguments are built on the supposition, that there is this conformity betwixt the future and the past," claimed Hume. Belief that humans are mortal, for instance, is based on the observation that no human being has managed to live beyond a hundred or so years. But, of course, these observations are always of the past. We cannot see what will happen to future human beings. We assume, however, that the future will be like the past, at least when it comes to basic laws of nature. We believe that Hume was kept on the ground in La Flèche by the same force of gravity that prevents us floating off today, that the process of fermentation that created the wines he would have drunk are the same as those that created the *petit vin* I took home after my trip there.

This is common sense and no one would seriously dispute it. But Hume points out that we can never *prove* this conformity of past and future. "This conformity is a matter of fact, and if it must be proved, will admit of no proof but from experience," he writes. "But our experience in the past can be a proof of nothing for the future, but upon a supposition, that there is a resemblance betwixt them. This therefore is a point, which can admit of no proof at all, and which we take for granted without any proof."[57]

This has become known as "the problem of induction." Induction is reasoning that generalizes from a limited number of particular, past cases to general rules that also hold in the future. The "problem" is that logically there is no way of getting from premises about the past to conclusions about the future. From a logical point of view, no argument that begins with claims about *what has been* can jump to conclusions about *what will be.*

Of course we believe, as Hume did, that "effects will always correspond to causes" and this is what gives us confidence that the future will indeed follow the patterns of the past.[58] But we do not have any *logical proof* of such a principle. The idea of a cause can always be separated from that of its supposed effect, and this shows that the denial of cause and effect "implies no contradiction nor absurdity; and is therefore incapable of being refuted by any reasoning from mere ideas."[59]

Some object to this by arguing that everything must have a cause "for if any thing wanted a cause, it wou'd produce itself; that is, exist before it existed; which is impossible."[60] But this argument begs the question. To say that without an external cause, a thing must be the cause of itself is still to assume that everything must have a cause. That is precisely what is being contested.

However, Hume's skeptical philosophy goes even deeper than this. We may accept that we go beyond what logic grants when we conclude that, for example, because striking a match has tended to cause a flame to ignite in the past that it will continue to do so in the future. We may also accept that we go beyond what logic grants when we conclude that every event is the effect of some cause. But surely we do not doubt that we have in fact observed causes and effects, such as the striking of a match causing fire, the taking of paracetamol to calm a fever, or the drinking of water to slake thirst?

Hume, however, argues that we have never seen any such thing. We have never observed cause and effect in action. All we have observed is one event following another. We can never see the "necessary connection" between the two that we call causation. "This deficiency in our ideas is not, indeed, perceiv'd in common life," wrote Hume. But we are "as ignorant of the ultimate principle" that binds cause and effect in everyday matters as we are "in the most unusual and extraordinary" ones.[61] The deficiency only becomes clear if we take a rigorous philosophical look. Try it: Hume wagers that all you will ever be able to see is one event following another. You never see the causal power itself. It is difficult even to imagine how such a power could be observed.

So why do we assume that we do see cause and effect in action? Because the mind instinctively fills in the gaps, attributing causal connections between events in a sequence that it cannot in fact observe. This is one of the most keenly contested issues in Hume scholarship, but it seems clear to me that Hume believes that we get our idea of causal power in the external world from a feeling of necessary connection that is part of the natural operations of the mind. The key sentence here is: "This connexion, therefore, which we feel in the mind, this customary transition of the imagination from one object to its usual attendant, is the sentiment or impression, from which we form the idea of power or necessary connexion."[62]

The power of necessary connection is thus "an illusion of the imagination." The word "illusion" here is potentially misleading. What Hume means is that the perception of causation arises out of the imagination. Whether what we imagine corresponds to something in the real world is another matter.

So the question for Hume is "how far we ought to yield to these illusions." Answering it presents us with "a very dangerous dilemma." We cannot be too quick to accept the illusions of the imagination because so many of them "lead us into such errors, absurdities, and obscurities, that we must at last become asham'd of our credulity. *Nothing is more dangerous to reason than the flights of the imagination, and nothing has been the occasion of more mistakes among philosophers.*"[63]

But on the other hand, if we resolved only to believe what we could demonstrate as certain by reason, we would be left in "total scepticism," unable even to assume the chair will hold our weight, that food will feed rather than poison us, or even that our home will still be where it was when we left it this morning.

Hume confessed that he found these and other skeptical thoughts such as "From what causes do I derive my existence?" and "On whom have I any influence, or who have any influence on me?" deeply troubling. "I am confounded with all these questions, and begin to fancy myself in the most deplorable condition imaginable, inviron'd with the deepest darkness, and utterly depriv'd of the use of every member and faculty." What provides the cure? No one has put it more eloquently than Hume:

> Most fortunately it happens, that since reason is incapable of dispelling these clouds, nature herself suffices to that purpose, and cures me of this philosophical melancholy and delirium, either by relaxing this bent of mind, or by some avocation, and lively impression of my senses, which obliterate all these chimeras. I dine, I play a game of back-gammon, I converse, and am merry with my friends; and when after three or four hour's amusement, I wou'd return to these speculations, they appear so cold, and strain'd, and ridiculous, that I cannot find in my heart to enter into them any farther.[64]

The Humean maxim we can extract from this is one borrowed from the nineteenth-century American pragmatist Charles Sanders Peirce: *"Let us not pretend to doubt in philosophy what we do not doubt in our hearts."*

It is easy to see why so many other philosophers have been troubled by Hume's diagnosis of the problem and his way out of it. Kant would later say that reading Hume shook him out of his "dogmatic slumbers," forcing him to try to seek a surer foundation for human knowledge than Hume had done. To many, it seemed Hume had posed a problem that philosophy could not solve and had merely shrugged his shoulders and carried on anyway.

This to me seems like a profound mistake that fails to fully appreciate the depth and subtlety of Hume's thinking. Accepting Hume's conclusions about the limits of logical reasoning requires us to give up the hope that reason alone can stand as the foundation of knowledge. Instead we have to rely on experience. But basing our conclusions on experience is no less philosophical than basing them on rational argument; it is simply philosophical in a way that hadn't previously been properly appreciated.

Hume's ideas about causation and the conformity of past and future are therefore not simply empty assumptions with no philosophical justification. Rather, they are philosophical conclusions with no *logical* justification. Instead, the justification comes from experience. We know by carefully attending to the world that without belief in cause and effect, no reasoning about matters of fact is possible. We also know, thanks to Hume, that belief in cause and effect is not justified by reason or observation. "Custom" or habit "is the great guide of human life. It is that principle alone, which renders our experience useful to us, and makes us expect, for the future, a similar train of events with those which have appeared in the past."[65]

Hume counts "the customary transition from causes to effects, and from effects to causes" among "the principles which are permanent, irresistible, and universal."[66] We therefore can only conclude that we *must* believe in cause and effect without having an ultimate justification for that belief. Hume's skepticism is therefore not a serious doubt about the power of cause and effect but a fatal doubt in our ability to rationally justify our belief in it other than by appealing to the absolute *necessity* of believing in it.

This was made clear in a reply to an all too common criticism, pressed most clearly in a review of the *Treatise* in an influential journal called *History of the Works of the Learned*. The reviewer claimed Hume had argued "That *any* thing may produce any thing."[67] Hume denied this absolutely. "I never asserted so absurd a Proposition as that *any thing might arise without a Cause*," he wrote. "There are many different kinds of

Certainty; and some of them as satisfactory to the Mind, tho' not so regular, as the demonstrative kind."[68] To be fair, Hume invited this misunderstanding by careless readers when he wrote, "Any thing may produce any thing. Creation, annihilation, motion, reason, volition; all these may arise from one another, or from any other object we can imagine." But this was preceded by the claim that "there are no objects, *which by the mere survey, without consulting experience,* we can determine to be the causes of any other; and no objects, which we can certainly determine in the same manner not to be the causes [my emphasis]."[69] When Hume wrote "any thing may produce any thing," we are to understand that this is qualified by "for all reason and observation alone tells us."

Hume's use of the word "certainty" in his defense is confusing, since elsewhere it seems clear that he is saying there is no certainty when it comes to matters of fact. The confusion arises because, in effect, Hume is rejecting the idea of certainty inherited from Plato, Descartes, and all rationalist philosophers. That kind of certainty claims strict, logical proof for fundamental principles of reason. With that notion discredited, however, it is possible to talk instead of a different kind of certainty, as a sufficiently warranted, strongly felt conviction. In that sense, we are and must always be certain that the world is governed by regular principles of cause and effect.

Nonetheless, some scholars maintain that Hume believes that cause and effect is in fact nothing more than something that we project onto the world. I think there is little doubt he believed it to be a real power. Early in *An Enquiry concerning Human Understanding* he responds to the objection that his practice refutes his expressed doubts about cause and effect. Hume says to his imaginary critic, "You mistake the purport of my question. As an agent, I am quite satisfied in the point; but as a philosopher, who has some share of curiosity, I will not say scepticism, I want to learn the foundation of this inference."[70] His whole discussion of free will later in the same work only makes sense if cause and effect are real. Indeed, he says there, "It is universally allowed, that matter, in all its operations, is actuated by a necessary force, and that every natural effect is so precisely determined by the energy of its cause, that no other effect, in such particular circumstances, could possibly have resulted from it."[71] Hume never seriously doubts that cause and effect are real. All he doubts is our ability to ground this belief in reason or observation.

There is more evidence for this interpretation in a notorious passage in the *Enquiry*, where he gives two definitions of cause and effect as though they were equivalent. In the first, a cause is defined as *"an object, followed by another, and where all the objects, similar to the first, are followed by objects similar to the second."* In the second it is *"where, if the first object had not been, the second never [would have] existed."*[72] Scholars protest that these are very different and that the first in no way implies the second. We need not enter into the technical details of the debate here but simply note that the very fact that he makes the second claim suggests that he thought there was a real necessary connection between events in the world and this is not merely a human fancy.

Indeed, he goes on in this passage to specify eight rules for identifying genuine causes, rules that would make no sense if causation were an illusion. The most important of these are that genuine causes are contiguous in time and space with their effects; causes come before their effects; causes and effects must have a "constant union"; like causes must produce like effects; where different objects produce the same effect it must be because they share a common quality; and where objects have different effects it must be because of their different qualities.

Some protest that if Hume allows that we are justified to believe in cause and effect without either logical proof or observation, what is to stop us being justified in believing in God, miracles, or any number of other unverified things or phenomena? The answer to this is simple and owes a great deal to Newton's scientific method, which stipulates, "We are to admit no more causes of natural things than such as are both true and sufficient to explain their appearances."[73] Belief in cause and effect is absolutely essential to make sense of the world; belief in God or any other supernatural force is not. Assume nothing and you're left in total skepticism, without any basis on which to reason and draw inferences about the world. Assume too much and you will end up believing falsehoods. The maxim to follow is: *Assume no more and no less than you have to assume.* The set of assumptions you end up with by following this maxim is very small, perhaps only that there is cause and effect, that the world is not a systematic illusion, and that we are not completely mad. Although we should at times doubt even these, we should not use our inability to prove their impossibility as a reason to stop making these assumptions.

Hume's argument is at once reassuring and deeply unsettling. Stopping for a coffee in La Flèche, I pondered its implications. For sure, everything I do assumes the reality of cause and effect, the regularity of nature. When the barista puts the coffee in the portafilter, attaches it to the espresso machine, and presses the button, pressurized hot water will extract an espresso shot, not milk or molten gold. When I sit down the chair will hold my weight, not throw me sixty feet into the air. Every little thing I take for granted about the world rests on the regularity of cause and effect. And yet I never see this causal power at work nor have any logical argument to tell me it is real. I have to trust that my instincts are attuned to nature. It's dizzying. But clearly it can be no other way. I bring the coffee cup to my lips, knowing entirely what to expect, but in a deeper sense not really *knowing* at all, just believing. *We have only a fragile grip on reality, one we cling to by custom, habit, and instinct.*

Reason

Just as Hume cuts the idea of "certainty" down to size, so he humbles reason without doing away with it. Hume rejects the rationalist idea that reason is a tool capable of proving matters of fact. As he puts it in a witty and incisive metaphor, "An experiment which succeeds in the air, will not always succeed in a vacuum."[74] The moral for philosophers might be even clearer if we inverted this: *An experiment which succeeds in a vacuum will not always succeed in the air.*

But for all his skeptical words about reason, in all his works Hume is very clearly reasoning. Indeed, it is only because he reasons so well that his skeptical doubts have any force. As Hume ironically notes, "It may seem a very extravagant attempt of the sceptics to destroy reason by argument and ratiocination; yet this is the grand scope of all their enquiries and disputes."[75] *You cannot even argue against reason without employing reason, since argument requires reason or it is nothing but ungrounded assertion.*

We have to change our understanding of what reason is, not reject it. Reason cannot provide us with the certainty that rationalists like Descartes believed it could. But nor can it lead us to complete Pyrrhonic skepticism, named after the Greek Pyrrho, whose ideas were transmitted to us via Sextus Empiricus's *Outlines of Pyrrhonism.* The key motto of the Pyrrhonic skeptic is "I suspend judgment" because "I am unable to say which of the objects presented I ought to believe and which I ought to disbelieve." In this state of suspension, the mind "neither affirms nor denies anything."[76]

Hume rejects this, not because he had a decisive rational argument against such skepticism but simply because "all human life must perish, were his principles universally and steadily to prevail. All discourse, all action would immediately cease; and men remain in a total lethargy, till the necessities of nature, unsatisfied, put an end to their miserable existence." This is not a serious possibility. *"Nature is always too strong for principle."*[77] Left to itself, reason would destroy all belief. Nature, not more and better arguments, is what "breaks the force of all sceptical arguments in time, and keeps them from having any considerable influence on the understanding."[78] The best remedy for skepticism is not philosophy but "carelessness and inattention."[79]

Used properly, reason therefore is neither the creator nor the destroyer of certainty. It is more of a guide through uncertainty. This form of reason Hume calls "mitigated scepticism" or "academical philosophy." It is what we end up with when we confront the excessive doubts of Pyrrhonism and "correct" them "by common sense and reflection." For Hume, *"To philosophise . . . is nothing essentially different from reasoning on common life; and we may only expect greater stability, if not greater truth, from our philosophy, on account of its exacter and more scrupulous method of proceeding."*[80]

This is a more modest form of reason but that is precisely its virtue. *We must be modest about and in our reasoning.* As Hume observed, "The greater part of mankind are naturally apt to be affirmative and dogmatical in their opinions; and while they see objects only on one side, and have no idea of any counterpoising argument, they throw themselves precipitately into the principles, to which they are inclined; nor have they any indulgence for those who entertain opposite sentiments." This is no less true today than when he wrote it. What is needed to counter this is a clearer sense of our intellectual limitations: "Could such dogmatical reasoners become sensible of the strange infirmities of human understanding, even in its most perfect state, and when most accurate and cautious in its determinations; such a reflection would naturally inspire them with more modesty and reserve, and diminish their fond opinion of themselves, and their prejudice against antagonists."[81]

Hume repeatedly encourages those who would philosophize to guard against arrogance. "Philosophers, that give themselves airs of superior wisdom and sufficiency, have a hard task, when they encounter persons of inquisitive dispositions," he warns. *"The best expedient to prevent this confusion, is to be modest in our pretensions; and even to discover the difficulty ourselves before it is objected to us.* By this means, we may make a kind of merit of our very ignorance."[82]

Modesty with regard to reason would also have another positive effect, namely "the limitation of our enquiries to such subjects as are best adapted to the narrow capacity of human understanding." We would stop speculating about matters of ultimate reality beyond our experience and instead focus on what it is within our ability to understand. *"A correct Judgment,"* says Hume, *avoids "all distant and high enquiries, confines itself to common life, and to such subjects as fall under daily practice and experience; leaving the more sublime topics to the embellishment of poets and orators, or to the arts of priests and politicians."*[83] This reminds me of Confucius's refusal to speculate about the nature of ultimate reality. "Does heaven speak?" he asks. "The four seasons pursue their courses, and all things are continually being produced, but does heaven say anything?"[84]

There is something very attractive and humane about this modest understanding of rationality. However, it might not seem clear exactly what this version of reason is. We know that it is not logical deduction. We also know that it is a kind of reasoning from experience. But the problem of induction—how we reason from limited experience to wider generalizations— does not seem to have been solved.

However, although Hume does not clearly *tell* us what the right kind of reasoning about experience is, he certainly *shows* us. From his example, we can extract several maxims for better reasoning. First, *before you begin to reason and draw conclusions, attend carefully to whatever it is you are seeking to understand.* This might seem obvious, but the history of philosophy suggests it is a rule more honored in the breach than in the observance. Hume's unusual capacity to first attend carefully is what leads him to conclude that we never actually observe cause and effect, nor, as we will see, are we ever aware of ourselves as distinct, thinking beings. Philosophy is often so fixated on the importance of sound reasoning that it forgets how important careful observation is. Seeing clearly is the precondition for thinking and understanding clearly: *"Obscurity, indeed, is painful to the mind as well as to the eye; but to bring light from obscurity, by whatever labour, must needs be delightful and rejoicing."*[85]

A second maxim of reasoning is that *a rational argument should offer compelling reasons for belief.* There are many ways an argument can do this. Philosophy tends to focus on those that involve logical steps. These can be positive or negative. A positive one is of the kind, *if this is true, that must be true.* For instance, if everything must have a cause then there must be a cause for this thing. A negative is of the kind, *if this is true, that cannot also be true.* For example, if time is infinitely divisible, then there cannot be a smallest unit of time. Note that in both of these examples, however, what we start with—the "if"—is not something that can be established philosophically, if at all. That is not accidental. It is partly for that reason that Hume places so little importance on deductive reasoning. A logical argument is only as good as its premises, and when it comes to how the world is, no premise is so secure as to allow us to make secure logical deductions from it.

Fortunately, there are other ways of offering compelling reasons for belief. One is that even though there can be no decisive way of showing which of two possible explanations must be right, we can show why one is more plausible than the other. That was how the argument against belief in miracles worked. It is simply more plausible that the experience of the vast majority of humankind the vast majority of the time is accurate than it is that one or a handful of people have accurately observed something that contradicts it. This is not a logical principle, but it is a rational one. Take it as a Humean maxim that *"rational" is not the same as "logical."*

Still, Hume's skepticism about the limits of reason goes very deep. There are many things we can do to test the reasonableness of a belief, but at bottom all we can ultimately depend upon is our own judgment. Hume puts this most starkly in the *Treatise* when he says that "all probable reasoning," that is, reasoning concerning matters of fact, "is nothing but a species of sensation. . . . When I am convinc'd of any principle, 'tis only an idea, which strikes more strongly upon me. When I give the preference to one set of arguments above another, I do nothing but decide from my feeling concerning the superiority of their influence." This is shocking since it suggests that ultimately *"'tis not solely in poetry and music, we must follow our taste and sentiment, but likewise in philosophy."* He is not saying we should follow our *unexamined* tastes and sentiments, but he is making it plain that when all reasoning is done, all we are left with to judge the quality of an argument is whether it seems to us to be strong.[86]

Ultimately, I think that Hume doesn't give us a precise account of what good reasoning consists in because no such clear and comprehensive account can be given. Although logic is algorithmic, meaning that it follows strict rules, reasoning in general is not. *There is no algorithm for good reasoning.* There are many examples of this, such as his comments on the principles that *"'tis lawful to take arms even against supreme power; and that **as government is a mere human invention for mutual advantage and security, it no longer imposes any obligation, either natural or moral, when once it ceases to have that tendency.**"* Although he believes this principle is true, he says it is "certainly impossible for the laws, or even for philosophy, to establish any particular rules, by which we may know when resistance is lawful; and decide all controversies, which may arise on that subject."[87] In other words, there are no moral algorithms we can use to help us decide when the general principle should be applied and when it should not. We are left relying only on our judgment.

That is not to say that reasoning has no structure or order at all. Hume criticized "modern orators," saying that their "great affectation of extemporary discourses has made them reject all order and method, which seems so requisite to argument, and without which it is scarcely possible to produce an entire conviction on the mind."[88] Good argument has to be thorough, careful, and systematic. It cannot leap from one point to another without establishing some connection between them.

But the requirement for order is not the same as a requirement for a formula.

Consider an analogy with music. A good piece of music is not a chaotic collection of notes. There will be a coherence of some sort, be that rhythmic, melodic, or thematic, and the piece will progress in a way that makes musical sense. But there is no way of generating a whole piece of music from its first bar. Try to capture musical composition in a finite set of principles and you will always come up against exceptions. A change in time signature can jar in one piece and delight in another. Or take the example of Mozart in Peter Shaffer's *Amadeus*. The genius composer describes a sequence from his work in progress, the opera *Figaro*. "Duet turns into trio. Then the husband's equally screaming valet comes in. Trio turns into quartet. Then a stupid old gardener—quartet becomes quintet, and so on. On and on, sextet, septet, octet! How long do you think I can sustain that?" Mozart is defying conventional ideas of what a pleasing piece of music can be. "Twenty minutes of continuous music. No recitatives." You can describe what has generally worked well in music before, but you cannot specify in advance what can and must work. Similarly, we know the most typical features of good arguments, but there is no complete set of rules that determine which work and which don't.

One way to see if an argument is a good one is simply to test it against other arguments. That is surely why Hume sought out intellectual friendships, even with people he did not agree with. Walking around the grounds of the College at La Flèche and talking with the monks was one way in which Hume could test his arguments. *You cannot judge a good argument by an absolute standard. The best argument is simply the one that has no better rival.*

This is a radical challenge to the dominant idea of rationality as something that is best exemplified in the private reasoning of individuals. Although there is a sense in which we have to be the ultimate judges of what seems most rational to us, in order to reach such a judgment we have to argue with others and hear contradictory viewpoints. As Annette Baier explains it, our notion of reason has to be "enlarged" so rationality is seen as "a social capacity, both in its activities and in the standards of excellence by which they are judged."[89]

If Hume seems to be anti-reason it is only because we have come to assume that reason is more powerful and more individualistic than it is. Interestingly, this more modest and social understanding of rationality has been given recent support by the cognitive scientists Hugo Mercier and Dan Sperber. They argue against the "intellectualist" assumption that "the job of reasoning is to help individuals achieve greater knowledge and make better decisions." They propose instead an "argumentative theory of reasoning" in which "the normal conditions for the use of reason are social, and more specifically dialogic. Outside of this environment, there is no guarantee that reasoning acts for the benefit of the reasoner."[90] It's not entirely coincidental that the subtitle of their book in the United Kingdom, *A New Theory of Human Understanding*, echoes that of Hume's seminal book on the subject.

It is not surprising that many find Hume's notion of reason too flimsy or weak. Hume knew the feeling all too well. At the end of Book I of the *Treatise*, looking forward to Books II and III, he says, "Methinks I am like a man, who having struck on many shoals, and having narrowly escap'd ship-wreck in passing a small frith, has yet the temerity to put out to sea in the same leaky weather-beaten vessel, and even carries his ambition so far as to think of compassing the globe under these disadvantageous circumstances." The cause of this misfortune is nothing less than the exercise of reason itself. *"Understanding, when it acts alone, and according to its most general principles, entirely subverts itself, and leaves not the lowest degree of evidence in any proposition, either in philosophy or common life."*[91]

Philosophers have tended to exalt reason. It is rare to find one so willing to admit that the tools of their trade are so ill-equipped for the ambition of their task. But Hume is full of doubt, both in the power of philosophy and in himself as a reasoner: "With what confidence can I venture upon such bold enterprizes, when beside those numberless infirmities peculiar to myself, I find so many which are common to human nature? Can I be sure, that in leaving all establish'd opinions I am following truth; and by what criterion shall I distinguish her, even if fortune shou'd at last guide me on her foot-steps?" *A truly ambitious philosopher must also be modest and as willing to doubt and question themselves as they are to doubt and question others.* "A true sceptic," says Hume, "will be diffident of his philosophical doubts, as well as of his philosophical conviction."[92]

Hume wrote a somewhat contrived allegory about modesty that nonetheless makes an important point.[93] Jupiter, the king of the Roman gods, initially created Virtue, Wisdom, and Confidence as a trio that belonged together, with their opposites being Vice, Folly, and Diffidence. Both groups set out along the road, but whereas Wisdom would always deliberate about which road to take, Confidence would stride on. So in time, Confidence became separated from Virtue and Wisdom. Similarly, Diffidence, "with her doubts and scruples," ended up being left behind by the more impetuous Vice and Folly. Confidence ended up blagging its way into the house of wealth, where it found Vice and Folly. Diffidence was given sanctuary in the home of Poverty, where Virtue and Wisdom had also taken shelter. So Confidence degenerated into Impudence and Diffidence mellowed into Modesty. The allegory is a warning that confidence should always be treated with suspicion and be guarded against. This is a somewhat countercultural message at a time when we are all encouraged to be confident. We are told that "confidence breeds confidence," but for Hume that is precisely the problem as it results in too much confidence. *Confidence should always be challenged, since if it is merited, it will withstand the challenge, and if it is not, it will justly crumble.*

When we challenge the confidence of philosophy, we find that it is largely unwarranted. However, the only alternative to pursuing philosophy in full awareness of its limitations is either to pretend the enterprise is more robust than it is or to give up on it altogether. The choice is "betwixt a false reason and none at all." The first path is dishonest, the second, says Hume, impossible. We cannot take it as "a general maxim, that no refin'd or elaborate reasoning is ever to be receiv'd." That would require us to "cut off entirely all science and philosophy" and proceed solely on the basis of gut instinct, imagination, or superstition. Nor can we simply give up on thinking about philosophical matters altogether because it is in our nature to think beyond our immediate needs, to question, to seek to understand. We have to embark on that quest and so "we ought only to deliberate concerning the choice of our guide, and ought to prefer that which is safest and most agreeable."[94] That, says Hume, is philosophy, meaning evidence-based reasoning of all sorts, which for all its imperfection is superior to anything else we might try instead. Adapting Winston Churchill, we might say *reason is the worst means of understanding except for all those other forms that have been tried from time to time.*

Impressions and Ideas

Before I went to La Flèche, I only had vague and fuzzy ideas of what it was like, composed of some generic images of French villages, wine valleys, and monasteries. While I was there, the town was made real. Now that I am back in Bristol, I retain some memories, more vivid than my prior ideas but less strong than my actual experience of being there. Commonsense observations like these about the contents of our minds formed the basis of one of the central arguments of Hume's *Treatise*.

For Hume, everything we are aware of is called a "perception of the mind." Such perceptions come in two varieties, *impressions* and *ideas*. The most natural way to distinguish the two is to say that impressions are firsthand perceptions whereas ideas are the mind's secondhand copies of them. So, before I went to La Flèche I had vague *ideas* about it, conjured by imagination. While I was there, I had *impressions* of the town and area, produced by the place itself. And when I returned, I retained *ideas* formed from these impressions about La Flèche in the form of my memories.

Hume believed the difference was obvious, being more or less the commonsense distinction "betwixt feeling and thinking." However, he did not primarily distinguish between ideas and impressions in this way. Rather, he made the distinction rest on how vivid or lively the perceptions of the mind were. Impressions strike us with "force and violence" whereas ideas are faint and weak in comparison. "The most lively thought is still inferior to the dullest sensation."[95] He did this, it seems, because he wanted to define ideas and impressions by their own nature, not on the basis of what typically caused them, in part because, atypically, impressions can actually be caused by ideas. Sympathy, for instance, is "the conversion of an idea into an impression." Emotions transfer by a kind of contagion: "The sentiments of others can never affect us, but by becoming, in some measure, our own."[96] We perceive someone as being in a particular emotional state, we form an idea of that, and from that idea is generated a similar feeling in ourselves. We can even generate such impressions from the mere thought of a feeling. "An idea of a sentiment or passion," says Hume, can "be so inliven'd as to become the very sentiment or passion." A poet or a novelist, for example, can convey the idea of, say, grief so powerfully that we are moved to tears reading it, genuinely feeling grief ourselves. This is possible because emotions are always generated from within, and so "they arise more naturally from the imagination, and from every lively idea we form of them."[97]

So the mind is filled with ideas, derived from impressions. In order for the mind not to become a mess of unrelated ideas, it has to organize them in some way. It does this by means of three "principles of association" that link ideas: contiguity in time and space, resemblance, and causation. There was, he argued, no association we make between ideas in the mind that is not based on some version of these three. Although Hume does a very good job of showing the plausibility of this theory, Baier questions how he could have been so sure there are three and only three principles of association. "Hume's own theories may have included dogmatic elements," she says, arguing that "there is some tension between Hume's official scepticism and the assurance of his own philosophy of mind."[98]

Many a reader has been deterred by the seemingly interminable discussion of ideas and impressions in Book I of the *Treatise*, and in the later *Enquiry*. I confess that I also find it tedious. So why did Hume devote so much time and space to it? The most obvious answer is that he thought it was the very foundation of his new system of philosophy. In essence, Hume wanted to base philosophy on the study of human nature. This meant he had to account for where we got our ideas from. He seemed to think it very important to show that the source of all our knowledge was experience.

To see why this was so important to him, we have to understand that Hume was working in a tradition where the argument about whether we had any knowledge independently of experience was an extremely hot one. The likes of Plato and Descartes had believed that we have innate ideas, that is to say, ideas that are in some sense already in our minds, waiting to be discovered, and which don't require experience to verify. For Descartes, this had theological significance. It meant that we could know that God exists purely by examining our idea of God and seeing that God's perfection entails that he exists. This is an example of how the concept of innate ideas was seen as part and parcel of a rationalist understanding, in which we could come to know some things about the nature of reality by thought and reasoning alone.

Hume, as an advocate of empiricism, thus wanted nothing to do with innate ideas. He followed John Locke, one of the first empiricists, who compared the human mind at birth to a *tabula rasa*: a blank slate or white sheet of paper. "Let us then suppose the mind to be, as we say, white paper void of all characters, without any ideas," he wrote. "How comes it to be furnished? Whence comes it by that vast store which the busy and boundless fancy of man has painted on it with an almost endless variety? Whence has it all the materials of reason and knowledge? To this I answer, in one word, from *experience*."[99]

This debate has rumbled on ever since. In its most recent manifestations it has mutated into the battle between nature and nurture: Are human beings fashioned by genes or life experiences? All reputable scientists, however, now accept that the war is a phony one. Human beings are shaped by nature *and* nurture. The only real dispute is what precisely each contributes, and how much.

The narrower question of the extent to which the human mind is a blank slate has similarly ceased to be an either/or dispute. In fact, it has been since at least 1912, when Bertrand Russell published his *The Problems of Philosophy*. "One of the great historic controversies in philosophy is the controversy between the two schools called respectively 'empiricists' and 'rationalists.'" Empiricists maintain "that all our knowledge is derived from experience" whereas the rationalists maintain that, "in addition to what we know by experience, there are certain 'innate ideas' and 'innate principles', which we know independently of experience."[100]

Russell claims that "it has now become possible to decide with some confidence as to the truth or falsehood of these opposing schools." The rationalists were right that the principles of logic which tell us whether our reasoning is constant or contradictory "cannot be themselves proved by experience, since all proof presupposes them." The empiricists were right, however, that even this knowledge cannot be obtained unless it is "elicited and caused by experience." Without experience, the principles of logic would never become evident to us. Hence Russell prefers to call logic "*a priori*"—from first principles, rather than "innate," since the strict meaning of innate is that which we are born with.

On another point, however, the empiricists were certainly correct: "Nothing can be known to *exist* except by the help of experience." This is what really matters for Hume's project. It is what is required to maintain the difference between matters of fact and the relation of ideas. As long as this distinction holds, Hume doesn't need to insist that *all* knowledge comes from experience. And if he doesn't need to do that, he doesn't need to show that all ideas are derived from impressions. However, it seems Hume was too caught up in the debate over innate ideas to see this clearly. He thought his empiricism required the rejection of all innate ideas, and so he spent too much time pointlessly trying to show how his theory of ideas and impressions accounted for all we could know.

However, there are at least three signs that Hume himself must have realized less was at stake than his protracted reasonings suggested. The first is a famous passage in which Hume imagines a person who had never seen a particular shade of blue. Now imagine that "all the different shades of that colour, except that single one, be placed before him." Could he, in his imagination, fill in the blank space? This question, known as the "missing shade of blue," is often taken to be a challenge to Hume's view that all ideas have their origins in impressions since most people think such a person *would* be able to fill in the gap by using their imagination. Perhaps surprisingly, Hume is one of them. "I believe there are few but will be of opinion that he can; and this may serve as a proof, that the simple ideas are not always derived from the correspondent impressions." It would seem then that Hume himself has come upon a decisive counterexample against his own theory. And yet far from taking it as terminal, he simply observes "the instance is so particular and singular, that 'tis scarce worth our observing, and does not merit that for it alone we should alter our general maxim."[101]

What explains Hume's nonchalant waving away of an apparently devastating challenge? The uncharitable answer is that he is displaying a vice he himself so acutely observed in others: that of being so enchanted by his own philosophy that he is blind to its failings. But that is not consistent with him drawing the problem to the attention of the reader. A more consistent interpretation is that Hume was here acknowledging that it does not matter whether literally every idea comes from experience, merely that all the major and important ones do. The fact that we can imagine a color very similar to one we have already seen does not in any way suggest that we can come to knowledge of things completely outside our experience by reason alone.

A second reason for thinking that Hume was less concerned that all knowledge comes from experience is his entire theory of cause and effect. On the one hand, it is precisely because we seem to lack an impression of causation that he spends so much time discussing the source of the idea. Many writers get so caught up in how Hume despairs of locating the source impression that they carelessly conclude Hume never found it. In fact, he clearly did, as he explains in *An Enquiry concerning Human Understanding*. We form the *idea* of necessary connection, on which cause and effect is based, from the *impression* we have of the mind itself moving from what we perceive to be the cause to what we perceive to be its effect. I've quoted the key sentence already but its importance makes it worth repeating: "This connexion, therefore, which we feel in the mind, this customary transition of the imagination from one object to its usual attendant, is the sentiment or impression, from which we form the idea of power or necessary connexion."[102]

On the one hand, this solves Hume's puzzle about the impression on which the idea of cause and effect is based. On the other, since it locates that impression in the mind and not in the world, it is an acknowledgment that not all of our ideas come from experience of the world, as pure empiricism would maintain. Hume's whole theory of causation entails that at least one key feature of how we understand the world comes from our minds, not from experience. Far from being a *tabula rasa*, the mind comes equipped at the very least with an instinct to perceive causation. Hume explicitly acknowledges this in the *Enquiry* when he says our inferences from cause to effect "are a species of natural instincts, which no reasoning or process of the thought and understanding is able, either to produce, or to prevent."[103]

The third and clinching piece of evidence that Hume fully accepted that not everything derives from experience is that he says in the *Treatise* that "reason is nothing but a wonderful and unintelligible instinct in our souls."[104] He reiterates this in *An Enquiry concerning Human Understanding*, saying, "The experimental reasoning itself, which we possess in common with beasts, and on which the whole conduct of life depends, is nothing but a species of instinct or mechanical power."[105]

For non-academic readers of Hume, his theory of ideas and impressions might seem technical and dull. The fact that two of his most important works spend much time setting them out is surely one reason why Hume is not more widely read than he is. But without getting bogged down in the details of theory, it should be possible to appreciate its spirit. Hume is telling us *the world of experience and our representations of it is the only world we can know, and so that has to be the world we seek to understand better.*

We can see why Hume believed his *Treatise* was philosophically revolutionary and was bound to cause a stir. He was initially satisfied with his work, and he left France believing he had expressed his opinions "with such Elegance & Neatness, as to draw to me the Attention of the World."[106] The epigram from Tacitus that he attached to the first two volumes speaks of his optimism: "*Rara temporum felicitate, ubi sentire quae velis, et quae sentias dicere licet*" ("It is the rare fortune of these days that one may think what one likes and say what one thinks"). Hume had dared to say what he thought, and he believed the time was right for his radical new philosophy to be received. After all, the old philosophies had proven themselves to be bankrupt. Philosophers had fallen in love with abstract speculation and had lost touch with reality. In a damning indictment of his predecessors and peers he said, *"Whatever has the air of a paradox, and is contrary to the first and most unprejudic'd notions of mankind is often greedily embrac'd by philosophers, as shewing the superiority of their science, which cou'd discover opinions so remote from vulgar conception."*[107]

For many years, the general consensus among scholars was that Hume had indeed done his best work in Anjou. Lytton Strachey expressed a common view when he claimed that "had Hume died at the age of twenty-six his real work in the world would have been done, and his fame irrevocably established."[108] Only recently has this view been widely challenged. It took much less time, however, for Hume's hopes for immediate success to be dashed.

CHAPTER THREE

The Meaning of Success

*How happens it that we Philosophers cannot as heartily despise
the World as it despises us?*

Dead-Born from the Press

When Hume returned to Britain in September 1737 he initially
lived in London. He lasted barely eighteen months there, perhaps, suggests his biographer Mossner, because "he was alien-
ated by London contempt for provincials and Scotsmen" and
"missed the cosmopolitanism of Paris and France, and even of
Edinburgh."[1]

More disappointing than London, however, was how his
Treatise was received: "Never literary attempt was more unfortunate than my *A Treatise of Human Nature*," he later recalled in
his memoir. This is an exaggeration. A writer in an Edinburgh
magazine said, "I was in Edinburgh soon after the original publication, and well remember how much and how frequently it
was mentioned, in every literary conversation."[2] Nonetheless,
the book was hardly a sensation and Hume was evidently
deeply disappointed by its lukewarm reception. "I am now out
of Humour with myself," he wrote to the judge and writer

Henry Home, on hearing of his sales, but hoped "not in a little time to be only out of Humour with the World, like other unsuccessful Authors." He chastised himself for the "folly" of his reaction since "I cou'd not expect any better from such abstract Reasoning, nor indeed did I promise myself much better."[3]

However, Hume was convinced that the problem was not the substantive content of the book but how he had expressed his ideas. "I had always entertained a notion," he recalled in his autobiography, "that my want of success in publishing the *A Treatise of Human Nature,* had proceeded more from the manner than the matter, and that I had been guilty of a very usual indiscretion, in going to the press too early." Over the coming years Hume therefore recast the arguments of the *Treatise* in *An Enquiry concerning Human Understanding* and *An Enquiry concerning the Principles of Morals.* Hume disowned the *Treatise* and asked readers to consult only these later works instead. Indeed, the *Treatise* was not included in any edition of Hume's collected writings published in his lifetime.[4] Posterity, however, reversed this judgment. The orthodox view is the one printed on the jacket of a 1987 edition I acquired as a student: "*A Treatise of Human Nature* is the major philosophical work of David Hume."

The real misfortune of the *Treatise* was not that it was ignored but that it was widely misunderstood and misrepresented. Thomas Reid was typical in dismissing the work as an entirely negative attempt to bring everything into doubt. "The ingenious author of that treatise," he wrote, "hath built a system of scepticism, which leaves no ground to believe any one thing rather than its contrary." He said the intention of the work was "to shew, that there is neither human nature nor science in the world."[5]

This reading of the *Treatise* would persist for decades. For instance, Dugald Stuart's entry in the 1815–17 edition of the

Encyclopaedia Britannica said Hume's "aim is to establish a universal scepticism, and to produce in the reader a complete distrust in his own faculties."[6]

In response to this widespread misunderstanding, Hume felt obliged to publish an abstract of the *Treatise* in 1740, the original title of which barely concealed his irritation: *An Abstract of a late Philosophical Performance, entitled A Treatise of Human Nature, &c. Wherein the Chief Argument and Design of that Book, which has met with such Opposition, and been represented in so terrifying a Light, is further illustrated and explain'd.* This suggests Hume may not have been quite as accepting of the book's fate as he later claimed to be when he wrote, "being naturally of a cheerful and sanguine temper, I very soon recovered from the blow."[7] However, he did calm down enough to remove the clause "*which has met with such Opposition, and been represented in so terrifying a Light*" from the title of the *Abstract* in its reprintings.[8]

Probably the most damaging attack on the *Treatise* was a pamphlet by Rev. William Wishart, Principal of Edinburgh University, called *Specimen of the Principles concerning Religion and Morality, said to be maintain'd in a Book lately published, intituled, A Treatise of Human Nature.* Hume felt obliged to publish a reply to this, called *A Letter from a Gentleman to his Friend In Edinburgh: Containing Some Observations on a Specimen . . . .* In this Hume makes it clear that he is bringing human reason down to earth, not dismissing it. The purpose of the skeptical doubts expressed in the *Treatise* is simply "to abate the Pride of mere human Reasoners, by showing them, that even with regard to Principles which seem the clearest, and which they are necessitated from the strongest Instincts of Nature to embrace, they are not able to attain a full Consistence and absolute Certainty. Modesty then, and Humility, with regard to the

Operations of our natural Faculties, is the Result of Scepticism; not an universal Doubt, which it is impossible for any Man to support, and which the first and most trivial Accident in Life must immediately disconcert and destroy."[9]

These controversies show that Hume's claim that the *Treatise* "fell dead-born from the press" was wide of the mark. As Mossner points out, it actually achieved such a notoriety as to make him deemed "unfit to teach the young."[10] Rasmussen also challenges Hume's complaint that the *Treatise* "had failed even to excite a murmur among the zealots," pointing out that his own decision to remove the most controversial chapters on religion made sure it didn't do so.[11] It was enough, however, to give him a reputation as a dangerous thinker. Wishart's unjust and inaccurate attack in particular probably cost Hume the appointment of the Chair of Ethics and Pneumatical ("Mental") Philosophy at Edinburgh University in 1745, an academic position that his talents surely merited. He was similarly thwarted when he was proposed for the chair in logic at Glasgow University in 1751. However, it is perhaps fortunate that he didn't get either job. Hume's own experience of university study was negative, and it is not obvious he would have relished the teaching and the other trappings of university life.

Chance, Choice, and Freedom

I have often been struck by how arbitrary Hume's path frequently was. So often, it took a turn here when it could just as easily have taken another there. It was far from inevitable that Hume's two candidacies for professorships were rejected. Had he been offered either, how would his life have been different? What would have happened if he had tried working for a more congenial merchant in Bristol? What if the *Treatise* had been more favorably received? Sometimes it only takes one influential figure to champion a work for its reputation to soar. There are many more such forks in the road to come, as we shall see.

There are two aspects of this that I find myself mulling over. One is the role of chance in life. Anyone who looks back at their own past will see that so many key changes in direction were the result of pure chance. The very existence of this book you are reading is owed more to luck than to any master plan on my part. This is something Hume does not discuss at any length in any of his writings. In his letters he often makes passing reference to his good fortune, mainly in having a cheerful temperament. In his philosophy, he deals with the concept of chance only to reject it. "Chance has no place, on any hypothesis, sceptical or religious," says Philo, presumably speaking for Hume in his *Dialogues concerning Natural Religion*. "Every thing is surely governed by steady, inviolable laws."[12] This is taken to be so uncontroversial that another character, Demea, also says, "*Chance is a word without a meaning.*"[13] For Hume, "what the vulgar call chance is nothing but a secret and conceal'd cause."[14] Nothing happens without a cause, but when we are ignorant of what that cause is, it seems to us that what happened could just as easily have *not* happened, and so it only happened by chance. But if we accept that everything has a cause and causes necessarily produce their effects, everything happens from necessity and there is no kind of "chance" in the universe that is an exception to this. (Even in quantum theory, randomness only occurs at the subatomic level, and even then only in some interpretations.) So "we conclude," says Hume, "that the chance or indifference lies only in our judgment on account of our imperfect knowledge, not in the things themselves, which are in every case equally necessary, tho' to appearance not equally constant or certain."[15]

However, this is not the only meaning of chance. When we talk of chance in the sense of "luck" or "fortune," we are not necessarily thinking about whether everything is ultimately the result of the necessary laws of causation. Rather, we are often simply thinking about how what happens to us is due to factors out of our control that have no interest in how our lives turn out. We are unlucky to be caught in a tsunami, even though there is a sense in which the wave was an inevitable consequence of an inevitable geological event and we were always going to be where it hit. We talk of ill fortune here because nothing we did made us more or less deserving of our fate than anyone else.

Hume certainly believed in this kind of chance and made passing reference to it in several places. Most notably, he seemed to accept that material wealth is more often down to chance than merit: *possession of a large fortune is largely dependent on fortune.* For instance, Hume noted that society required "the stability of possession," meaning that there have to be secure rights of ownership governed by rules. These rights have to start by granting ownership to what people already have in their possession and then govern what is theirs by right of "occupation, prescription, accession, and succession." Hume notes that "these depend very much on chance," which is frequently "contradictory both to men's wants and desires."[16] Even the fruits of our hard work are in part determined by chance because innovation is rewarded but "good fortune frequently contributes to all this, by discovering the effects that result from the different mixtures and combinations of bodies."[17]

Hume evidently thought that the importance of this kind of chance was not widely appreciated. When it came to their own characters, for instance, people liked to believe anything good was due to merit rather than fortune. Hence he said of clergymen that "if by chance any of them be possessed of a temper more susceptible of devotion than usual, so that he has but little occasion for hypocrisy to support the character of his profession; it is so natural for him to over-rate this advantage, and to think that it atones for every violation of morality, that frequently he is not more virtuous than the hypocrite."[18] The general point is that *our tendency to overrate our own virtues leads us to overlook our own vices.*

Hume also believed that it was a vice of philosophers and intellectuals not to admit that they do not know why certain things happen. They are therefore reluctant to put it down to chance, in the sense of the causes being unknown. Such an admission would leave "the writer in the same state of ignorance with the rest of mankind." If, however, he can claim to describe the exact causes, "he may then display his ingenuity, in assigning these causes; and as a man of any subtilty can never be at a loss in this particular, he has thereby an opportunity of swelling his volumes, and discovering his profound knowledge, in observing what escapes the vulgar and ignorant."[19] I think of this when reading op-eds by many pundits, confident that their analysis makes sense of events in the world that, in reality, no one fully understands. I also try to remember it when I am in the position of writing such an op-ed, hoping to catch myself before offering an analysis that testifies more to my ability to impose an order on the subject than it does to any order it really possesses.

Hume's beliefs that chance in the strict sense doesn't exist but that chance in the looser sense does are intimately connected. It is precisely because the world moves inexorably forward according to principles of cause and effect that we can never be in full control of our destinies or be entirely responsible for our successes or failures. *To believe that the universe is governed by laws, not chance, is to believe more strongly in the reality of luck in everyday life.* That should engender the core Humean virtue we come back to again and again: modesty.

There is, however, another aspect of this period of Hume's life and the way in which it could have taken a different direction that resonates particularly with me. Hume missed out on becoming a professor but in the long run that seems to have done him no harm, and perhaps some great benefit. He always valued his independence, and that would have been compromised by the formal duties of a university job and by the informal obligation to conform and avoid any controversy. Those were among the reasons why he allowed himself to be put forward for both the Edinburgh and Glasgow posts somewhat reluctantly—"contrary to my opinion and advice" in the latter case. He was tempted, however, because such a post would have provided a stable income, access to a good library, and recognition from the establishment. This latter advantage is one we have every reason to believe Hume desired, no matter how much his philosophical mind told him it was worthless. When he was elected to the more modest office of keeper of the Advocates' Library, he wrote to John Clephene that "I have been ready to burst with vanity and self-conceit."[20] How much prouder would he have been to have become a university professor?

So there were clearly pros and cons of becoming a professor, and it would have been difficult to judge where the balance of benefits tipped. But Hume did not have to decide. "Chance," meaning events outside of his control and not strictly determined by his merits, saw to it that he continued down the road of independent scholarship.

Given what Hume wrote about pride, however, we should not expect him to be entirely against it, nor free of it himself. He argued that a proper degree of pride was natural and benign, as long as it doesn't descend into vanity. Regardless of what Christianity might say, "the world naturally esteems a well-regulated pride, which secretly animates our conduct without breaking out into such indecent expressions of vanity, as may offend the vanity of others."[21]

He thought it "unjust" that people routinely downgraded the virtue of any action which carries with it any hint of pride, as though that contaminated it and rendered any other motive null and void. "Vanity is so closely allied to virtue," he argued, "and to love the fame of laudable actions approaches so near the love of laudable actions for their own sake, that these passions are more capable of mixture, than any other kinds of affection; and it is almost impossible to have the latter without some degree of the former."[22] The reason for this is that by "our continual and earnest pursuit of a character, a name, a reputation in the world, we bring our own deportment and conduct frequently in review, and consider how they appear in the eyes of those who approach and regard us. This constant habit of surveying ourselves, as it were, in reflection, keeps alive all the sentiments of right and wrong, and begets, in noble natures, a certain reverence for themselves as well as others; which is the surest guardian of every virtue."[23] *Proper pride is taking satisfaction from having done what you judge to be right or of value, without the vanity of believing that makes you superior or special.*

But if chance plays such an important role in life and so little of what we do is due to our own choices, what right do we have to feel any pride (or shame) at all? This leads us to the perennially controversial topic of free will. Hume's treatment of this subject was radical and skeptical. He defined a position that is, in broad terms, still the most popular among professional Western philosophers today.

A human being is, for Hume, as much a part of the natural world as anything else. Therefore our actions must also be subject to the same laws of cause and effect as everything else. Yet it is commonly supposed that humans have a capacity of free will that allows us to make choices that are undetermined by prior causes. If this were the case, human choices would be causes but not effects. Were this true, it would make them unique among everything else in the universe. On this view, says Hume, "it is pretended, that some causes are necessary, some not necessary."[24]

For Hume, this would make free choice something of a miracle, an exception to the laws of nature. As we have seen, Hume did not believe in miracles, let alone ones that we perform every minute of every day. So he believed that human actions were as much determined by prior causes as anything else. "The conjunction between motives and voluntary actions is as regular and uniform," he claimed, "as that between the cause and effect in any part of nature." Hume maintained that far from being controversial, "this regular conjunction has been universally acknowledged among mankind, and has never been the subject of dispute, either in philosophy or common life."[25]

As evidence for this, he explains how our everyday actions depend upon the regularity of human behavior as much as they do the regularity of nature. When we drive, we need to assume that drivers as well as cars will behave as they usually do. Hume gives a more colorful example of a prisoner who "discovers the impossibility of his escape, as well from the obstinacy of the gaoler, as from the walls and bars with which he is surrounded; and in all attempts for his freedom chuses rather to work upon the stone and iron of the one, than upon the inflexible nature of the other." The prisoner perceives the same necessity and inevitability in the behavior of people as he does in buildings. So "the same prisoner, when conducted to the scaffold, foresees his death as certainly from the constancy and fidelity of his guards as from the operation of the ax or wheel."[26]

Although it is true that we depend on a certain regularity in human behavior, people do not generally think this is entirely mechanistic, as nature's workings are. This is largely because we do not appear to behave with the same predictable regularity as plants and animals. But Hume argued this is simply because the determinants of human behavior are more complicated and therefore less predictable than many other aspects of nature. That does not mean they are less determined by prior causes. Unexpected behaviors are not uncaused; their causes are simply less obvious. If we understood the full circumstances better we would easily see why they occurred. "The most irregular and unexpected resolutions of men may frequently be accounted for by those, who know every particular circumstance of their character and situation." For instance, "A person of an obliging disposition gives a peevish answer: But he has the toothake, or has not dined."[27] In my own case, I can testify that such conditions are as certain to cause peevishness in me as water is certain to dissolve sugar.

In claiming this is no more than common sense Hume is being either optimistic or disingenuous. Many people, perhaps most, do believe that they have a kind of free will, which means their choices and actions are not determined by any prior causes but originate in their own volition. Why do so many believe this "doctrine of liberty" that Hume says is both "absurd" and "unintelligible"? One reason is that we find it hard to believe that we are "governed by necessity, and that it was utterly impossible for us to have acted otherwise." This idea of necessity seems "to imply something of force, and violence, and

constraint." Since we *feel* none of this, we assume our actions
are not in any way necessary, and we have freedom. Unaware of
all the hidden causes of our actions, it feels to us as though the
only thing causing our actions is our willing them. Indeed, this
feeling that we are the originating causes of actions is the source
of the concept of the will. "By the will," says Hume, "I mean
nothing but *the internal impression we feel and are conscious of,
when we knowingly give rise to any new motion of our body, or new
perception of our mind.*"[28]

Hume thinks one source of our muddled thinking about free
will is a failure to distinguish between "the liberty of spontaneity"
and "the liberty of indifference."[29] Liberty of spontaneity is simply the ability of an agent to act uncoerced, without being
forced to act in a certain way by an external agent. Liberty of
indifference is the ability to act free from the necessity of cause
and effect. The latter is an impossibility. Freedom of spontaneity is the only true freedom we have. The only possible true
sense of liberty is therefore "*a power of acting or not acting, according to the determinations of the will*; that is, if we chuse to
remain at rest, we may; if we chuse to move, we also may. Now
this hypothetical liberty is universally allowed to belong to
every one, who is not a prisoner and in chains."[30]

A common objection to this account of human liberty is that
it is a threat to morality. If we are not the ultimate causes of our
actions, how can we be held responsible for them? For Hume,
however, the threat is only to religious morality. Its need for
absolute responsibility in order to make the rewards of heaven
and the punishments of hell just is one reason why the false
doctrine of liberty has been so dominant. "There is no method
of reasoning more common, and yet none more blameable,
than in philosophical debates to endeavour to refute any hypothesis by a pretext of its dangerous consequences to religion

and morality," says Hume. *"When any opinion leads us into absurdities, 'tis certainly false; but 'tis not certain an opinion is false, because 'tis of dangerous consequence."*[31]

But even the non-religious often protest that if there is a real sense in which, "if it was utterly impossible for us to have acted otherwise," how can we be held accountable for our actions? Hume turns this objection on its head. He argues it is only because "our motives have a regular and uniform influence on the mind" that we can have any notion of moral responsibility at all.[32] "Where would be the foundation of *morals*, if particular characters had no certain or determinate power to produce particular sentiments, and if these sentiments had no constant operation on actions?"[33]

The best way to make this case is negatively: think of cases where actions are *not* the result of settled and stable causes in a person's character. When people's actions are random and capricious, we don't believe they have free will; we think they are mad or careless. Their actions "have less regularity and constancy than the actions of wise-men, and consequently are farther remov'd from necessity."[34]

Hume makes his case clear and persuasively in a short paragraph in *An Enquiry concerning Human Understanding*:

> Actions are, by their very nature, temporary and perishing; and where they proceed not from some *cause* in the character and disposition of the person who performed them, they can neither redound to his honour, if good; nor infamy, if evil. The actions themselves may be blameable; they may be contrary to all the rules of morality and religion: But the person is not answerable for them; and as they proceeded from nothing in him, that is durable and constant, and leave nothing of that nature behind them, it is impossible he can,

upon their account, become the object of punishment or vengeance.[35]

He goes on to add, "Actions are objects of our moral sentiment, so far only as they are indications of the internal character, passions, and affections; it is impossible that they can give rise either to praise or blame, where they proceed not from these principles, but are derived altogether from external violence."[36]

Hume's skepticism about free will can be read in two ways. The first is that he is entirely demolishing the idea, plain and simple. In the *Treatise*, this negative mission is more pronounced, as he denounces the "fantastical system of liberty."[37] In his later *An Enquiry concerning Human Understanding*, however, which reworked the arguments of the *Treatise*, he describes his philosophy of free will as a "reconciling project."[38] The idea here is that he is showing us that we can have everything we want and need from the idea of free will without a mistaken belief in "liberty of indifference." This general approach has been called "compatibilism" and remains the most popular position on free will held by philosophers in the English-speaking world today.

The Middle Station

In February 1739, Hume left London and returned to live at Ninewells. At this point in his life Hume was neither rich nor poor, famous nor obscure. An essay published three years later suggests he was more than content enough like this, in what the essay's title called "the middle station of life." Hume quotes Agur's prayer:

> Two Things have I requir'd of thee, deny me them not before I die, Remove far from me Vanity and Lies; Give me

neither Poverty nor Riches, feed me with Food convenient for me: Lest I be full and deny thee, and say, Who is the Lord? Or lest I be poor, and steal, and take the Name of my GOD in vain.

Hume takes this as the perfect expression of the idea that the extremes of neither poverty nor riches are conducive to a virtuous and happy life. "The Great are too much immers'd in Pleasure; and the Poor too much occupy'd in providing for the Necessities of Life, to hearken to the calm Voice of Reason." If someone in the middle station realizes this, they can even get some pleasure from "comparing his Situation with that of Persons above or below him." This is an intriguing contradiction of the almost universal advice *not* to compare yourself to others if you want to be happy. But the comparison Hume encourages fosters the very opposite of envy. If we genuinely believe we are better off *not* being as well off as some others are, comparing ourselves to the wealthy becomes a form of affirmation rather than jealousy and avarice.[39] There is an almost riddle-like maxim here: **Although the worst is to be among the worst off, and it's better to be among the best off, it's best merely to be better off.**

Perhaps Hume overstated his belief in the merits of the middle station. It is striking that in the *Treatise* he says, "Nothing has a greater tendency to give us an esteem for any person, than his power and riches; or a contempt, than his poverty and meanness."[40] Perhaps these were the words of a young man still bedazzled by worldly goods. He clearly did still have ambitions at this time. The relative failure of the *Treatise* led him to try his hand at a different literary form: the essay. These required greater concision and clarity, a discipline that Hume appeared to relish. These essays were his first genuine success as a writer, and they were published in two volumes of *Essays, Moral, Political, and Literary* in 1741 and 1752.

Hume spent most of the next twelve years at Ninewells, with a hiatus between the springs of 1745 and 1749 occupied with a series of somewhat eccentric diversions.[41] He was briefly a tutor to the young Marquess of Annandale, but soon discovered he was insane and the whole household was dysfunctional. His escape came via an acceptance of an invitation from his cousin, Lieutenant-General James St. Clair, to join a military expedition in Quebec as his secretary. Given that this would doubtless have involved death and killing, it seems odd that such a genial *bon viveur* as Hume viewed the prospect as "Such a Romantic Adventure."[42]

The maritime winds, however, did not favor the fleet and the expedition was canceled. Hume wrote a short account called "Descent on the coast of Brittany" that reveals what happened next.[43] Pondering how they might avoid wasting the collected resources and manpower, the general suggested to the secretary of state, "Why may you not send the squadron and troops to some part of the coast of France, and at least frighten and alarm them as they have done us?" To which the answer should have been, "How long have you got?" For a start, the general "had no single map of any part of France on board with him; and what intelligence he may be able to force from the people of the country can be but little to be depended on, as it must be their interest to mislead him. . . . The ignorance of the country, and want of guides, was a desperate evil, for which the General could provide no remedy."

Despite these not insignificant hurdles, they went ahead with their "plan for annoying the French" and were initially successful, landing their troops and having sight of the town. The engineers informed the general that they could "destroy the town, by laying it in ashes in twenty-four hours." It turned out, however, that the chief engineer was incompetent, placing the cannons too far away and at the wrong angle, and forgetting to light a furnace for the supposedly devastating "red-hot balls." They had no choice but to retreat.

Hume's account and subsequent writings suggest that he had only ever lamented the incompetence of the Lorient raid, never doubting its rightness, even though to contemporary eyes it seems both pointless and lacking any principled justification. Hume exonerates St. Clair from any blame, saying the general "neither proposed it, nor planned it, nor approved it, nor answered for its success" and "had no pilots, guides, nor intelligence, afforded him." He concludes with the stark statement that the expedition ended with "the loss of near twenty men killed or wounded, on the whole enterprise," as though that were a trifling number and that it was not even necessary to distinguish the dead from the wounded.

This military interregnum reminds us that for all his genius, Hume was a still a man of his time. In philosophy, his skepticism was acute, but he often failed to use that skeptical eye to question many of the social mores and conventions of the time. Fighting the French was something that the British just did, and a gentleman would take his place on a military expedition without question. *Even the keenest eye has blind spots: no one's field of vision is entirely in focus.* This is a hard lesson to learn. We may believe we are above simplistic hero worship and never put people on pedestals as though they were more divine than mortal. But even when we don't succumb to absolute idolatry, we are never comfortable to admit serious flaws in the people we most admire. We tend instead to either ignore evidence that they have any or explain them away as less serious than they really are.

Such a tendency is one any admirer of David Hume should resist. We appreciate Hume for his honest, clear intellect and so should apply that same intellectual rigor to his life and character as much as anything else. When we do, however, we find some things that most of his modern aficionados find uncomfortable, such as his racism. More generally, he is much loved by academics, who tend to be liberal in their political outlooks. But the evidence is that, although Hume was fairly liberal for his time, he tended toward the conservative.

For example, a recent biographer, James Harris, describes in some detail an incident in 1768 in which an MP, John Wilkes, was imprisoned for "outlawry." Wilkes was something of an opportunist agitator and he turned his cause into one about free speech and liberty, winning the support of many of London's merchants and tradesmen, who had understandable grievances of their own. Wilkes whipped up public indignation and during the rioting that then erupted, soldiers opened fire on a crowd, killing twenty people and wounding many others.[44] Hume, however, showed no sympathy for the crowd. In fact, he seems to be contemptuous of the "rascally mob," saying that they "roar liberty" even though they had "more liberty than any people in the world; a great deal more than they deserve; and perhaps more than any men ought to have."[45]

This fits a pattern in which Hume frequently expressed skepticism at the wisdom of greater democracy that would put more power into the hands of ordinary men and women. "Nothing indeed can be a stronger Presumption of Falsehood than the Approbation of the Multitude," he once wrote to Adam Smith.[46] Although he once described "the consent of the people" as "surely the best and most sacred of any" foundation of government, consent is very different from rule *by* the people.[47] The people should have their say, but they should not always get their way. "The people," wrote Hume, "would want wisdom, without the senate: The senate, without the people, would want honesty."[48] Indeed, after the Wilkes affair he even revised his essay "Of the Liberty of the Press," removing the section arguing that this titular right "is attended with so few inconveniences, that it may be claimed as the common right of mankind." It would seem his fear of the "mob" had made him less inclined to reform, and he made no comments in support of proposals to expand the voting class or even Edmund Burke's more modest proposals to make the cabinet less powerful.[49]

He was also opposed to republicanism, which he thought was only suitable for small states and in one like Britain would "only produce anarchy, which is the immediate forerunner of despotism."[50] In an essay on British government he made his support for monarchy quite clear. "Here I would frankly declare, that, though liberty be preferable to slavery, in almost every case; yet I should rather wish to see an absolute monarch than a republic in this island," he wrote. Any such republic would not be the utopia republicans envisaged since in order even to establish it, the leader of the republic would have to take so much power as to be, in effect, an absolute monarch. This would be much worse than the actual form of British monarchy, where the sovereign is held in check by Parliament. "Thus, if we have reason to be more jealous of monarchy, because the danger is more imminent from that quarter; we have also reason to be more jealous of popular government, because that danger is more terrible. This may teach us a lesson of moderation in all our political controversies."[51]

Hume also believed it was necessary "to know our rank and station in the world, whether it be fix'd by our birth, fortune, employments, talents or reputation," which offends most of us today who believe that "rank," even if it has to exist in some form, should certainly not be fixed by birth.[52]

Those keen to find traces of political progressivism in Hume's life and work can only focus on his support for American independence, although as Harris points out, this was far from unqualified. In 1771 he clearly said that America "cannot long subsist" as a colony, but in 1774 he added that since Americans were "still in their nonage" the time for independence was not yet ripe. Eighteen months later, however, he was finally persuaded that the colony should "be left entirely to themselves." His reasons, however, were pragmatic rather than based on any rights of self-determination. It was simply militarily and financially unfeasible to keep America against its people's will, especially given the huge ocean separating it from the mother country.

Hume's conservatism was not just a result of blind prejudice. It had reasonable philosophical foundations. First, he shared Burke's pessimism that the way to construct a better society is to work out abstract general principles and then try to apply them. Reformers tend to be too confident that they can see what is for the best and that they know how to put it into practice. Hume suspected, however, "that the world is still too young to fix many general truths in politics, which will remain true to the latest posterity. . . . It is not fully known, what degree of refinement, either in virtue or vice, human nature is susceptible of; nor what may be expected of mankind from any great revolution in their education, customs, or principles." For example, Machiavelli was an example of someone who thought he had uncovered general principles, but these had turned out to be "extremely defective" because he "confined his study to the furious and tyrannical governments of ancient times, or to the little disorderly principalities of Italy."[53]

Hume expressed his Burkean conservatism most explicitly in an essay "Idea of a Perfect Commonwealth," an idea he warned against. "An established government has an infinite advantage, by that very circumstance of its being established," he wrote. "To tamper, therefore, in this affair, or try experiments merely upon the credit of supposed argument and philosophy, can never be the part of a wise magistrate." Any sage reformer will "bear a reverence to what carries the marks of age; and though he may attempt some improvements for the public good, yet will he adjust his innovations, as much as possible, to the ancient fabric, and preserve entire the chief pillars and supports of the constitution."[54]

This outlook made him resistant to the whiggish view that, through the advance of science and reason, we will inevitably arrive at a better future. He mocked his friend Turgot's "laudable, if not too sanguine hope, that human society is capable of perpetual progress towards perfection, that the encrease of knowledge will still prove favourable to good government, and that since the discovery of printing we need no longer dread the usual returns of barbarism and ignorance."[55]

Connected to this was Hume's strong commitment to the rule of law as a necessary source of peace and stability. Like Aristotle, he thought that too much democracy threatened this, as it would give a new majority government a mandate to rip up whatever laws already existed and implement the so-called "will of the people," which in reality is at best only the will of a majority of the people. Hence Hume tended to err on the side of stability against reform. So, for example, he commends the principle "*Salus populi suprema Lex*, the safety of the people is the supreme law," arguing that "common sense teaches us, that, as government binds us to obedience only on account of its tendency to public utility, that duty must always, in extraordinary cases, when public ruin would evidently attend obedience, yield to the primary and original obligation." Nonetheless, he sides with those who put great stress on our allegiance to the state and its laws and consider the abandonment of it as "the last refuge in desperate cases, when the public is in the highest danger, from violence and tyranny."[56] As he put it in the *Treatise*, "The common rule requires submission; and 'tis only in cases of grievous tyranny and oppression, that the exception can take place."[57]

Hume was correct to see that liberty is not an unqualified good and that it needs to be in balance with the rule of law, which he saw as resting on authority. Hence "in all governments, there is a perpetual intestine struggle, open or secret, between Authority and Liberty; and neither of them can ever absolutely prevail in the contest. A great sacrifice of liberty must necessarily be made in every government; yet even the authority, which confines liberty, can never, and perhaps ought never, in any constitution, to become quite entire and uncontroulable. . . . liberty is the perfection of civil society; but still authority must be acknowledged essential to its very existence."[58]

Hume's weakness in his political analysis is deeply connected to his philosophical strengths, in ways we would do well to remember. Hume was cautious in his thinking and advocated caution in others. *"A scrupulous hesitation to receive any new hypothesis is so laudable a disposition in philosophers, and so necessary to the examination of truth, that it deserves to be comply'd with,* and requires that every argument be produc'd, which may tend to their satisfaction, and every objection remov'd, which may stop them in their reasoning."[59]

This kind of philosophical temperament avoids extremes. It can see "on the one side this, on the other side that" and so tends to end up in moderate positions. However, the maxim Hume's life suggests is that *moderation too must be moderated.* When moderation becomes a habit, it can be hard to see the exceptions, when moderation becomes a vice rather than a virtue. It tends us toward too much acceptance of the status quo, so skeptical of radical reform that we forget that *to have reasons for suspicion is not to have reasons for pronouncing guilt.* So, for example, when Hume wrote about monarchy and republicanism and said, "Matters . . . must be trusted to their natural progress and operation," this was not an absolute rule but at best a general truth, one that arguably did not apply to the case in question. Similarly, in his essay "Of the First Principles of Government," he concludes, "Let us cherish and improve our ancient government as much as possible, without encouraging a passion for such dangerous novelties."[60] But when "as much as possible" is not enough, we must also consider novelties, without dismissing them out of hand because change always carries risk. Conservatives tend to forget that *the certain harms of the status quo are sometimes more real than the uncertain dangers of reform.*

A Shape-Shifting Bundle

Hume's military experience certainly didn't seem to weaken his affection for St. Clair, since in 1747 Hume again accompanied him, this time on a more pacific diplomatic mission to Vienna and Turin. On this trip he was struck by the poverty and bad government of Italy. "Alas poor Italy!" he wrote. "The poor Inhabitant Starves in the midst of Nature's Plenty curst: And in the loaded Vineyard dyes for thirst. The Taxes here exorbitant beyond all Bounds."[61]

By this time Hume had grown into the body shape he would keep all his adult life. "My Belly has swelled so enormously," he wrote. "Alas! that is not an Infirmity like grey hair to be disguis'd with Powder & Pompon."[62] His income had also grown, not to the same excess but enough to give him the sense of security and independence he craved. As he put it in *My Own Life*, "My appointments, with my frugality, had made me reach a fortune, which I called independent, though most of my friends were inclined to smile when I said so; in short, I was now master of near a thousand pounds."[63]

Hume's new, stouter self was the most visible sign of change. But, of course, every person changes over a lifetime. Yet through that change, we think the same person endures. How is this possible? This question of personal identity was one Hume directly addressed.

Consider first the commonsense notion of selfhood. To write this book I have followed in Hume's footsteps. It seems obvious that this means tracking the life and thought of a single person, David Hume, who was essentially the same in Edinburgh, Bristol, La Flèche, back in Britain, in Paris, and finally back to Edinburgh again. And I was the same person who started out on this journey who is now writing it up. In some sense, this is uncontroversial. Hume had no problem with the idea of considering a person as the same over a lifetime. His short autobiography, *My Own Life*, only makes sense if there was an entire life that was indeed his. Nor would he deny that he made choices. But what he understood by self and choice were radically different from received opinion, then and now.

Take the nature of the self first. Here I am, standing at my desk, writing. But what is it to say that *I* am here? Descartes's answer is that "I" am a thinking thing, not a material one. My essential nature is that of an immaterial *res cogitans* that has no mass or spatial dimensions. This "I" is simple and indivisible.

Descartes not only believed this, he argued he could be certain of it. The existence of the "ego" was the only thing he could not doubt.

Hume surely had Descartes in mind when he began the section of the *Treatise* on personal identity by saying, "There are some philosophers, who imagine we are every moment intimately conscious of what we call our Self; that we feel its existence and its continuance in existence; and are certain, beyond the evidence of a demonstration, both of its perfect identity and simplicity."

Hume, however, was not so sure: "For my part, when I enter most intimately into what I call *myself*, I always stumble on some particular perception or other, of heat or cold, light or shade, love or hatred, pain or pleasure. I never can catch *myself* at any time without a perception, and never can observe any thing but the perception. When my perceptions are remov'd for any time, as by sound sleep; so long am I insensible of myself, and may truly be said not to exist."[64]

Hume was on to something. Take, for example, me walking around in Hume's room in La Flèche. If I pay close attention to myself, what do I find? There are my perceptions: the sight of the marble fireplace, the slightly musty, dusty smell of a room older than the people who live in it, the sound of my footsteps and those of the people I am with, a slight ache in my calves. Then there are the thoughts that buzz through my head: my attempts to imagine Hume at work here, wondering how much time our host will grant us, fleeting ideas about what we'll have for lunch, the stubborn, irritating tune that refuses to stop going around my head. Then there are emotions: a strange, humbling sense of two lives finding a connection across the centuries, an awe at how a person can persist through nothing more than the bequest of their ideas.

Add all of these things up and there is nothing else with any awareness where I stand. There is no *self* in addition to these thoughts and feelings: the self simply *is* all these thoughts and feelings. To put it another way, we say the self *has* experiences but the self *is* actually just an ordered collection of experiences. When we truly realize this, the self becomes so light as to almost vanish. What we thought to be permanent, unified, and enduring actually turns out to be a flux of transient experiences.

This might sound extraordinary, but Hume is clear that in this respect personal identity is no different from any other kind of identity. Every object is made up of parts that change over time and we never perceive any permanent unchanging essence of it. That is why Hume rejected the idea of "substance." Since Aristotle, most philosophers had distinguished between a substance and its properties, qualities, or "modes." So, for example, the College at La Flèche has certain properties of shape, color, solidity, and so on. All these properties are the things we perceive but "behind" them, in some sense, is the "stuff" the college is made of, its substance.

Hume, however, thought that it made no sense to talk of such substance. "We have . . . no idea of substance, distinct from that of a collection of particular qualities, nor have we any other meaning when we either talk or reason concerning it."[65] "Substance" is an empty word, meaning nothing more than "whatever the thing is independently of its properties." But a thing *just is* all its properties. We may not know what all its properties are, so a thing is obviously not just the sum of all its *observed* properties. But unobserved properties are still properties; they are not something else called "substance."

Hume's theory of the self is really just an extension of this idea. The self simply is all the properties of the self, which are essentially psychological ones: perception, memory, desire, and so on. There is no "self-substance" in addition to this.

If it is true that there is no abiding substance which is the self, then what we call identity is not the strictly logical property of "=" but is nothing more than the perception of a "succession of parts, connected together by resemblance, contiguity, or causation."[66] We call something the "same" when these relations are strong enough to create the sense of sameness, but there is no rule that tells us when there is enough continuity for sameness.

There are, however, several factors to consider. For example, the proportion of change matters. We don't say that a house is no longer the same building when a roof tile falls off, even though it is now slightly different. When "some very small or inconsiderable part to be added to the mass, or subtracted from it," says Hume, "tho' this absolutely destroys the identity of the whole, strictly speaking; yet as we seldom think so accurately, we scruple not to pronounce a mass of matter the same, where we find so trivial an alteration."[67]

As well as the *proportion* of change, so too the *pace* of change matters too. "A change in any considerable part of a body destroys its identity," writes Hume, "but 'tis remarkable, that where the change is produc'd *gradually* and *insensibly* we are less apt to ascribe to it the same effect."[68] Hume's point stands even when such changes are not insensible. To give one example, consider a rock band. Of the five original members of Deep Purple when it formed in 1969, only one is currently in the band. There have been several times when there have been more ex–Deep Purple members in other bands, such as Rainbow and Whitesnake, than there were in Deep Purple itself. Yet Deep Purple has an identity as a single band that changes over time, an identity that is distinct from other bands its members went on to join.

One reason for this is another factor Hume considers important for the very notion of identity: when the parts form "a combination to some common end or purpose." Hume here borrows from Thomas Hobbes the example (though unnamed and uncredited) of Theseus's Ship.[69] A ship may return to dock for repairs and have parts replaced, sometimes several times. But throughout the lifetime of the ship its parts remain part of a ship of the same form, with the same general purpose. Because it remains functionally the same, we think of it as the same object.

In all these cases it is clear that context is important when determining whether something is considered to be the same or not. So, "where the objects are in their nature changeable and inconstant, we admit of a more sudden transition, than wou'd otherwise be consistent with that relation" of identity.[70] The water in a river changes very quickly, but because that is of the nature of rivers, we don't think this turns it into a different river. Football clubs inevitably change their players and managers, not least because a professional can only maintain a top level for a decade or so. Therefore, we don't have any problem thinking of a football team as being the "same" even though it has none of the players it used to have. Which criteria of sameness we use can also depend on our particular interest. If I am a worshipper, I can think of a church as the same even after it has been extensively refurbished. If I am an architectural historian, the removal of the original elements might be critical.

Hume says that in all these cases we are not talking strictly about *identity* but of *individuation*: what we do when we pick out an object as an individual entity, at a time or over time. If we understand properly how this works in general, the question of personal identity loses any sense of mystery. It does not consist in any unchanging essence, because nothing has such an essence. It is consistent with change because as we grow up, change is natural and part of what it means to be a person. A person remains the same person just as long as there is sufficient relation of "resemblance, contiguity, or causation" over time, and what counts as "sufficient" cannot be specified by a strict rule.

Of all the factors that enable these relations, Hume singles out memory "chiefly, as the source of personal identity." Hume is clear that he really does mean "chiefly" and not "entirely." (As someone with a poor memory I find this reassuring, as I do Hume's remark that "'tis so far from being a virtue to have a good memory, that men generally affect to complain of a bad one; and endeavouring to persuade the world, that what they say is entirely of their own invention, sacrifice it to the praise of genius and judgment.")[71] Without memory there is nothing to make us aware of the "continuance and extent of this succession of perceptions." But memory has a curious double role here. In one sense, "memory not only discovers the identity, but also contributes to its production, by producing the relation of resemblance among the perceptions." Memory helps create the sense of sameness over time by unifying the "bundle of perceptions." However, it is also the case that we do not remember everything, yet what we count as our past does not consist only of what we remember. In this sense, then, "memory does not so much produce as discover personal identity, by shewing us the relation of cause and effect among our different perceptions."[72]

Hume's account of personal identity is a good example of the kind of modest reasoning he commended. First, it is a kind of reasoning that accepts the absence of any definitive criteria for making judgments of identity. "We have no just standard, by which we can decide any dispute concerning the time, when they acquire or lose a title to the name of identity," says Hume.

"All the disputes concerning the identity of connected objects are merely verbal."[73] Hume thought many philosophical arguments were like this. "We find few disputes, that are not founded on some ambiguity in the expression," he wrote in an essay. "When I am present, therefore, at any dispute, I always consider with myself, whether it be a question of comparison or not that is the subject of the controversy; and if it be, whether the disputants compare the same objects together, or talk of things that are widely different."[74] We would do well to remember: *What appears to be a fundamentally philosophical disagreement is often simply a matter of different people using the same terms differently (and also legitimately).*

Second, at its heart this reasoning is not an argument that proceeds logically from step to step but consists in a close attention to the nature of experience. It is by attending to what is happening when we are conscious that we observe the absence of a unified self, or rather fail to observe its presence, which is the only evidence of absence we can ever have. Because his case rests on an observation, Hume happily concedes that "if any one upon serious and unprejudic'd reflection, thinks he has a different notion of himself, I must confess I can reason no longer with him. All I can allow him is, that he may be in the right as well as I, and that we are essentially different in this particular." Of course, Hume doesn't believe that human beings could be so radically different, nor does he expect his readers to. He is simply openly acknowledging the fact that the final judge in this case is experience, not reason. He teases those who disagree with him, saying, "setting aside some metaphysicians of this kind, I may venture to affirm of the rest of mankind, that they are nothing but a bundle or collection of different perceptions, which succeed each other with an inconceivable rapidity, and are in a perpetual flux and movement."[75]

Hume only used the word "bundle" to describe the self once, but the word stuck and many now use the term "bundle theories" to describe a family of positions similar to Hume's. One reason it stuck is that a "bundle" sounds chaotic and disorganized and so it conveys a sense of the idea's implausibility that critics exploited. The same could be said of Hume's phrase "nothing but a heap or collection of different perceptions," but "bundle" is pithier.[76] One of Hume's contemporaries, Thomas Reid, critically attributed to him the view that "what we call the mind, is only a bundle of thoughts, passions, and emotions, without any subject."[77] The key word here is "only." For many, it just seems incredible that we can be nothing more than a mere bundle of perceptions. But there is nothing "mere" about it. The universe is no less incredible because it is "only" a vast collection of atoms. Indeed, perhaps it is more so. Nor are we any less remarkable because we are made up of our thoughts, feelings, memories, desires, and sensations.

Hume's self is no more or less remarkable or mysterious than everything else in this physical universe. I am often struck with awe when I stop to consider what this world of ours is fundamentally made of, especially when traveling, since that is when we most notice our surroundings. Looking out from where Hume worked over La Flèche and the Loire valley, I see a landscape that has been carved in part by millennia of natural evolution and in part by centuries of human intervention. I am staggered at what nature and human beings have done and how it is even possible that I, a creature made up of the same fundamental stuff as stones and grass, can be conscious of it all. More remarkably still, the moment I die this universe of experiences that I inhabit will vanish completely too.

Aristotle said that "it is owing to their wonder that men both now begin and at first began to philosophise." But if wonder (or astonishment) is the beginning of philosophy, it is very rarely its end. Philosophers tend to strive to lose their wonder, to make what seems incredible perfectly understandable. Anything strange is tamed by bringing it under a theory. "When a philosopher has once laid hold of a favourite principle, which perhaps accounts for many natural effects," wrote Hume, "he extends the same principle over the whole creation, and reduces to it every phænomenon, though by the most violent and absurd reasoning."[78] Hume is not completely immune to this vice but he suffered from it less than most. His view seems to be that *accepting an astonishing mystery is better than believing an incredible explanation.* A bad explanation is worse than no explanation at all. It is better to accept that cause and effect are real but lack rational or evidential warrant than it is to deny causation exists. It is better to accept that the self is an astonishing bundle of perceptions than to posit a unified soul that not only defies experience but raises more problems than it solves.

Hume made this even clearer in an appendix to the *Treatise*, admitting that "upon a more strict review of the section concerning personal identity, I find myself involv'd in such a labyrinth, that, I must confess, I neither know how to correct my former opinions, nor how to render them consistent." More specifically, "all my hopes vanish, when I come to explain the principles, that unite our successive perceptions in our thought or consciousness. I cannot discover any theory, which gives me satisfaction on this head." Hume believed that his theory left too much mysterious to be entirely satisfactory, but was clear that in essence it had to be right and that there was no enduring, substantive "self." So all he could do with intellectual honesty was to embrace the imperfection and hope that "others, perhaps, or myself, upon more mature reflections, may discover some hypothesis, that will reconcile those contradictions."[79]

Hume's view of the self was radical in a Europe where ideas of the self were tied up with Platonic and Christian ideas of immortal, immaterial souls. In Asia, however, they have been mainstream for millennia. Hume's view is actually very close to that of the Buddha, who argued that there was no "*ātman*" (*attā* in Pali), the immaterial essence of self postulated by all orthodox Indian schools of philosophy. Instead, there were only the "aggregates": body, feelings, perception, mental formations, and consciousness. The permanent, abiding self was an illusion. This doctrine is known as *anattā*, not-self.

The close similarity between the Humean and Buddhist conceptions of the self is all the more remarkable because, as far as we know, Hume had no knowledge of Buddhist thought. Recently, however, it has been speculated that Hume might have come across Buddhist ideas after all, thanks to his sojourn at La Flèche. The professor of psychology and philosophy Alison Gopnik has done some detective work that shows more than one possible way for Indian ideas to have made their way to Scotland, via France.

One possible route was via the Jesuit missionary Ippolito Desideri, who in 1728 completed what Gopnik calls "the most complete and accurate European account of Buddhist philosophy to be written until the 20th century." His book was based on research conducted on an extensive trip to Nepal that began in 1714 with a grueling eighteen-month trek from Delhi across the Himalayas to Lhasa, where he announced to the king that he intended to convert him and his subjects to Catholicism. Far from being offended, the king simply suggested that if he wanted to do that, he ought to study Buddhism so that he could explain why Christianity was superior. If he could do that, they would be happy to convert.

So for the next five years Desideri studied in the Buddhist monasteries in the Nepalese mountains. He even composed Christian tracts in Tibetan verse, which he wrote on scrolls and presented to the king. War then pushed him even farther into the mountains, where he translated the work of the Buddhist philosopher Tsongkhapa into Italian. The book he eventually completed covered a lot of Buddhist thought, including the denial of the abiding self. Although the Vatican did not allow a book about such heathen ideas to be published, manuscripts did circulate among some monks. More significantly, in his book he wrote, "On the 31st (August) around noon I arrived at our Royal College at La Flèche. There I received the particular attention of the rector, the procurator, Père Tolu and several other of the reverend fathers. On the 4th I left La Flèche." Records show that twelve Jesuit fathers who had been at La Flèche when Desideri visited were still there when Hume arrived. One of them, P. Charles François Dolu, had traveled to the French embassy in Siam and also had firsthand experience of a Buddhist country.

None of this evidence proves anything more than that Hume *might* have read or heard about the Buddhist philosophy of not-self. Given that he makes no mention of it, this is slender reason to think that he actually did. The similarities might seem too striking to be coincidental, but there are two reasons to think they might be. The first is that Hume's ideas on the self are a logical progression from those of John Locke, a step forward that requires no external stimulus. The second is that if Hume and the Buddha are right, then anyone who paid close attention to their experience would notice the absence of an abiding self. This absence was always hiding in plain sight, in France as well as in India.

Return to Edinburgh

Despite the success of his essays he was "still little known in the world of letters," as Mossner put it.[80] However, a change of abode was about to herald a change of fortune. Hume's brother got married, leading Hume and his sister Katherine to move to Edinburgh. "I lived several years happy with my brother at Ninewells," he later recalled, "and had not his marriage changed a little the state of the family, I believe I should have lived and died there."[81]

I'm not sure whether we should believe Hume. In his letters, he often offered contradictory opinions about the best place to live. Even as he tells us how content he would have been to remain at Ninewells, he also expresses the view that Edinburgh was "the true scene for a man of letters."[82] Hume was a man who valued both solitude and good company and seemed conflicted as to which was preferable. He agreed with Aristotle that a human being is a "social animal," writing, *"We can form no wish which has not a reference to society. A perfect solitude is, perhaps, the greatest punishment we can suffer."*[83] But perhaps a perfect, complete absence of solitude would be just as bad, especially when the quality of the company cannot be guaranteed. "One that has well digested his knowledge both of books and men, has little enjoyment but in the company of a few select companions. He feels too sensibly, how much all the rest of mankind fall short of the notions which he has entertained."[84] As a result, he tended to oscillate between the two, getting the best of both worlds.

The house in Edinburgh that Hume and his sister moved to was in Riddle's Land, just off the south side of the Lawnmarket. The building still stands in what is now called Riddle's Court, though it has been much altered. It was already historic in Hume's time, having been built as a merchant's house in the 1590s and playing host to two royal banquets in 1598, hosted by King James VI and his wife, Queen Anne of Denmark, in honor of the visit of Anne's brother, Ulric Duke of Holstein.

Today it has a somewhat claustrophobic courtyard, hemmed in by five stories. This is because originally there was no courtyard at all: the space was opened up in the 1890s when buildings on either side of the passageway leading into it from Lawnmarket were demolished. This required building a new staircase on the outside of the building to allow access between the first and second floors. At this time, the building was used by the University of Edinburgh before being taken over by the City of Edinburgh Council after World War II, to be reopened as an adult education center in 1964.

When I visited, it was still something of a building site, but with good reason. It was undergoing extensive conservation and refurbishment by the Scottish Historic Buildings Trust, with support from Edinburgh World Heritage. Rooms have been refurbished in different styles to reflect the building's history and can now be rented for weddings, meetings, conferences, and parties. Its main use, however, is the home of the Patrick Geddes Centre. It was Geddes who turned the building into university halls for students in the 1880s, also running summer schools open to people from less privileged backgrounds. Geddes is a little-known polymath, described by the center today as a "Biologist, Geographer, Sociologist, Environmentalist, Philosopher, Town planner, Cultural champion, Anarchist, Free Churchman, Educator."

While the spirit of Geddes is kept very much alive at Riddle's Court, that of Hume's is somewhat thin. He is mentioned as a former inhabitant on the center's website, and one of the many courses offered by the center is on the Scottish Enlightenment. Of course, Geddes has a stronger and more recent connection with the building than Hume. But Geddes was also more of a man of the people, someone who was always concerned with the ordinary person. Perhaps one reason why Hume is not as well-known as his impeachable philosophical stature suggests he should be is that he does not conform to the standard heroic model of most civilizations. "Great men" (since women have lamentably rarely been granted greatness) have been either powerful leaders or self-sacrificial saints. To be exceptional is to be more godlike than most, whether that is a powerful deity of myth or the God who died on the cross of Christianity. Hume's kind of exceptionality is the opposite: he was more fully human than most, nothing more, nothing less. The virtues he exemplified were not extreme ones of daring or courage but quiet ones of amiability, modesty, generosity of spirit, hospitality. Lest this sound like little, consider how difficult it is to live our lives consistently expressing such virtues.

Celebrating such a life is difficult because it undeniably depends upon privilege. So many struggle even to stay alive, so many live in war zones, that no wonder we prefer to praise those whose self-sacrificial acts help others. But the Humean good life, like that of Aristotle, points to what all that altruism is supposed to lead to. We want to eliminate poverty, disease, and war so that people can get on and live flourishing, productive lives, like that of David Hume. In a better world, we would have no need of heroes like Geddes. In the world we do have, it is understandable that we celebrate those who fight its present injustices more than we do those who show us what a better one looks like.[85]

Edinburgh at the time was expanding fast. It had a population of a little over 50,000 when Hume moved there, but this had risen to 80,000 by 1775. Not surprisingly, with this dynamism came a certain sleaze. The city had plenty of "Bawdy-Houses," as the brothels were known. One soldier remarked that a common question asked by their frequenters was "if they have got a Pair of Canon-Gate Breeches, meaning the Venereal Distemper, which rages here."[86]

Nonetheless, Hume was certainly correct to say that Edinburgh was the true scene for men of letters. A contemporary account reported, "Here I stand at what is called the Cross of Edinburgh, and can, in a few minutes, take fifty men of genius and learning by the hand. . . . In London, in Paris, and other large cities of Europe, though they contain many literary men, the access to them is difficult; and, even after that is obtained, the conversation is, for some time, shy and constrained. In Edinburgh, the access of men of parts is not only easy, but their conversation and the communication of their knowledge are at once imparted to intelligent strangers with the utmost liberality."[87]

The "Cross of Edinburgh" is the Mercat's (Market) Cross, situated a few hundred yards down the Royal Mile from Riddle's Court, in Parliament Square next to St. Giles's Cathedral. This is where market stalls would have been set up and many civic events were held. The current cross is several yards from the one that stood when Hume lived nearby, which was demolished in 1756. An octagonal arrangement of cobblestones now marks where it stood. I'm not sure you can take "fifty men of genius and learning by the hand" there now, but Edinburgh remains a city of unusual intellectual vigor.

One manifestation of this is the annual International Book Festival, which claims with some justification to be "the largest public celebration of the written word in the world." I've spoken there many times and can testify that it is not mere PR-speak when the festival says that the approximately one thousand writers and thinkers who come there "rub shoulders" with the audience. The festival is one of the most egalitarian in spirit I know. All speakers, from the most famous to the most obscure debutante, mingle in the famous writer's yurt and are treated exactly the same. Audiences are similarly generous. My first ever book festival talk was at Edinburgh, when I was virtually unknown and my book even less so. Knowing that in addition to competing events at the book festival there were dozens of other things going on in the city as part of the arts festival and its even larger fringe, I wondered who on earth would turn up. I was relieved to find a healthy audience and learned there and then that in Edinburgh people will turn up for a talk on an interesting subject even if the speaker is not famous. I don't think it is too fanciful to trace a continuity and connection between the open-minded intellectual curiosity of Edinburgh today and the thriving capital of letters it was in the eighteenth century. Fine minds grow best in a rich intellectual culture, something those responsible for education policy would do well to remember. Philosophy is a vital part of any culture's creative ecosystem. "The same age, which produces great philosophers and politicians, renowned generals and poets, usually abounds with skilful weavers, and ship-carpenters. We cannot reasonably expect, that a piece of woollen cloth will be wrought to perfection in a nation, which is ignorant of astronomy, or where ethics are neglected."[88] In other words, *a vibrant economy requires a society rich in intellectual as well as economic capital.*

Hume threw himself enthusiastically into this literary life, which centered on several intellectual clubs that thrived during the Scottish Enlightenment. In 1751, he was elected joint secretary of the Philosophical Society, a post he held for twenty years. This has become the most august of the intellectual societies. It was founded in 1731 and went on to become the Royal Society of Edinburgh in 1783. In its early days it seems to have been peripatetic, and it has been based in several locations over the centuries. Since 1909 it has occupied a rather grand building that used to be the headquarters of the Edinburgh Life Assurance Company. It's on George Street, in the New Town of Edinburgh that was built during Hume's lifetime. With its grand staircase, dark wooden pillars, leather armchairs, and portraits of former grandees, the society exudes a pride in the intellectual history of the city. But this gives a false impression of what the society must have been like in Hume's day. Then there were no past glories to bask in, no permanent endowments or buildings. The society was at the vanguard of new ways of thinking, looking forward to the future.

In 1752 Hume also became Keeper of the Advocates Library, "a genteel office, though of small revenue."[89] The key advantage of this was that it gave him access to the library's great collection of books, which, as we will see shortly, was essential for his major literary endeavor in this period of his life. The library is one of the few buildings from Hume's era that still stands, so I was eager to pay it a visit. It is not open to the public as it is within Parliament House, part of a complex that houses the Supreme Courts of Scotland. It is hardly even visible to outsiders. You can only get a peek at it by standing on George IV Bridge and peering down the strip of grass between the Institut français d'Écosse and the National Library of Scotland to the windowed wall at the far end, beyond the Signet Library on your left. However, Hume's successor as keeper, Mungo Bovey QC, kindly granted me access and I was given a tour by Sara Berry, a senior librarian.

FIGURE 12. Exterior view of the Advocates Library, at the far end of the grass.

To get to the library you have to go through the grand Parliament Hall, completed in 1639, with its striking oak hammer-beam roof. It only functioned as a parliament until the Act of Union in 1707, which merged England and Scotland into a single kingdom of Great Britain. Now it is a meeting place for lawyers who maintain the tradition of walking up and down as they talk, in order to prevent eavesdropping.

The modern library is a quiet, working space for lawyers. To see where Hume worked you have to go down a level to a long hall with stone arches running across the middle of its length. These used to be entrances to partitioned rooms but have been long removed, and the hall is now a single space. One area of it has the sign "Devils may sit here," which would surely have amused the religiously skeptical Hume. A "devil" is in fact simply the argot for a pupil undertaking the period of apprenticeship necessary to become an advocate.

A large stone fireplace sits out of commission and one can imagine how the room would have been heated—probably inadequately—from this single source. The space has been modernized in several respects, from the laminated floors to the modern bookshelves, but its eighteenth-century version remains more than just a palimpsest. This would have been an exceptional study space: quiet, spacious, and incredibly well resourced. It is little wonder Hume sought the office of keeper.

However, his election was not without controversy. "The violent cry of Deism, atheism, and scepticism was raised against me," he wrote, "and 'twas represented that my election would be giving sanction of the greatest and most learned body of men in this country to my profane and irreligious principles."[90] It was then perhaps inevitable that the appointment would not end happily. In 1754 he ordered seventy-four items and the curators ordered that three "be struck out of the Catalogue of the Library, and removd from the Shelves as indecent Books & unworthy of a place in a learned Library." All three were French. Hume wrote to Robert Dundas, saying, "The expelling of these books I could conceive in no other light than as an insult on me, which nothing can repair but the re-instating them. . . . If all worse than *Bussi Rabutin* or *Crebillon*, be expelled, I shall engage that a couple of porters will do the office."[91]

However, resigning his office would both hurt his pocket and, more importantly, restrict his access to the books. But, as he wrote to Adam Smith, he saw that it was "impossible to succeed." His way out of the dilemma was to retain the office but hand over his salary and duties to Blacklock, a blind poet. It worked for two years before he judged that the curators had so

FIGURE 13. Hume by Allan Ramsay (1754).

compromised his position that he had to resign.[92] There is a moral in this tale: *To never compromise is a mark of excessive rigidity, to always compromise an even surer sign of having no standards at all.*

There is some evidence, however, that Hume might have partially prevailed in his choice of books after all. Much of the historical contents of the Advocates Library is now in the hands of the National Library of Scotland. Its catalogue of the Advocates Library collection reveals that it contains a copy of the *Histoire amoureuse des Gaules par le comte de Bussy Rabutin* from 1722, one of the books that Hume had ordered. Crebillon's earliest edition in the collection is a 1779 edition of his *Collection complete des oeuvres*, while there is a 1751 edition of an English translation of *The adventures of Capt. De la Fontaine, late an officer in the service of the States-General*. So Hume was either only partially thwarted or soon vindicated.

In 1754 he became one of the founders of the Select Society, which Mossner says "included most of the important figures from the law, the university, and the church, with a few choice selections from the social world."[93] No doubt thanks to Hume's position, they met at the Advocates Library on Wednesday evenings at 6:00 p.m. between the middle of November and the middle of August. In March 1755, "An Account of the Select Socieit [*sic*] of Edinburgh" was published in *The Scots Magazine*, informing the public that: "The intention of the gentlemen was, by practice to improve themselves in reasoning and eloquence, and by the freedom of debate, to discover the most effectual methods of promoting the good of the country."[94]

Hume was also active in the Poker Club, a more informal gathering where the discussion was particularly forthright. For a shilling, members enjoyed robust conversation and dinner, accompanied by sherry or claret. Historian Roger L. Emerson says Hume preferred the "plain roughness" of the Poker Club to the gentility of the other societies.[95] The odd name of the club was proposed by Adam Ferguson to suggest its role as a provocateur on the then pressing political issue of whether there should be a standing militia. They met at Thomas Nicholson's tavern (on West Bow, according to one source).[96]

In addition to these more or less formal clubs, the philosopher, satirist, and essayist Thomas Carlyle tells us that Hume gave "little suppers now & then to a few select friends . . . and best of all, he furnished the entertainment with the most instructive and pleasing conversation, for he assembled whosoever were most knowing and agreeable among either the laity or clergy. . . . For innocent mirth and agreeable raillery I never knew his match."[97]

In 1753 Hume and his sister moved to a new home in Jack's Land that no longer stands.[98] This proved to be one of the most difficult locations to track down. A description by James Grant in his *Old and New Edinburgh*, published in the 1880s, describes it as "a lofty stone tenement" standing "opposite to the archway leading into St. John Street."[99] If that is right, the original building certainly no longer stands today. Today it is the building that sits over the arched entrance to Sebald Walk, built tastefully in the local pale yellow stone to fit in, but clearly a very recent structure. Once again, nothing attests to Hume's association with the site.

By this time Hume had a life that lacked nothing. "With frugality I can reach, I find, cleanliness, warmth, light, plenty, and contentment," he wrote. "What would you have more? Independence? I have it in a supreme degree. Honour? that is not altogether wanting. Grace? that will come in time. A wife? that is none of the indispensable requisites of life. Books? that *is* one of them; and I have more than I can use. In short, I cannot find any blessing of consequence which I am not possessed of, in a greater or less degree; and without any great effort of philosophy, I may be easy and satisfied."[100]

The Philosopher's End?

What Hume did next has dismayed his philosophical admirers for centuries. He wrote a six-volume history of Great Britain, published between 1754 and 1762. Hume picked up the narrative with the reign of James I in 1603, with volume two ending with James II in 1688. The reception of these first two volumes led him to start working backward, filling in the gaps, with two more on the history of England under the House of Tudor (1485–1603) followed by two more from the invasion of Julius Caesar in 54 BCE to the accession of Henry VII in 1485.

Although the first volume initially sold slowly, the second sold well and the series became an enormous success, much more than his philosophical works. It became the best-selling history to be published in Britain until Gibbon's *Decline and Fall of the Roman Empire* in the 1780s. Gibbon himself called Hume the "Tacitus of Scotland." To the French, he was the "English Tacitus," the inaccurate national adjective something the proud Scot would have appreciated less.[101] This is praise he would have enjoyed given his own admiration of the Roman historian. In his essay "Of the Standard of Taste," Hume talks about how our preferences change with age, saying "at twenty, Ovid may be the favourite author; Horace at forty; and perhaps Tacitus at fifty."[102]

"Nothing can be added to the fame of this History, perhaps the best ever written in any language," wrote Voltaire in 1764. "Mr Hume, in his History, is neither parliamentarian, nor royalist, nor Anglican, nor Presbyterian—he is simply judicial."[103]

That was just the praise Hume was looking for. In *My Own Life* he wrote, "I was, I own, sanguine in my expectations of the success of this work. I thought that I was the only historian, that had at once neglected present power, interest, and authority, and the cry of popular prejudices; and as the subject was suited to every capacity, I expected proportional applause." But Voltaire's appreciation of his evenhandedness was far from universal. A cheerleader for none, he ended up being criticized by all. "I was assailed by one cry of reproach, disapprobation, and even detestation; English, Scotch, and Irish, Whig and Tory, churchman and sectary, freethinker and religionist, patriot and courtier, united in their rage against the man, who had presumed to shed a generous tear for the fate of Charles I."[104]

But just as he was willing to "castrate" his *Treatise* to calm the ire of his religious critics, so he was willing to make pragmatic deletions to his histories. Most notably, in the first edition of the first volume on the Stuarts, Hume denounced early Protestantism as enthusiasm and Roman Catholicism as superstition. This led some to dismiss the whole work as atheistic. To avoid having people not read the book for this reason he took these passages out of subsequent editions.[105]

Controversies such as these did not stop the histories from becoming best sellers. His essays had also done well and continued to sell after his death. An editor of his letters, Eugene Miller, notes that sixteen editions of his *Essays and Treatises on Several Subjects* were published from 1777 to 1894, and in his lifetime many were translated into French, German, and Italian, and appeared in America. His friend John Home observed years after Hume's death, "His Essays are at once popular and philosophical, and contain a rare and happy union of profound Science and fine writing."[106]

By 1757, Mossner says he "was generally acknowledged to be the leading man of letters, not only of North Britain, but of South Britain as well." He was also celebrated in France, and in 1762 Boswell called him "the greatest Writer in Britain."[107] But although his contemporaries judged him well for the work, posterity has been harsher. The standard view for some time has been that when Hume turned his attention to his histories, he effectively gave up the vocation for philosophy that most suited his talent. As James Harris, Hume's intellectual biographer, puts it, the general view was that "as early as mid-1751 . . . Hume's philosophical oeuvre was all but complete."[108] That was the year

Hume published the new version of Book III of the *Treatise*, recast as the *Enquiry concerning the Principles of Morals*.

Typical of this view is a preface to an edition of Hume's essays published in 1889, in which T. H. Grose wrote: "On reviewing the history of Hume's literary and philosophical works, we are at once struck by the suddenness with which his labours in philosophy came to an end." In Grose's opinion, Hume's work on metaphysics ended when he completed the *Treatise* in 1736, when he was just twenty-five, and by the time he was thirty-nine he had completed his contribution to the philosophy of religion. Philosophically speaking, "after this date he added nothing." Grose's explanation of this betrays the common perception that Hume's skeptical philosophy was wholly negative. Having torn everything down, Hume had to either build it up again or walk away from the devastation. For the former, thought Grose, "Hume certainly lacked the disposition, and probably the ability."[109]

There are several things that are questionable in this narrative of philosophical abandonment. The first is that it is anachronistic to divide up the various subjects on which Hume wrote into the subject silos that we currently use. As we have seen, a "man of letters," which Hume always wanted to be, would study what we call history, philosophy, and politics as aspects of the same subject, not different ones. As Harris says, "He is best seen not as a philosopher who may or may not have abandoned philosophy in order to write essays and history, but as a man of letters, a philosophical man of letters, who wrote on human nature, on politics, on religion, and on the history of England from 55BC to 1688."[110]

This is not simply a matter of using a different taxonomy of disciplines. For Hume, doing history was part of doing philosophy. ***Philosophy is either continuous with other disciplines or it*** *is sterile, lifeless, and alone.* As he set to work on the histories, he told the Abbé le Blanc that "the philosophical spirit, which I have so much indulg'd in all my writings, finds here ample materials to work upon."[111] As Rasmussen explains, Hume's lifelong project, which began in the *Treatise*, was to apply the experimental method to human nature in order to make our understanding of it more scientific.[112] Although you cannot experiment on human beings by putting them in radically different environments, you can observe how they behave in different conditions by the study of history. History is therefore a means to discover what is constant and unchanging in human nature and what is subject to alteration by our cultures and political situations. "The advantages found in history seem to be of three kinds," Hume wrote, "as it amuses the fancy, as it improves the understanding, and as it strengthens virtue."[113]

The idea that Hume's essays marked a departure from philosophy is even more questionable. It seems Hume paid the price of many serious writers who have tried to express themselves plainly and concisely, addressing the concerns of everyday life. But *never confuse a lightness of touch in the writing with a lightness of mind in the thinking.* Hume's essays are actually often little gems of wisdom. Many have aged, but only because they addressed particular issues of the day that are of little interest to us now.

In his essays, Hume arguably achieved a marriage between what he calls in the first book of *An Enquiry concerning Human Understanding* "easy and obvious" and "accurate and abstruse" philosophy. Hume seemed fond of making such distinctions and had several variants. In another essay, he claims that *"the greater part of mankind may be divided into two classes; that of shallow thinkers, who fall short of the truth; and that of abstruse thinkers, who go beyond it."*[114] In yet another he distinguishes between the "learned" and the "conversible," the latter being more concerned with sociability and "an Inclination to the easier and more gentle Exercises of the Understanding." Although Hume said that the latter were "the most rare" but also "by far the most useful and valuable," Hume is critical of both. Abstruse philosophy tends to concern abstractions that "cannot enter into business and action" and so "vanishes when the philosopher leaves the shade, and comes into open day." By neglecting the passions and feelings that make us what we are, it fails to give a proper account of life and action. But the easy and obvious does little more than "represent the common sense of mankind in more beautiful and more engaging colours," and "an author is little to be valued, who tells us nothing but what we can learn from every coffee-house conversation."[115] It also leads people to "the absolute rejecting of all profound reasonings," since they find anything of this kind too difficult in comparison.[116]

Hume's ambition was to combine the intellectual rigor of accurate and abstruse philosophy with the clarity of style and humane focus of the easy and obvious. He was very keen to write in an attractive style. In one letter he criticizes a sermon on the basis that the author "does not consult his Ear enough, nor aim at a Style that may be smooth and harmonious; which next to Perspicuity is the chief Ornament of Style."[117] But style always had to be in the service of substance. *"Happy, if we can unite the boundaries of the different species of philosophy, by reconciling profound enquiry with clearness, and truth with novelty!"*[118] Arguably, Hume never did this as well as in his essays. In "Of Essay-Writing" he explicitly said this was his ambition for them. Developing the metaphor of the worlds of learning and conversation as two nations, he said, "I cannot but consider myself as a Kind of Resident or Ambassador from the Dominions of Learning to those of Conversation; and shall think it my constant Duty to promote a good Correspondence betwixt these two States, which have so great a Dependence on each other."[119]

The absurdity of making a distinction between Hume's essays and his supposedly more serious work is exposed by the fact that his *An Enquiry concerning Human Understanding,* largely a reworking of the material in Book I of the *Treatise,* is considered a major philosophical work. Hume himself asked readers to consider this and not his juvenile efforts his definitive statement of the philosophical views contained in them, an instruction scholars have blithely ignored. Yet this *Enquiry* was first published as *Philosophical Essays concerning Human Understanding,* with each of its twelve chapters presented as a self-contained essay. One wonders whether the prejudice against this short form of writing would have prevented the work being taken seriously had it not been renamed. Hume shows us that *the best writing combines rigor of thought with clarity of expression, difficulty of substance with ease of style.*

One final reason to reject the view that Hume effectively gave up on philosophy is that he continued to revise and correct his work until he died. In a letter to his publisher, William Strahan, he wrote, "One half of a man's life is too little to write a book, and other half too little to correct it."[120] As Harris says, "Correction was as important a part of Hume's literary life as composition was."[121] In philosophy, surely, second, third, and fourth thoughts are at least as important as first ones, and a willingness to revise and correct is a sign of a diligent philosopher, not a person who has given up on thinking. Hume recognized this early on. In the Appendix to Book I of the *Treatise* he wrote, "A man, who is free from mistakes, can pretend to no praises, except from the justness of his understanding: But a man, who corrects his mistakes, shews at once the justness of his understanding, and the candour and ingenuity of his temper."[122] In other words, *being right shows the quality of your intellect; being wrong but able to acknowledge and learn from your mistakes shows the quality of your character.*

The success of the histories probably led Hume to write more volumes than he initially planned to do. In 1759 he seemed reluctant to write what would be the last two volumes, telling Smith that he accepted the contract, "chiefly as a Resource against Idleness. . . . For as to Money, I have enough: And as to Reputation, what I have wrote already will be sufficient, if it be good: If not, it is not likely I shall now write better."[123] Indeed, Strahan wanted him to write more volumes than he eventually did. Around 1768 Hume candidly explained why he would not: "Because I am too old, too fat, too lazy, and too rich."[124]

In 1762, after a few years in London, he returned to Edinburgh, buying the third story of James Court, on the north side of Lawnmarket. What strikes me most about this move is simply how close this, Jack's Land, and Riddle's Court all are. Hume's first three homes in the Scottish capital were never farther than half a mile apart. Edinburgh was indeed a compact city where every intellectual would know every other.

James Court was a prestigious address and would have had views both across the city of Edinburgh and over the port of Leith, the Firth of Forth, and the hills of Fife. Hume said he had "a View of Kirkaldy from my Windows."[125] It was arranged around a generous square courtyard and had the luxury of its own private muck collector, so residents did not have to rely on the council to have their excrement removed. It is extraordinary to think how such a service showed how much Hume was moving up in the world.

By the end of the century, however, the area had gone into decline after the wealthy of the city had moved to the New

FIGURE 14. James Court, Edinburgh, where Hume moved to live in 1762.

Town. A plaque tells us the original building Hume lived in was destroyed by fire in 1857 and that Boswell lived there after Hume. However, a sense of its former grandeur remains and it is certainly once again a prime address. Like Riddle's Court, which is barely fifty feet away on the other side of the Lawnmarket, it is entered via a narrow passageway from the main road. You emerge from this to be surrounded by seven stories (including the basement) of gray-stoned tenements, in the company of a number of small trees. It is an oasis in the heart of the city where office workers and laborers in fluorescent tabards come to sit and have their sandwiches or drink their coffee. The recovered salubrity of the square is once again due to Patrick

Geddes, who seems to have a habit of saving Hume's former addresses from dereliction. In 1886 he and his family moved into James Court and began to renovate it as part of their vision of bringing town and gown, university and working people, together.[126]

During these years Hume made friends and acquaintances with some of the most significant minds of the era. He was friends with the conservative thinker and politician Edmund Burke and also Benjamin Franklin, whom he probably first met at the London home of William Strahan. According to Rasmussen, in 1759 Hume hosted Franklin in Edinburgh for nearly a month.[127]

Three years later Franklin wrote a paper for the Edinburgh Philosophical Society, at Hume's request, although it seems it was read by someone else in his absence.[128] The paper concerned a method of protecting houses from lightning strikes by means of conductors.[129] It reads like an entry from a DIY manual. "Let the big end of the rod have a strong eye or ring of half an inch diameter: Fix this rod upright to the chimney or highest part of the house, by means of staples, so as it may be kept steady. Let the pointed end be upwards, and rise three or four feet," and so on.[130] Hume wrote back with improvements suggested by two members, one of whom died eight days later. When Mary Midgley argued that philosophy is like plumbing, I don't think this is what she had in mind. But it reminds us that as late as the eighteenth century philosophy was not a discrete subject, separate from the sciences and other humanities. A philosopher could discuss the design of lightning rods as well as designer gods.

But "the Socrates of Edinburgh" as he became known had enemies as well as friends; pretty much all of them opposed him for theological rather than personal reasons. By 1761, the index

FIGURE 15. Hume's bookplate for his personal library, from the collection
of William Zachs.

of prohibited books of the Roman Catholic Church contained the entry Hume, David. *Opera omnia* (all works).[131]

Hume seemed to be fulfilled, content, and settled. In 1761, he wrote "in reality a book and a fireside, are the only scenes for which I am now qualified."[132] The same day he wrote in another letter that he was "a Recluse and an Ascetic, who retains no Ambition, who has lost his Relish for Pleasure, and who is becoming every day unqualify'd for any Pursuit but Sauntering & Study & Indolence."[133] But far from settling down, Hume was soon to give up his domestic bliss for a second extended sojourn in France.

CHAPTER FOUR

Retaining Our Humanity

Generally speaking, the errors in religion are dangerous; those in philosophy only ridiculous.

Paris Calling

Despite being apparently settled, Hume clearly retained an affection for France, with Paris in particular holding a special appeal. In the late 1750s he wrote of the French capital, "I believe it will be safer for me not to go thither, for I might probably settle there for life."[1] Since he first arrived in Rheims en route to La Flèche, he had held France and its people in high esteem. His Francophilia might not have been unusual for a Scot at the time. The two nations seemed to have some affinity. The English journalist and playwright Captain Edward Topham wrote a few decades later that "the air of mirth and vivacity, that quick penetrating look, that spirit of gaiety which distinguishes the French, is equally visible in the Scotch." That very un-English custom of exchanging kisses in the street when seeing friends was common in both.[2]

In 1763, the opportunity to live awhile in France presented itself when Hume was invited to accompany the ambassador

Lord Hertford to Paris as his secretary. France and Britain had not long been at war, and Lord Hertford was to be the first peacetime British ambassador since the outbreak of the Seven Years' War in 1756. By this time many of Hume's works had been translated into French and he was already a celebrated thinker in France.[3] For example, one of the old books I have had the privilege to handle is two volumes of the *Discours Politiques de Monsieur Hume, traduits de l'anlgois*. This translation of his political essays was published in Amsterdam in 1754, a decade before Hume's return to Paris. By 1764 most editions of his works were reprints. A volume of *Essais Moraux et Politiques* (moral and political essays) from that year was a second edition, while another was a new edition of Hume's *Oeuvres Philosophiques* (philosophical works). Hume was widely published and republished.

A wine merchant, John Stewart, reported to Hume in 1759 that in France "under the title of your friend I have been more caressed here than ever stranger was by people of distinguished merit and a high rank in life." Andrew Stuart Torrance reported that Hume "is so much worshipped here that he must be void of all passions if he does not immediately take post for Paris." Lord Elibank wrote, "No author ever yet attained to that degree of Reputation in his own lifetime that you are now in possession of at Paris."[4]

The prospect of Hume coming to their country clearly excited many of the French. One especially encouraged him. Mme. de Boufflers was one of the leading salon hostesses, a *salonnière*. The salons were a distinctive Parisian Enlightenment institution. Intellectuals and artists would meet, usually in the homes of women hosts, who would act as facilitators of discussion. Being a *salonnière* was one of the few opportunities intelligent women had to be involved in serious, intellectual affairs, and many seized the opportunity with relish.

Mme. de Boufflers was by many accounts the hostess of the finest salon in Paris.[5] She was a great reader and became an admirer of Hume. Her first letter to him in 1761 is effusive in its praise. "I can assure you, Sir, with unquestionable sincerity, that I have found none which, in my judgment, unites so many perfections as yours," she wrote. "It enlightens the mind by showing that true happiness is closely united with virtue and discovers, by the same light, what is the end, the sole end, of every reasonable being."

Interestingly, she adds the comment, "All these sublime qualities are so far above the understanding of a woman, that it is fitting I should say little about them."[6] It seems extremely unlikely that Mme. de Boufflers really believed that women were incapable of fully understanding the philosophical writings of men. We can only assume that the comment is meant to reflect the belief common at the time that women's minds were not fit for metaphysical and philosophical speculation. In most cultures for most of human history, women have been considered the intellectual inferiors of men, and eighteenth-century France was no exception.

I was reminded of this when I had lunch at Le Procope, the oldest café in Paris still operating. Here, many philosophers would come to drink coffee and talk. Although there is no record of Hume having come here, it would have been remarkable if he had not been through its doors at least once during his time living in Paris. Today, the bar and restaurant lives off this history, luring in tourists keen to dine alongside the ghosts of Voltaire, Victor Hugo, and the *encyclopédistes*. The food is very good, but its price is somewhat inflated by a kind of "nostalgia tax" the owners can easily get away with adding. But it's worth paying to wallow in the history. Head upstairs to the toilets and you'll pass a Voltaire quote painted onto the wall: "*Les femmes*

sont comme les girouettes: elles se fixent quand elles se rouillent"—
Women are like weathervanes: they set when they rust. Misogyny was rife, even among the most enlightened thinkers of
the time, friends of demonstrably smart women.

But why did de Boufflers feel the need to acknowledge this
received wisdom? Given this letter was their first contact, it
seems unlikely she spoke in jest, confident that Hume would
detect the irony. Did she feel that she had to acknowledge her
lower status, so that Hume did not feel she was being presumptuous in writing to him about his philosophy? She was, after all,
not only a woman but fourteen years his junior. Or was she perhaps testing Hume, to see whether he would take her confession
of inadequacy at face value or treat her as an intellectual equal?

We cannot know. In his reply to Mme. de Boufflers, Hume
does not address the nature of her femininity directly. He does
pay tribute to her intellect by saying how flattered he was to be
praised by "a person, who could write so well, herself" and so
"must be a good judge of writing in others."[7] From his other
writings, we can conclude that Hume respected women of
learning and intelligence. In "Of Love and Marriage" he also
says it would be better if "everything was carry'd on with perfect
equality, as betwixt two equal members of the same body."[8]
However, equal does not mean the same, and Hume believed
women's strengths were different from those of men. Sometimes, this made them superior. "Women of Sense and Education," he claimed, "are much better Judges of all polite Writing
than Men of the same Degree of Understanding." "Polite" writing refers more to style than content, suggesting that women's
strengths as writers lie in their aesthetic sensibility, not intellectual rigor. The compliment might therefore seem somewhat
backhanded. But Hume follows up this remark with the observation that "in a neighbouring Nation, equally famous for good

Taste, and for Gallantry," which surely meant France, "the Ladies are, in a Manner, the Sovereigns of the learned World, as well as of the conversible; and no polite Writer pretends to venture upon the Public, without the Approbation of some celebrated Judges of that Sex." Indeed, he goes on to say that "there is only one Subject, on which I am apt to distrust the Judgment of Females, and that is, concerning Books of Gallantry and Devotion."[9]

However, it would be too charitable to Hume to suggest that he believed the sexes were different but equal. In the *Treatise* he claims that women's greater propensity to pity "makes them faint at the sight of a naked sword" and also "pity extremely those, whom they find in any grief or affliction." But since he describes this as an "infirmity" shared by "women and children," the implication that men are stronger and so superior in this regard is clear.[10] In one essay, he says bluntly, "Nature has given *man* the superiority above *woman*, by endowing him with greater strength both of mind and body."[11] In the essay "Of the Immortality of the Soul" he says that "the inferiority of women's capacity is easily accounted for. Their domestic life requires no higher faculties, either of mind or body."[12] Elsewhere he claims that because "the Fair Sex have a great Share of the tender and amorous Disposition" this "perverts their Judgment."[13]

Perhaps his most condescending remarks toward women are that "there is nothing which I would recommend more earnestly to my female readers than the study of history, as an occupation, of all others, the best suited both to their sex and education, much more instructive than their ordinary books of amusement, and more entertaining than those serious compositions, which are usually to be found in their closets."[14] Hume himself may have doubted the wisdom of these lines because the essay was withdrawn from later editions.

It has been suggested that the French philosophers had a more enlightened view of women. However, the entries on "Woman" in the *Encyclopédie* suggest otherwise. One states that "men, according to the prerogatives of their sex and the force of their temperament, are naturally capable of all sorts of employment and activities; whereas women, due to the fragility of their sex and their natural delicacy, are excluded from many functions and incapable of certain activities." Another says that "even when she speaks the truth, it is an equivocal one" and "women are vindictive." It's true that Diderot wrote an essay on how men mistreated women, blaming education for a lot of the social inequality. But even then he wrote that "they are rarely systematic, always dictated by the moment." A woman has "none of the firmness, natural or acquired, that prepares us for life."[15]

In some of his writings, Hume shows himself capable of more enlightened thinking. In his essay "Of Polygamy and Divorces" he insists "it is mere superstition to imagine, that marriage can be entirely uniform, and will admit only of one mode or form," accepting that "as circumstances vary, and the laws propose different advantages, we find, that, in different times and places, they impose different conditions on this important contract."[16] He also questions the "sovereignty of the male," calling it "a real usurpation" that "destroys that nearness of rank, not to say equality, which nature has established between the sexes." Who today cannot but cheer when he concludes that "courtship, the most agreeable scene in life, can no longer have place, where women have not the free disposal of themselves, but are bought and sold, like the meanest animal."[17] He even argues for divorce, saying that "nothing can be more cruel than to preserve, by violence, an union, which, at first, was made by mutual love, and is now, in effect, dissolved by mutual hatred."[18]

Read on, however, and it transpires that Hume is simply making the best case for changes to his age's mores. Although he thinks they are all excellent reasons, he concludes that they are decisively outweighed by three other considerations. First, marriage must be maintained for the sake of the children. Second, we need to constrain our own freedom in order for fickle passion to grow into the kind of calm friendship that long marriage requires. Third, unless a married couple completely throw their lots in with each other, there will be conflicts of interest and division. Marital harmony requires a strong, binding commitment. Hence he concludes that "the exclusion of polygamy and divorces sufficiently recommends our present European practice with regard to marriage."[19] Once again, Hume's more conservative instincts ultimately won out.

We cannot be in any doubt that Hume broadly endorsed the patriarchal attitudes of his time, believing them to be natural rather than socially constructed. For instance, in the *Treatise* he advances the thesis that "the imagination naturally turns to whatever is important and considerable; and where two objects are presented to it, a small and a great one, it usually leaves the former, and dwells entirely upon the latter." So, for instance, the crowds notice the singer much more than the backing musicians, the tallest peak more than the smaller ones around it, and so on. Although there is some truth in this, Hume possibly overstates it. But he is surely just wrong when he adds as examples our greater tendency to notice the husband rather than his "consort" or "a stronger propensity to pass from the idea of the children to that of the father, than from the same idea to that of the mother."[20] To the extent that this is true, it simply reflects a deep-rooted misogyny in society rather than any actual superiority in the male. Hume's failure to notice this adds to the case against him that he was not as aware of his own misogyny as he perhaps could and should have been. In the first chapter of his *An Enquiry concerning Human Understanding* he wrote, "Be a philosopher; but, amidst all your philosophy, be still a man."[21] The maxim is, fortunately, easily updatable: *Be a philosopher; but, amid all your philosophy, be still a human being.* But the gendered nature of the original suggests a mischievous twist: *He may be a philosopher, but amid all his philosophy, he is usually still all too much a man.*

Whatever Mme. de Boufflers eventually made of Hume's attitude to women, she was so keen to meet Hume that in April 1763 she actually went to London with the prime motivation of doing just that. Hume, however, was at Ninewells. She extended her stay beyond the intended two months in the hope of meeting him but he did not oblige her with a visit.[22] This might seem like a slight but de Boufflers appeared to take it well. (Remember that by stagecoach the trip from Edinburgh would have taken Hume at least two days, usually more.) There was certainly no sign of any offense in the warm welcome she gave Hume when he finally arrived in Paris.

Hume's decision to accept Lord Hertford's invitation seemed to be based on the judgment that he had nothing to lose and a lot potentially to gain from a new adventure. Before leaving for France he wrote to Adam Smith, "I thought it ridiculous at my years to be entering on a new scene, and to put myself in the lists as a candidate of fortune. But I reflected that I had in a manner abjured all literary occupations; that I resolved to give up my future life entirely to amusements; that there could not be a better pastime than such a journey, especially with a man of Lord Hertford's character."[23]

However, there are signs that he remained ambivalent about his decision even as he was putting it into action. As the time to go neared he was at first excited. "I go to a Place of the World which I have always admird the most," he wrote.[24] But in London, a month before he was due to leave, he confided to Smith, "I repine at my Loss of Ease & Leizure & Retirement & Independence, and it is not without a Sigh I look backwards nor without Reluctance that I cast my Eye forwards."[25] Barely a week later, writing to Mme. de Boufflers, he again seemed confident he was doing the right thing: "I ought to esteem myself extremely obliged to Lord Hertford, as upon many other accounts, so particularly for rousing me from a state of indolence and sloth, which I falsely dignified with the name of philosophy. . . . I now find . . . that it is better for a man to keep in the midst of society."[26] Perhaps he already had reservations and hid them from all but his closest confidantes. More likely, he was genuinely torn. As we have already seen, throughout his life he found himself both craving a quiet life of relative solitude and enjoying intelligent, convivial company. What was attractive about Paris was also what made him nervous of going there: such an abundance of good company that escaping it would be difficult.

Le bon David

Lord Hertford and his entourage left London on October 13, 1763, setting sail from Dover the following day. Because of a strong southeasterly wind, they had to land in Boulogne instead of Calais.[27] Once again, it seems Hume, a poor sailor, was unfortunate in his channel crossing.

In Paris, Hume was received with adulation. After just three days in the capital and two at the royal palace in Fontainebleau, thirty-five miles south of central Paris, he wrote to Smith, "I have every where met with the most extraordinary Honours which the most exorbitant Vanity cou'd wish or desire."[28] In another letter to Adam Ferguson two weeks later, still with the royal court at Fontainebleau, he reported with a combination of pride and embarrassment that "the Royal Family downwards seem to have it much at heart to persuade me, by every expression of esteem, that they consider me as one of the greatest geniuses in the world."[29] Although he seemed to take some satisfaction in this, he was also genuinely troubled by what Mossner calls the "indiscriminate flattery" heaped upon him and the relentless schedule of large social gatherings. "I suppose this, like all other violent Modes, will pass," he wrote wearily, "and in the mean while, the Hurry & Dissipation, attending it, gives me more pain than Pleasure."[30] In March 1764 he would look back and regret that "I allowd myself at first to be hurry'd into too great a Variety of Company, and find a Difficulty to withdraw and confine myself to one Society, without which there is no real Enjoyment."[31]

Hume also struggled with his French, which had never been fluent in the first place. Such was the inadequacy of his linguistic skills that he worried they were not sufficient for his job and considered resigning his post. But he found it soon came back, while the errors and Scots accent that remained only seemed to endear him to the adoring French.[32] Despite his Francophilia, Hume never fully mastered the language. Mossner says, "Even in later life, Hume's conversational French was not fluent, and he always retained a Scottish burr which either disgusted or delighted the listener."[33]

Soon, it seems, the balance of pain and pleasure had tipped decisively toward the positive. He managed to narrow his social circle to people he found most agreeable, ridding himself of the "silly, distant admiration." The result was blissful. "I eat nothing but Ambrosia, drink nothing but Nectar, breathe nothing but Incense, and tread on nothing but Flowers."[34] By November 23 he could tell his friend Rev. Wedderburn, "I daily reconcile my-self more to this place, and expect soon to be a Parisian."[35] He was still as enthusiastic in June 1764 when he reported, "I con-tinue to live here in a manner amusing enough, and which gives me no time to be tir'd of any Scene. What between public Busi-ness, the Company of the learned and that of the Great, espe-cially of the Ladies, I find all my time fill'd up."[36]

His admiration for the French people was in stark contrast to the dim view he took of the inhabitants of the British capital, whom he called "the factious barbarians of London."[37] That harsh judgment seemed to be a settled opinion rather than an angry outburst as he repeated it in another letter praising Paris in which he said, "The Taste for Literature is neither decayd nor depravd here, as with the Barbarians who inhabit the Banks of the Thames."[38] He told Smith in 1765 that "London is the Capi-tal of my own Country; but it never pleased me much. Letters are there held in no honour: Scotsmen are hated: Superstition and Ignorance gain ground daily."[39] He took a dim view of the cultural sophistication of the English as a whole, saying that they are not in general "remarkable for delicacy of taste, or for sensibility to the charms of the muses."[40] He told his London publisher Strahan that "you grow every day madder in England: There is a Prospect that that worthless Generation will soon bring themselves to ruin, by their own folly."[41] As he got older his judgment seemed ever harsher. In a letter from 1773 he ex-pressed the opinion that until the beginning of the seventeenth century, England was an uncultivated nation. Ever the gour-mand, his evidence for this was partly gastronomic: "even When good Queen Elizabeth sat on the Throne, there was very little good Roast Beef in it, and no Liberty at all." As for poor Queen Catherine of Aragon, the first wife of Henry VIII, when "she had a Fancy to eat a Sallad, she could not find one in all England."[42]

Paris, he wrote, was "the Center of Arts, of Politeness, of Gallantry, and of good Company."[43] Much of his delight in Parisian intellectual life came from the salons. Mossner paints a romantic, attractive picture of this unique institution and the virtues it displayed: "In the *salon* all were expected to learn gracefully and unobtrusively; all were accepted as artistic, intellectual, or social equals. The artificial aristocracy of birth bowed to the natural aristocracy of talent; to patronise talent was the privilege of birth and wealth."[44] It is hard to imagine a setting more suited to the temperament of David Hume.

As we have already noted, these salons were hosted and run by women. Hume attended those of Mme. de Boufflers, Mme. Geoffrin, Mme. du Deffand, and Mlle. (Julie) de Lespinasse. These were all middle-aged women, "past thirty" as Hume put it, "Women of Sense and Knowledge." They did not tolerate the kind of bawdiness and vulgarity all-male meetings could descend into. "Scarce a double Entendre ever to be heard; scarce a free Joke," said Hume. However, that does not mean that they were paragons of traditional feminine virtues of chastity and purity. "What lies below this Veil is not commonly supposed to be so pure," wrote Hume, somewhat cryptically.[45]

The women themselves were less circumspect than Hume, doing little to disguise their refusal to play the demure role society had allocated them. Lespinasse became the mistress of d'Alembert, said to be Hume's favorite *philosophe*.[46] Their combined intellectual heft along with her strong personality helped her salon to surpass Mme. de Boufflers's as the most popular in Paris.[47]

In the case of Mme. de Boufflers, her rejection of traditional mores was hardly a secret. She drew up quite stern "Rules of Conduct" for her salon, which included "propriety and decency." But it is clear that she was not as pure as her tenets suggested. Her rival *salonnière* Mme. du Deffand said somewhat bitterly, "What is amusing, though a little annoying, is that this lofty morality is not perfectly in accord with her conduct; what is more amusing is that the contrast does not startle her." In his *Confessions,* Rousseau suggested she made improper advances to him and was even more forthright in private correspondence.[48]

Although these remarks report mere hearsay and reputation, she was openly living apart from her husband as the mistress of the Prince de Conti, seven years her senior. He was a libertine in an age of libertines but having only one mistress at a time counted as tame.

Hume became a devotee of Mme. de Boufflers, and many shared the opinion of Mme. de Verdelin, who told Rousseau that he was "madly in love" with her.[49] Greig, the editor of Hume's letters, is not so sure, convinced only that "there are signs that at one time Mme de Boufflers tried her best to make him fall in love with her." According to Greig, Hume found himself "distracted, flattered, and at length frightened" by this because "it threatened what he cherished more than life itself— his independence."[50]

We cannot know exactly what passions did or did not stir in Hume's breast, but there is a great deal of affection in his letters to her that sometimes bubbles over into passion. One of the most striking examples of this came after she wrote him a quite angry letter, stung by what she perceived as cold indifference in his last correspondence. His reply is visceral and heartfelt. "You may cut me to pieces, limb by limb," he wrote, "but like those pertinacious animals of my country, I shall expire still attached to you, and you will in vain attempt to get free."[51] A later letter is hardly less ardent. "I shall never, I hope, be obliged to leave the place where you dwell," he wrote. "No one can bear you a more tender and more sincere friendship or desire more earnestly a return of like sentiment on your part."[52] Over time, however, the correspondence cooled. Although he maintained their friendship for the rest of his life, such extremes of passion vanished from his letters. Once he left Paris, he never actually saw her again.[53]

Among themselves, the *salonnières* were often less than sisterly. Deffand detested Geoffrin and Lespinasse, and at one point demanded that Hume had to choose between coming to her salon and that of Lespinasse. Unsurprisingly, this most unfactious of men objected. "How many times have I told you, that I was ready to espouse the loves of my friend, but that I find it repugnant to embrace her hatreds?" he pleaded. (There is a maxim contained in this: *be as willing to share your friends' loves as you are reluctant to embrace their hatreds.*) But Deffand would not relent, so he had to choose Lespinasse, adding himself to Deffand's list of enemies.[54]

Given the historic importance of the salons, I was surprised to discover that so little has been done to mark their locations. Only that of Mme. Geoffrin at 374 rue Saint-Honoré merits a somewhat tarnished bronze plaque, noting that her salon was known as "Le Royaume de la rue Saint-Honoré" (The Kingdom of la rue Saint-Honoré). Now a much refurbished office block, the salon once hosted the likes of Fontenelle, Montesquieu, Voltaire, Grimm, d'Alembert, Helvetius, Marmontel, d'Holbach, and Diderot.

Just along the road at 239 rue Saint-Honoré is the site of the first salon of Louise d'Épinay, from 1748 to 1762, shortly before Hume's arrival. But there is nothing to tell the visitor this, nor at 5 rue de la Chaussée d'Antinon, where her salon moved to, which is now the delivery entrance to the Paris Opera. Another blank is drawn at the site of the salon of Mme. du Deffand, which was her suite at the Convent of St. Joseph at what is today

14 rue St. Dominique. This building is now used by the French Ministry of Defence and so is highly fortified. A peek through a gap in the gates reveals a building that certainly looks as though it could have been a former convent. Mlle. Lespinasse's salon was further down the corner with rue de Bellechasse, again unmarked.[55]

The Psychologist

Another Enlightenment site that no longer stands is the Paris residence of the Prince de Conti, the Temple, a medieval fortress built by the Knights Templar. According to Mossner, Conti assigned de Boufflers a house facing north on the rue Notre-Dame-de Nazareth with a simple garden to the south, and that was where she held her salon.[56] However, this would seem to be an impossibility because the site of the Temple, long demolished, does not adjoin the rue Notre-Dame-de Nazareth. This might not be an error on Mossner's part, since street names have changed over the years in Paris, particularly after Haussmann's vast renovation of the city from 1853 and even beyond his dismissal as prefect of the Seine in 1870. Haussmann turned the site of the Temple into one of the city's many new squares. Square du Temple is today a peaceful, green haven but once again, its role in France's history of ideas is unacknowledged.

Wandering around the Temple area I was amused to find it was home to many psychotherapists. Hume was in many ways a great psychologist and so in this respect, at least, his legacy remains. Hume made several observations almost as asides that experimental psychology has since vindicated.

For instance, he remarks that "an experiment, that is recent and fresh in the memory, affects us more than one that is in some measure obliterated; and has a superior influence on the judgment, as well as on the passions."[57] This has come to be known as the *recency effect,* a source of much error of judgment. For instance, when 9/11 was still fresh in Americans' memories, more people avoided planes and drove cars instead, even though driving is much more dangerous than flying. The memory of the recent catastrophe made the fear of flying weigh more heavily than it rationally should have done. Hume's own "experiments," based on nothing more than acute observation of everyday life, often yielded results as good as those of later, more controlled ones.

A related cognitive bias is *hyperbolic discounting,* the tendency to prefer immediate rewards over future ones, even when the future rewards are much greater. Hume describes this precisely when he writes that *"there is no quality in human nature, which causes more fatal errors in our conduct, than that which leads us to prefer whatever is present to the distant and remote, and makes us desire objects more according to their situation than their intrinsic value."*[58] Even when we are fully convinced that the more distant is much more valuable than that which is nearer, "we are not able to regulate our actions by this judgment; but yield to the sollicitations of our passions, which always plead in favour of whatever is near and contiguous."[59] It is for this reason that we need legally binding laws and contracts. Both these biases are based on the common principle that *imagination, not reason, reigns sovereign in the human mind and it can only be overthrown by great effort.*

A third great psychological insight is that "there is a principle of human nature, which we have frequently taken notice of, that men are mightily addicted to *general rules,* and that we often carry our maxims beyond those reasons, which first induc'd us to establish them." Hume is here describing what contemporary psychologists call *heuristics.* Human beings are cognitive misers, meaning that we expend as little brain power as possible, since our mental resources are finite and valuable. Therefore we do not go to the effort of calculating the optimal way to act in any given case but rely instead on "rules of thumb." If we couldn't do this we would be unable to act, forever stuck calculating the best way ahead. But the price we pay for using heuristics is that we sometimes end up applying a rule to a case that is an exception to it. Hume believes this is a price worth paying. Indeed, it is a principle as useful in politics as it is in human psychology. In matters of government, Hume argues it is essential that we follow general rules and do not make any exceptions at all. The law only works because it applies to everyone in the same way, irrespective of the specifics of their case. Even advocates of civil disobedience accept this: they break the law prepared to suffer from its sanctions in order to highlight its injustice.

Hume was also a shrewd observer of our tendency both to overestimate our own abilities and to attribute more of what happens to us to our characters than to chance or outside events, a bias known as *fundamental attribution error*. Hume argued that although it is good to know our own abilities accurately, "were it allowable to err on either side, twou'd be more advantageous to overrate our merit, than to form ideas of it, below its just standard. Fortune commonly favours the bold and enterprizing; and nothing inspires us with more boldness than a good opinion of ourselves." Here, Hume identifies both the bias and the explanation for its prevalence, since it is indeed the case that people who overestimate their own abilities a little tend to perform better than those who have "an over-weaning conceit of our own merit," which he condemns, or those who have excessive modesty, which he says "produces often uneasiness in the person endow'd with it."[60]

Yet another great psychological insight is that although we like to think we are reasonable people who base our conclusions on sound arguments, a lot of the time we simply use our intellects to rationalize what we already believe. This is often thought of as one of modern psychology's great revelations, but Hume was there nearly three hundred years ago. "The passion for philosophy," he says, "though it aims at the correction of our manners, and extirpation of our vices, it may only serve, by imprudent management, to foster a predominant inclination, and push the mind, with more determined resolution, towards that side, which already draws too much, by the biass and propensity of the natural temper." Our "natural indolence . . . seeks a pretence of reason, to give itself a full and uncontrouled indulgence."[61] *Do not be fooled by the apparent ubiquity of rational thought: we use reason more than we are governed by it.*

Hume was also a pioneer of what we now call *evolutionary psychology*, before there was even a theory of evolution. Without the specific insights of Darwin, he had a sense that certain principles of thought had developed over the course of human history in response to certain needs that emerged purely out of our biological and social situation. In one striking passage he suggests that our ideals of beauty are linked to what we would now call, in evolutionary terms, *fitness for survival.* "'Tis certain, that a considerable part of the beauty of men, as well as of other animals, consists in such a conformation of members, as we find by experience to be attended with strength and agility, and to capacitate the creature for any action or exercise. Broad shoulders, a lank belly, firm joints, taper legs; all these are beautiful in our species, because they are signs of force and vigour, which being advantages we naturally sympathize with, they convey to the beholder a share of that satisfaction they produce in the possessor."[62] Hume wrote this when he was young and relatively slender. Interestingly, he retained the example of the lank (flat) belly when he rewrote Book I of the *Treatise* as the *Essay concerning Human Understanding*, by which time the sight of his own stomach would not, by his own account, have given others much pleasure.[63]

Our natural history even explains the emergence of moral norms, another idea that has become popular in recent years, centuries after Hume. Perhaps the clearest example of this is his account of the moral norms concerning female chastity. Why is it that sexual promiscuity has been condemned more in women than in men? Hume offered a version of an argument that many evolutionary psychologists use today. It starts with the observation that "men are induc'd to labour for the maintenance and education of their children, by the persuasion that they are really their own; and therefore 'tis reasonable, and even necessary, to give them some security in this particular." As Hume delicately explains, "If we examine the structure of the human body, we shall find, that this security is very difficult to be attain'd on our part." The most efficient means that evolved to ensure this was for women themselves to internalize society's condemnation of infidelity. "In order, therefore, to impose a due restraint on the female sex, we must attach a peculiar degree of shame to their infidelity, above what arises merely from its injustice, and must bestow proportionable praises on their chastity."[64]

Combine this insight with those he had about heuristics, and it's easy to see how the usefulness of norms of chastity for married women of childbearing age generates a general rule that "carries us beyond the original principle, and makes us extend the notions of modesty over the whole sex, from their earliest infancy to their extremest old-age and infirmity."[65]

Hume's genius as a psychologist should come as no surprise to anyone who recognizes his genius as a philosopher. The two disciplines only formally separated in the late nineteenth century, when the German Wilhelm Wundt founded the first experimental psychology laboratory at the University of Zurich in 1879. But perhaps this amicable divorce has not served philosophy well. *To understand how you should best think, you need to understand how you actually think.* Doing philosophy without psychology is like trying to sail around the world with no knowledge of how boats work.

The Company of Atheists

The women-run salons did not have a monopoly on Parisian intellectual life. One of the most intellectually fecund locales was the Café de la Régence on rue Saint-Honoré. Originally known as the Café de la Place du Palais Royal, this was a particularly important meeting point for the *encyclopédistes* and their associates, such as Voltaire, Diderot, d'Alembert, Rousseau, Marmontel, and Benjamin Franklin. Diderot immortalized the café by making it the setting for the first scene of his satire *Neveu de Rameau* (*Rameau's Nephew*) in 1762. "If the weather is too cold or too rainy, I take refuge in the Regency Café," writes the narrator. "I like to watch the games of chess. The best chess players in the world are in Paris, and the best players in Paris are in the Regency Café." This was fact not fiction: from 1715 the café had played host to some famous chess tournaments. It was also the place where on August 26, 1844, Marx and Engels met for only the second time.[66]

There is no concrete evidence that Hume ever visited the café, but it would be extraordinary if he never stepped inside such a regular meeting place for Parisian intellectuals. Once again, however, pinpointing the exact location is difficult. A Paris history website places it at 155 rue Saint-Honoré. At that address, however, is a bookshop, Librairie Delamain, which knows nothing of this supposed history. Nor does this fit the description I found elsewhere of it lying on the west corner of Place Colette and rue Saint-Honoré. To add to the confusion, there is an extant Café de la Régence at 167 rue Saint Honoré, but since this doesn't even claim to be the original it seems it is simply trading on the historic resonance of its name. Indeed, even the original café was peripatetic, relocating temporarily to the Hôtel Dodun, 21 rue de Richelieu in 1852 before moving to 161 rue Saint-Honoré in 1854.

One place we know Hume did visit was the home of Paul-Henri Thiry, Baron d'Holbach. Here leading intellectuals gathered every Sunday and Thursday, when discussion would take place over lavish dinners and fine wines. Horace Walpole called d'Holbach "the host of Europe."[67]

D'Holbach's house is one of the few buildings which hosted salons that is still standing, on what was the rue Royale, Butte St. Roche but is now 8 rue des Moulins. When I visited Paris it was divided into several different commercial offices. The one that interested me was on the second floor, home to Trebosc + van Lelyveld, a gallery specializing in European sculpture from the Renaissance to the beginning of the twentieth century. The owners, Alfred van Lelyveld and Olivier Trebosc, showed me around what is almost certainly the space in which d'Holbach received his visitors. The building has a typical eighteenth-century layout in which the high-ceilinged story would have been the one used to entertain guests. This was the floor of the gallery, which has three small but elegant rooms. The largest is accessed directly from the stairwell and is where the dining table would have been set up, although van

Lelyveld told me dining rooms as such did not exist at the time. The room has French windows all the way to the floor and a large marble fireplace. One could imagine up to twelve people comfortably in this space, but no more, suggesting a certain intimacy in the salons held there. Off that was a smaller, similar room, also with a fireplace and French windows. The third room off this was the smallest of them all. Overall, it is a modest home for such a rich man, without ostentation, suggesting that his priorities were good company, intellectual endeavors, and fine food and drink.

It was at a dinner in this house that one of the most famous incidents of Hume's sojourn in Paris took place, recounted by Diderot. The first time Hume sat the Baron's table, he remarked that he did not believe in atheists, since he had never seen one. The Baron replied, "Count how many we are here. We are eighteen. It isn't too bad a showing to be able to point out to you fifteen at once: the three others haven't made up their minds."[68]

This incident has subsequently grown into a widely promulgated myth of the famous d'Holbach dinner in which Voltaire and all the other greats of the time were sitting around the same table. This isn't possible since Hume never met Voltaire, who had left Paris in 1759 to live in Ferney, France, near the Swiss border. Nevertheless, the gist of the story certainly rings true. The Baron and his associates were fervent atheists who believed Christianity would be abolished in Europe before the century was out.[69] Hume, for all his skepticism, never identified as an atheist, believing it to be too dogmatic a position.

In many ways, Hume was not at home among these atheists. The British historian Edward Gibbon said they laughed at his skepticism, while Sir James Macdonald wrote from Paris to London saying, "Poor Hume, who on your side of the water was thought to have too little religion, is here thought to have too much." Hume substantiates the existence of such mockery, writing much later that Lord Marischal and Helvétius "used to laugh at me for my narrow way of thinking in these particulars."[70] Hume mischievously called d'Holbach's coterie the "Sheikhs of the rue Royale."[71]

However, there is little evidence of any deep discomfort, let alone animosity, in Hume's relationship with the *philosophes*. The Hume family maintained that the atheistical club even presented Hume with a gold medal but that his grand-niece, atoning for his heresies, gave it to an Edinburgh church that melted it down and had a Parisian craftsman make into a censer, a container in which incense is burned during a religious ceremony.[72] If true, it would be a meticulously planned revenge, turning a souvenir of camaraderie with atheists into an instrument of the kind of superstitious religion Hume disliked the most, in the foreign city he loved above any other. However, one suspects Hume would have been more amused than irritated by this display of righteous indignation.

But why did Hume and the *philosophes* disagree at all? Today, Hume is a philosophical hero to many atheists who still use his arguments against religion. It seems clear he had no religious faith and believed in no god. Many of his published words about religion are overtly hostile. He says that "terror is the primary principle of religion."[73] He frequently deplores the intolerance religion breeds, unfavorably comparing the "bigotted jealousy, with which the present age is so much infested," with the "freedom and toleration" in ancient Greece and Rome that allowed philosophy to first flourish.[74] In some private letters he was overtly sacrilegious. He told Captain James Edmonstoune that "I believe I shall write no more History; but proceed directly to attack the Lord's Prayer & the ten Commandments & the single Cat [catechism of the Anglican Church]; and to recommend Suicide & Adultery; And so persist, till it shall please the Lord to take me to himself."[75] So why did he resist the label of atheist?

To answer this question, we need to look at Hume's writings on religion. But first, they need to be put in their historical context. In 1727, when Hume was sixteen years old, the last woman to be convicted of witchcraft in Scotland was burned alive. Her "crime" was turning her daughter into a pony. By 1777 Hume was able to write:

> There has been a sudden and sensible change in the opinions of men within these last fifty years, by the progress of learning and of liberty. Most people, in this island, have divested themselves of all superstitious reverence to names and authority: The clergy have much lost their credit: Their pretensions and doctrines have been ridiculed; and even religion can scarcely support itself in the world. The mere name of king commands little respect; and to talk of a king as GOD's vicegerent on earth, or to give him any of those magnificent titles, which formerly dazzled mankind, would but excite laughter in every one.[76]

Hume could only commend this development. But we should not confuse his pleasure at the decline of the worst aspects of religion with any glee over the decline of religion itself. Hume consistently made his main target not religion per se but *superstition* and *enthusiasm*. Superstition was primarily a Roman Catholic vice, manifest in the rituals of communion, wide belief in miracles, prayers to saints, and belief in the holiness of blessed water and sacred relics. Enthusiasm was more of a Protestant vice, displayed by puritanical ethics and an excessive zeal that allowed no dissent and led to the persecution of infidels and nonconformists. In one essay, Hume identified the sources of superstition as "weakness, fear, melancholy" and those of enthusiasm in "hope, pride, presumption, a warm imagination," while both were equally rooted in "ignorance."[77] He had no good word to say about either of them. "Nor does the wolf molest more the timid flock, than superstition does the anxious breast of wretched mortals," while "enthusiasm produces the most cruel disorders in human society."[78]

So while Hume vociferously opposed superstition and enthusiasm, he simply didn't believe in the other aspects of religion. His reason for this was straightforward: there is no evidence to suppose that the claims of religion are true. Therefore he didn't believe them. But nor could he prove that they are false. Hence he stopped short of declaring himself an atheist. The place of God in Hume's thought was rather like the one it had in the cosmology of the mathematician Pierre-Simon Laplace. When asked by Emperor Napoleon I why he had not mentioned God in his explanation of the orbits of Saturn and Jupiter, he is said to have replied, "I had no need of that hypothesis."

That made Hume an agnostic rather than an atheist. But the ways in which these two terms are used make that potentially misleading. Bertrand Russell captured this difficulty in a 1947 essay in which he said, "As a philosopher, if I were speaking to a purely philosophic audience I should say that I ought to describe myself as an Agnostic, because I do not think that there is a conclusive argument by which one can prove that there is not a God. On the other hand, if I am to convey the right impression to the ordinary man in the street I think I ought to say that I am an Atheist, because when I say that I cannot prove that there is not a God, I ought to add equally that I cannot prove that there are not the Homeric gods."[79]

One way of thinking about this is that for true agnostics, the question of God's existence is a live question, whereas for atheists it is not. That is why Hume did not approve of atheism. But there are two ways in which we might consider a question not to be a live one. One is that we think there is no doubt as to its answer. That is too strong for a question such as God's existence. But many people who describe themselves as atheists—including myself—do not go so far. We accept that we can never know for sure that God doesn't exist. But we point out that, as Hume himself argued, when it comes to matters of fact, nothing is absolutely certain. That does not mean we suspend belief about them. Some things seem so overwhelmingly probable that, while we accept it is possible new evidence will lead us to change our minds, for now we consider the issue settled. God's nonexistence is one such almost-certainty, along with the belief that the Earth was not created six thousand years ago, that smoking causes cancer, and that the Nazis murdered millions of Jews, homosexuals, Romanies, and dissidents in concentration camps in the 1940s.

Still, it might seem somewhat disingenuous that Hume refused to make his own disbelief more explicit. We can't be sure why he was so coy, but two reasons at least seem quite clear. The first is simple pragmatism. He had enough trouble with his reputation as an "infidel" without going the whole hog and declaring himself an atheist. We've already seen how his reputation cost him two professorships in Edinburgh and Glasgow. In the mid-1750s, there was a very real risk that the Church of Scotland would seek his prosecution as an infidel. In 1755 the General Assembly of the Church passed a motion calling for stern action on the purveyors of "Infidelity and Immorality," with Hume the unnamed but widely known target of the attack. In 1756 a written "overture" was presented calling for a committee to formally investigate him. Hume was defended by the young Rev. Wedderburn, who urged them to "trust to reason and scripture for the refutation of his errors." Wedderburn played down the risk Hume posed to public piety saying that his views were "of an abstract and metaphysical nature—not exciting the attention of the multitude—not influencing life or conduct." He asked the Assembly, "What advantage do you really expect from the course that is proposed?"[80] Wedderburn carried the day.

Hume was off the hook but not yet out of the woods. In 1757 he told Smith, "I expect the next Assembly will very solemnly pronounce the Sentence of Excommunication against me: But I do not apprehend it to be a Matter of any Consequence."[81] If Hume meant he wouldn't have been burned like the poor women convicted for witchcraft in his lifetime, he was right. But he must have known that being convicted by the church would have been damaging, which is surely why he abandoned plans to publish the heretical essays "Of Suicide" and "Of the Immortality of the Soul" as part of a planned book *Five Dissertations*.[82] The essays were circulated privately but were not included in his collected essays until 1783, several years after his death.

Mossner believes that however dire the consequences of a prosecution would have been for Hume, they would have been worse for the Church itself, which is why it never happened. Scotland had a well-deserved reputation as a free and open society. Had Hume been persecuted for his freethinking, "Scotland would have become the laughing-stock of England and Britain would have become the laughing-stock of Europe. Hume himself would have become the martyred hero of both Britain and Europe."[83]

This whole episode is in sharp contrast with the way in which another of the great Western philosophers dealt with religious persecution. The charge of "Infidelity and Immorality" is strikingly similar to that leveled against Socrates in fifth century BCE Athens. Socrates faced two charges: corrupting the youth of the city and refusing to recognize its gods. For Socrates, however, the penalty was much more severe: he was condemned to death by drinking the mortal poison, hemlock. Unlike Hume, Socrates refused to save himself either by saying the right things or by fleeing the city, as he could easily have done.

Socrates had two reasons for doing this. First, he believed in the immortality of the soul, which meant he did not believe his bodily death would be the end of him. Hume did not share this reassuring belief. Hume considered two varieties of argument for the soul's immortality and found them both wanting. Metaphysical arguments claim that minds must be distinct from matter, since matter is inert and minds are conscious. Hume's objection was that if it defies explanation to believe that matter is capable of thought, why is it any less incredible that a different kind of substance can be conscious? The deep philosophical problem—if there is one—is how can *any* kind of substance think? As Hume put it, "Matter . . . and spirit, are at bottom equally unknown, and we cannot determine what qualities inhere in the one or the other."[84]

Even if the soul were immortal, that would not mean that the person it currently animates is immortal. This is essentially a reiteration of an argument put forward by John Locke in *An Essay Concerning Human Understanding*. Locke asked whether having the same soul as, say, Nestor or Thersites at the siege of Troy would make the current bearer of the soul the same person as either of these men, even though it had no memory of their lives and experiences. Locke believed we would all say no.[85] Having the same soul as someone who lived before no more makes you the same person as them as having the liver, heart, or legs of a deceased person would. Hume concludes that *"the*

soul, . . . if immortal, existed before our birth: And if the former
state of existence no wise concerned us, neither will the latter."[86]
So even if souls are immortal, that wouldn't mean that Socrates
would be right to calmly believe *he* would live on after his death,
merely that his soul would.

Hume also dismisses the moral argument for life after death,
namely that it is necessary for justice to be done, since in this
mortal life, the wicked sometimes die unpunished and the good
die in misery. Hume doesn't give the answer many would give
today: "Life is not fair—get used to it." Rather, he argues that
the vision of the afterlife portrayed by Christianity is even less
fair. "Punishment," he wrote, "should bear some proportion to
the offence. Why then eternal punishment for temporary of-
fences of so frail a creature as man?" The whole idea of heaven
and hell supposes "two distinct species of man, the good and
the bad," but *"the greatest part of mankind float betwixt vice*
and virtue." Furthermore, if there were an eternal life to come,
this present one would be a "barbarous deceit" unworthy of a
"beneficent and wise" God. "What cruelty, what iniquity, what
injustice in nature, to confine thus all our concern, as well as all
our knowledge, to the present life, if there be another scene still
awaiting us, of infinitely greater consequence?"[87] The high in-
fant mortality rate makes the existence of this world as a precur-
sor of another even more absurd. "The half of mankind dye
before they are rational creatures."[88]

Finally, Hume considers an argument for the soul's mortality.
The study of nature shows us that *"nothing in this world is per-*
petual, every thing however seemingly firm is in continual flux
and change, the world itself gives symptoms of frailty and dis-
solution." The mind is no exception to this rule. "The last symptoms which the mind discovers are disorder, weakness, insensibility and stupidity, the fore-runners of its annihilation."[89]

Although Hume's arguments were heretical, he was bold enough to suggest that even theologians are "really infidels in their hearts, and have nothing like what we can call a belief of the eternal duration of their souls."[90] Despite what anyone might say, the vast majority of us try to avoid death and are heartbroken when those we love die. Nor can we really imagine life after death as a reality. Hume's maxim here is: *Belief in an eternal life is a lie we comfort ourselves with, knowing in our hearts it is a lie, but preferring the comfort to the truth.* This is a specific instance of a more general principle: *"All doctrines are to be suspected, which are favoured by our passions."*

Belief in an immortal soul was only one of Socrates's reasons for not giving in to his accusers. The other was that he believed there was no higher value than truth, not even life. Noble though this sounds, for Hume this is absurd. The only truths we can know for certain are trivial ones, things that are true by definition such as $1 + 1 = 2$ or that all bachelors are unmarried men. All matters of fact are uncertain. Why would the certainty of death be a fair price to pay to uphold any of them? Of course, we talk of people being willing to die for the truth, but more often than not what they are really dying for is other people. People lay down their lives so the truth of oppression can come out. It is not because the truth matters more than life but that life matters and protecting it requires protecting the truth. *Truth is not worth dying for, but some things worth dying for demand that we uphold the truth, no matter what.*

In refusing to suffer unnecessary hardship because some people wanted to persecute him for his views, Hume was following another great Athenian, Aristotle. Like Socrates, Aristotle faced charges of impiety and possible death. Unlike Socrates, he took the opportunity to flee and so had another year of

FIGURE 16. The site of the now drained Nor' Loch into which Hume fell.

precious life. "I will not allow the Athenians to sin twice against philosophy," Aristotle is supposed to have said. He did not believe that death should mean nothing to a philosopher. The more a person is "possessed of virtue in its entirety and the happier he is, the more he will be pained at the thought of death; for life is best worth living for such a man, and he is knowingly losing the greatest goods, and this is painful."[91]

Hume's attitude is perhaps best illustrated in one of the most famous stories of his life, albeit one that is possibly apocryphal. As part of the development of Edinburgh's New Town, the Nor' Loch (a lake) was drained, leaving a bog. Hume walked by it one day on the way from his James Court home in the Old Town to the site of his new one, still under construction. He slipped and fell in, calling out to an old fishwife for help. She recognized him as Hume the atheist and refused.

"But my good woman," protested Hume, "does not your religion as a Christian teach you to do good, even to your enemies?"

"That may well be," she replied. "But ye shallna get out o' that, till ye become a Christian yoursell, and repeat the Lord's Prayer and the Belief!"

Hume wasted no time in following her instruction, later saying she was the most acute theologian he had ever encountered—less to praise her than to mock theologians.[92] This was not hypocrisy but good, logical sense: if you believe that religious doctrines are nothing but nonsense and superstition, what is the harm in parroting them if doing so saves your life? There is an important Humean maxim here: *if philosophy is indeed part of a good life, no philosophy should tell us to treat life as though it were not good.*

If some of Hume's reluctance to embrace atheism was tactical or strategic, much was far more principled. Hume was simply too reasonable and skeptical to take a hard line, and far too forgiving of human folly to despise those who were more gullible in matters of religion. He was friendly with many liberal-minded clergy, as Thomas Carlyle attested years after Hume's death: "He took much to the company of the younger clergy, not from a wish to bring them over to his opinions, for he never attempted to overturn any man's principles, but they best understood his notions, and could furnish him with literary conversations."[93] Hugh Blair was one such clerical friend, and when Hume was in Paris he sent him "common letters" to be read by "my Protestant Pastors."[94] He was also great friends with Rev. John Home (no relation), a moderate cleric who after retiring even invited Hume to live with him.[95] Lord Hertford, whom he willingly served as secretary, was famously pious.[96] To the Rev. Robert Wallace he once wrote, "Why cannot all the World entertain different Opinions about any Subject, as amicably as we do?"[97]

Despite this, it seems some were determined to portray Hume as a militant anti-cleric. When Hume met the famous novelist Rev. Laurence Sterne in Paris in May 1764, where he delivered his last sermon, reports circulated that they had clashed. Sterne sternly denied this. "Mr. *Hume* and I never had a dispute—I mean a serious, angry or petulant dispute, in our lives:—indeed I should be exceedingly surprised to hear that David ever had an unpleasant contention with any man; and if I should ever be made to believe that such an event had happened, nothing would persuade me that his opponent was not in the wrong, for in my life did I never meet with a being of a more placid and gentle nature." What really happened was no more than "a little pleasant sparring . . . nothing in it that did not bear the marks of good will and urbanity on both sides. . . . David was disposed to make a little merry with the *Parson*; and, in return, the Parson was equally disposed to make a little mirth with the *Infidel*; we laughed at one another, and the company laughed with us both."[98]

Today, Hume's willingness to respect and engage with liberal believers is criticized by some atheists as "accommodationism." Their argument is that by taking moderates seriously, skeptics legitimize religion, which makes it easier for extremists. The moderates in effect provide cover for the radical fundamentalists. This is the logic of "the friend of my enemy is my enemy" or "you're either with us or against us."

Hume seemed alive to this danger, arguing that no matter how liberal a religion might be, there will always be those who take it to further extremes. "It is certain," he wrote, "that, in every religion, however sublime the verbal definition which gives it its divinity, many of the votaries, perhaps the greatest number, will still seek the divine favour, not by virtue and good morals, which alone can be acceptable to a perfect being, but either by frivolous observances, by intemperate zeal, by rapturous exstacies, or by the belief of mysterious and absurd opinions."[99] This did not, however, lead him to the conclusion that all religion needs to be fiercely challenged. Hume set an example: *refuse to meet intolerance with intolerance, religious extremism with secular extremism.*

His outlook seems to be best captured in a passage in his *Dialogues concerning Natural Religion*. This book was never published in his lifetime, even though many friends read it and some, he wrote, "flatter me, that it is the best thing I ever wrote."[100] At times, he seemed frustrated at his inability to publish them. To one of the people who strongly discouraged him to publish, Gilbert Minto, he wrote with teasing overstatement, "Is it not hard & tyrannical in you, more tyrannical than any act of the Stuarts, not to allow me to publish my Dialogues?"[101] Hume made great efforts to ensure they were published after his death. He had wanted Adam Smith to take on the task of executor, but Smith refused, fearing it would bring him too much trouble. He instead left it to his publisher, William Strahan, on the condition that if after two and a half years from his death they had not been published, they would be returned to his nephew, David, who would then be charged with publishing them.[102]

For some time, the scholarly consensus has been that Hume was too cautious. After all, he had published *The Natural History of Religion* as part of a collection titled *Four Dissertations* in 1757 without apparently making his reputation as a dangerous infidel any worse. In some ways, the *Natural History* is a more audacious work, in that it dares to examine the development of religion as a human creation. In that sense, it is similar in ambition to Daniel Dennett's *Breaking the Spell: Religion as a Natural Phenomenon*, which was controversial when published in 2006.

Hume's book certainly contains some provocative claims, notably that monotheistic religions are in general less tolerant than polytheistic ones. Near its end it concludes, "Examine the religious principles, which have, in fact, prevailed in the world. You will scarcely be persuaded, that they are any thing but sick men's dreams: Or perhaps will regard them more as the playsome whimsies of monkies in human shape, than the serious, positive, dogmatical asseverations of a being, who dignifies himself with the name of rational."[103]

But perhaps what saved the *Natural History* is that its target was widely seen to be Catholicism rather than religion in general. He makes fun of Catholic superstition in a story about a convert who was given the sacrament of Holy Communion, in which Catholics believe bread and wine become the body and blood of Christ. But when his new priest asks him the next day, "How many Gods are there?" the man answers, "None at all" because "You have told me all along that there is but one God: And yesterday I eat him."[104] Reviewing the book, the Rev. Caleb Fleming praised it, saying Hume "has finely exposed superstition and popery: professeth himself an advocate of pure theism, and so far as he is theist, he cannot be an enemy to pure Christianity."[105]

Fleming could credibly reach this conclusion because Hume made sure he included a few sentences that unambiguously supported religion. "Look out for a people, entirely destitute of religion," he warned. "If you find them at all, be assured, that they are but few degrees removed from brutes." The problem with religion, he suggested, is simply how some have abused it.

"What so pure as some of the morals, included in some theological systems? What so corrupt as some of the practices, to which these systems give rise?"[106]

Although the *Natural History* did receive critical reviews too, it hardly created a scandal that caused Hume any problems, and it has become received wisdom that when the *Dialogues* were finally published there wasn't much fuss either. Dennis Rasmussen, however, claims that "an inspection of the periodicals of the time suggests otherwise." The *Critical Review* described Hume's ideas as "pernicious," arguing that were they to prevail they would "terminate in the blind amazement, the diffidence and melancholy of mankind." The *Monthly Review* said Hume's principles meant that "the wicked are set free from every restraint but that of the laws" and "we are chained down to a life full of wretchedness and misery." The book should "shock the sense and virtue" of its good readers.[107] It is also telling that the first editions, one of which I had the opportunity to inspect personally, do not include the name of either the printer or the publisher, information that was standardly printed in all books at the time. It would seem that neither wanted to be associated with the work, suggesting that negative consequences were anticipated if they were.

Hume did his best to cloak his work in a veil of piety. At the beginning of the *Dialogues* he has their narrator, Pamphilus, say, "What truth so obvious, so certain, as the being of a God, which the most ignorant ages have acknowledged, for which the most refined geniuses have ambitiously striven to produce new proofs and arguments?"[108] At the very end, Pamphilus concludes that Cleanthes, the natural theologian who attempts to establish religion on evidential grounds, comes closest to the truth. He even has Philo approvingly cite the famous saying from the Bible, in the Book of Psalms, that "the fool hath said in his heart, There is no God."[109] He also says that "true religion" is innocent of all the charges he brings against "religion, as it has commonly been found in the world," although it is all too clear that mainstream Christianity is closer to the common than the true type.[110]

Today, the *Dialogues* are notable for their lack of zealotry and the respect they grant to religion. Hume's aim was to avoid *"that Vulgar error . . . of putting nothing but nonsense into the Mouth of the Adversary."*[111] The dialogue is introduced as though it were a record Pamphilus wrote down and sent to his friend Hermippus. This allows Hume to give Pamphilus a letter introducing the dialogues in which the advantages of the dialogue form are spelled out:

> "Any question of philosophy . . . which is so obscure and uncertain, that human reason can reach no fixed determination with regard to it; if it should be treated at all; seems to lead us naturally into the style of dialogue and conversation. Reasonable men may be allowed to differ, where no one can reasonably be positive: Opposite sentiments, even without any decision, afford an agreeable amusement: and if the subject be curious and interesting, *the book carries us, in a manner, into company, and unites the two greatest and purest pleasures of human life, study and society.*"[112]

Hume was willing to criticize irrational superstition and enthusiasm where he saw it, but he was also keen to find common ground shared by all reasonable people, of faith or none. For instance, in the dialogues he has Philo say, "The Theist allows, that the original intelligence is very different from human reason: The Atheist allows, that the original principle of order bears some remote analogy to it. Will you quarrel, Gentlemen, about the degrees, and enter into a controversy, which admits not of any precise meaning, nor consequently of any determination?"[113]

Hume seems to be arguing that when faith is reasonable, and atheism equally so, there is little to distinguish the two. The rational believer has to accept that the nature of the creator is mysterious, beyond human comprehension. The atheist has to accept that the universe bears some relation to a creation. Both then are left in a state of ultimate ignorance—at least pre-Darwin—unable to ignore the signs that the universe was created but equally unable to say anything meaningful about its supposed creator. His strategy is *when people strongly disagree, try to find what they haven't noticed unites them, not what they already know divides them.*

This would seem to take Hume close to the most popular alternative to theism at the time: Deism. Voltaire, Bayle, Montesquieu, Rousseau, Paine, and Franklin were all Deists. They believed that there was some kind of divine creator God but it did not involve itself with human affairs and its nature was unknowable. This looks close to the kind of God Philo describes as being shared by theists and atheists, at least if they were to think properly about it.

This is not the only place where Hume seems to push rational believers toward deism. In a letter from 1743 he argues that a God who possessed the "Attributes of highest Perfection" is not "the natural Object of any Passion or Affection."[114] That is because affection requires some sympathy—some sense of shared feeling. But such a God, due to its "Invisibility & Incomprehensibility," would simply be beyond our comprehension. The only way to make God lovable would be to "degrade him into a resemblance" with ourselves, which is a kind of blasphemy.

However, Hume was not a Deist because even that required us to say more about the attributes of God than we could ever have any grounds for doing. "Our ideas reach no farther than our experience," says Philo in the *Dialogues*. "We have no experience of divine attributes and operations: I need not conclude my syllogism: You can draw the inference yourself."[115] Deists, however, believe that God can at the very least be ascribed the properties of a creator. Hume thought that even that is beyond our capacity to judge.

In short, as Philo puts it, "we have no *data* to establish any system of cosmogony."[116] One of Hume's most powerful and enduring arguments based on this general principle is against the idea that the universe must be the product of some kind of intelligent purpose. This "argument from design" claims that just as we can infer the existence of a watchmaker from the existence of a watch, so the intricacy of the universe requires that we posit a creator.

However, any argument from *analogy is only as strong as the similarity between the two cases being compared.* They work on the principle of "from similar effects we infer similar causes."[117] That means "where-ever you depart, in the least, from the similarity of the cases, you diminish proportionably the evidence; and may at last bring it to a very weak analogy, which is confessedly liable to error and uncertainty."[118] Hume argued that the analogy between God and the kinds of creators we have experience of is simply too weak and does not hold. We can only infer the existence of a watchmaker from a watch because we already know that watches are human artefacts. We have no such experiences that tell us what kinds of things produce universes. Such cases "are single, individual, without parallel, or specific resemblance."[119] If we did dare to make a comparison between the original of the universe and things we actually understand, the best analogy would not be one theists would be happy with: "The world plainly resembles more an animal or a

vegetable, than it does a watch or a knitting-loom," says Philo.
"Its cause, therefore, it is more probable, resembles the cause of
the former. The cause of the former is generation or vegetation.
The cause, therefore, of the world, we may infer to be something
similar or analogous to generation or vegetation."[120]

Actually, we don't even know that the universe has a cause at
all. Given that even theists accept that God, as a necessary
being, has no cause, "why may not the material universe be the
necessarily-existent Being?"[121] Even if we decided we had good
reason to believe the universe does have a cause, we could say
nothing about it. *"When we infer any particular cause from an
effect, we must proportion the one to the other, and can never be
allowed to ascribe to the cause any qualities, but what are exactly sufficient to produce the effect."*[122] So even if we could establish that the universe has a creator, "beyond that position he
cannot ascertain one single circumstance, and is left afterwards
to fix every point of his theology, by the utmost licence of fancy
and hypothesis."[123] As soon as we describe the cause of the universe as a god of any kind, we are attributing more properties
to that cause than is rationally warranted.

So, for example, even to think of God as a kind of "mind" is
mistaken. Hume allows Demea, a rationalist theist, to make this
case. Demea repeats a version of Hume's theory of the self, saying that "the soul of man" is "a composition of various faculties,
passions, sentiments, ideas; united, indeed, into one self or person, but still distinct from each other." God, on the other hand,
has the properties of "perfect immutability and simplicity." That
must mean that if God has a mind, it is one "whose acts and
sentiments and ideas are not distinct and successive; one, that
is wholly simple, and totally immutable; is a mind, which has
no thought, no reason, no will, no sentiment, no love, no hatred" and that, "in a word, is no mind at all."[124] (Philo, however,

goes on to show that even Demea's belief that God is a perfect unity is unfounded, since we can know nothing of the nature of the deity.)

Hume repeatedly tried to present this view as being genuinely pious. The impious are those who dare to know the nature of the Almighty and so deny his greatness and mystery. The greatest example of this vice is anthropomorphism: seeing God in our own image. "By representing the Deity as so intelligible, and comprehensible, and so similar to a human mind," argues Philo, "we are guilty of the grossest and most narrow partiality, and make ourselves the model of the whole universe." The only problem is, of course, that mainstream Christianity *does* attribute human-like characteristics to God, and so Hume's claim that this is presumptuous ends up being a criticism of the dominant religion of his time, not a defense of it.

This is perhaps most evident when he has Philo attack the idea of god as omniscient (all-knowing), omnibenevolent (all-loving), and omnipotent (all-powerful). He dismisses this as yet another form of anthropomorphism, one that is not even consistent, as Epicurus showed with his old, "yet unanswered" questions: "Is he willing to prevent evil, but not able? then is he impotent. Is he able, but not willing? then is he malevolent. Is he both able and willing? whence then is evil?"[125] This has become known as the "problem of evil," and Hume leaves us in no doubt that he takes it very seriously indeed. No one, he argued, who looked at the world with all its suffering would reach the conclusion that it was made by a good God. Worse, "the true conclusion is, that the original source of all things is entirely indifferent to all these principles, and has no more regard to good above ill than to heat above cold, or to drought above moisture, or to light above heavy."[126]

Hume's religious skepticism goes very deep. He believes we know nothing at all about the ultimate ground of being. This not only distances him from the Deists, it also makes Hume significantly different from most atheists today. Modern atheism is mostly a kind of *naturalism*. Naturalism is the view that the natural world is all there is. The only things that exist are made of the stuff described by science. This can give rise to things that have properties not found in physics or chemistry, such as love or aesthetic beauty, but there is nothing that exists that does not consist of matter.

Hume was in many ways a good naturalist. His argument against miracles rests on the belief that we always have more reason to believe in natural causes than supernatural ones. He was also against superstition, which essentially means the ascription of supernatural powers. But a genuine naturalist has to accept the limits of what natural philosophy—what we call science—can actually tell us. Hume warns that our science is young and incomplete so "what new and unknown principles would actuate her in so new and unknown a situation, as that of the formation of a universe, we cannot, without the utmost temerity, pretend to determine."[127]

But as his unwillingness to embrace atheism illustrates, Hume did not go as far as to assert that the natural world is definitively *all that there is*. Rather, the natural world is *all that we know* and we should confine what we believe to what we know about it. Whenever there is anything else we do not know, we should remain agnostic about it. "A very small part of this great system, during a very short time, is very imperfectly discovered to us: and do we thence pronounce decisively concerning the origin of the whole?"[128] We could then call him a metaphysical agnostic, suspending judgment about the ultimate nature of reality. As Wittgenstein put it two centuries later, *"Whereof one cannot speak, thereof one must be silent."*[129]

Hume's lack of animosity toward religion was so sincerely felt that he did not hesitate to credit religion when credit was due. Most strikingly, although he was clearly of the view that enthusiasm was almost always harmful, in his histories he was willing to allow that at least during the Tudor and Stuart eras, religious fanaticism fueled the resistance to absolute monarchy and so advanced the cause of civil liberty. Hume wrote, "So extensive was royal authority, and so firmly established in all its parts, that it is probable the patriots of that age would have despaired of ever resisting it, had they not been stimulated by religious motives, which inspire a courage unsurmountable by any human obstacle."[130]

Perhaps more surprisingly still, he was in favor of an established church: a Church of England that had a special, protected constitutional role. His rationale was that in the absence of an established church, different religions or denominations would end up competing to attract followers, and that would inspire extremism and fanaticism. It is much better when the government pays salaries of clergy to "bribe their indolence" and render it "superfluous for them to be farther active, than merely to prevent their flock from straying in quest of new pastures."[131]

Such moderation was not the style of the *philosophes*. Perhaps this fundamental difference of both opinion and temperament helps explain one of the strangest features of Hume's second stay in France. As Harris points out, Hume's decision to accept Lord Hertford's invitation "was, as it turned out, in one sense the end of Hume's career as an author. He wrote only a handful of short and minor pieces during the remaining thirteen years of his life. . . . Nothing there [Paris] inspired him to write anything new."[132] Given the intellectual ferment of France, this seems extraordinary. Surely if anywhere were to inspire a person of ideas it would be Paris, populated by so many great minds. But these thinkers offered Hume nothing new, nothing worthwhile. Anything the French Enlightenment had to offer the Scottish Enlightenment had already been given, more calmly, more rationally, more humanely. There would be no terror in Scotland, no guillotine in Glasgow. If anything, the French philosophers would have cautioned Hume against the dangers of a kind of freethinking that is too free and not thoughtful enough.

Diplomatic Life

For philosophical pilgrims such as myself, Paris today provides thin gruel. Hume lived in various parts of the city and although it is possible to stand where they were, none are publicly accessible or even acknowledge that the great Scot was once there. Lord Hertford and his entourage first resided at the Hôtel de Grimberg in rue St. Dominique, later at Hôtel de Beaupréau (now 3 rue de l'Université), and then at the Hôtel du Parc royal, rue du [now Vieux] Colombier.[133] Nothing today attests to these historical facts.

One residence, however, very much remains. From March 1764 the Hôtel de Brancas served as the British Embassy, where Hume had a separate apartment. It is now the Residence of the President of the National Assembly on 126–128 rue de l'Université. To get inside, you need to arrange an appointment via a deputy of the French Parliament. With the help of some French colleagues and the cooperation of the Chief of Staff of the President of the National Assembly, I was able to have a look around.

FIGURES 17 AND 18. The Hôtel de Brancas, where Hume resided in Paris.

From the moment I set eyes on it I could believe Mossner's claim that it was "certainly the most luxurious that the man of letters had ever had."[134] It was built for the Marquis de Lassay between 1726 and 1730. After Lassay's death in 1750, the hotel passed into ownership of the Brancas by way of marriage to the Marquis's grand-niece. It was during this period that Hume and Hertford used the building. It would later be sold to the Prince de Condé, grandson of the Duchess of Bourbon, before being confiscated by the state of France in 1792. It has remained a national property ever since, except for a short period when it was restored to the house of Condé from 1815 to 1843.

The original single-story building (with servants' rooms in the basement) was built in an Italian style, the upper floor being an addition that postdates Hume's time there. During that era it was in a relatively undeveloped area of Paris, virtually the countryside. Its gardens extended to the banks of the Seine rather than the few hundred yards to the busy Quai d'Orsay street.

From the outside it has an unpretentious grandeur, extending along a wide gravel driveway-cum-courtyard. Long windows extend almost to street level with a small central staircase leading to triple front doors. Inside, however, understatement turns to ostentation. The entry hall is simple enough, but the gilded dining hall to the right gives a taste of the luxuriant decoration of the quartet of rooms that comprise the main interior space. The ceilings and their elaborate moldings are richly painted, with a lot with gold leaf. Gold is also the color used to decorate the architraves, the doors themselves, and the panels that cover the lower sections of the walls. Chandeliers and mirrors add to the glitz. A sense of trying too hard is given by some of the mirrors, which comprise two panes inside the same frame, the join between them all too clear, because it simply wasn't possible to make a big enough mirror in one piece at the time.

My guide was very knowledgeable about most of the building's history but said that there was a gap in their records between Lassay's and the state's ownership from 1750 to 1792. Hence he had no idea that it had ever been used as a British ambassadorial residence. No other source reveals where Hume's quarters would have been. There are some small rooms at the far end of the building, now used for storage, which could have served as bedrooms. The most likely room, however, would seem to be what is now known as the departure room. It is from here that the President of the National Assembly leaves with great ceremony twice a week to be present at the chamber of the French Parliament's lower chamber. It now adjoins a later extension, the *salle des fêtes* or ballroom, that links the hotel to the semicircular Assembly chamber. It is smaller than the other rooms but just as gilded.

One wall is now dominated by a tapestry reproduction of Raphael's famous painting *The School of Athens*, which depicts many of the great ancient Greek philosophers—an unknowing nod to the room's philosophical past. It is also, however, the site of some very un-Humean superstitions. The president's table is said to be the one on which Napoleon signed his letter of surrender in 1814, and so it is considered unlucky to sign anything on it—a serious inconvenience for a presidential table. One president in a hurry who forgot this one day supposedly tripped soon afterward and fractured his leg. There are also two statue candelabras on either side of the large double doors leading out to the *salle des fêtes*. The one on the right is more worn because it is considered lucky for the president to rub it before leaving to face the Assembly. This echoes the new tradition of rubbing the toe of Hume's statue in Edinburgh, which is supposed to bring good luck, especially to scholars. It seems statue-rubbing follows Hume wherever he goes, something which would no doubt have amused the superstition-debunking Scot.

Au Revoir

Hume would leave France at least as celebrated as he arrived. He turned up in a somewhat purple poem by Claude-Joseph Dorat in which the writer ends by apologizing for rhapsodizing about the man in his songs, the "light children of my delirium," and neglecting to see him as a thinker, the "respectable Philosopher." Hume becomes "only the lovable man who will forgive me."[135]

More memorably, he was painted by Charles-Nicholas Cochin, a profile that was later engraved by S. C. Miger, sometimes looking left, sometimes right. It is perhaps significant that this is one of the more flattering pictures of Hume, showing him serious, seemingly in deep but calm thought, his double chin there but not overly pronounced.

He was also painted by Louis Carrogis, called Carmontelle, in a picture held in storage by the Scottish National Portrait Gallery. It is a shame this is not on permanent public view, because to me it seems the most natural and honest depiction of the philosopher ever painted.

Hume is shown sideways on, his girth neither disguised nor emphasized, seated at a black, gilded desk on a terrace facing a tall building. He is dressed in a red tunic, white stockings, and black shoes, with a white wig and cravat. His clothes and the setting suggest a man of some standing, as he was in Paris. A manuscript is held upright on the desk in front of him, but Hume is not looking at it. Instead, he is staring into the distance, his

FIGURE 19. Portrait by Louis Carrogis (Carmontelle),
c. 1764.

hands in his pockets as though to emphasize that whatever he
is doing, it is not work. His expression is curious and hard to
read. He seems to be neither concentrating hard nor daydream-
ing, neither bored nor deeply engaged. He is simply thinking,
as though indifferent to his surroundings and the painter, who

can show us everything except what is in his mind. A good portrait is often said to capture the essence of a person, and this one does exactly that by making us realize that nothing we can attend to in Hume's outward appearance and situation really gets to his essence at all. The picture pulls off the clever trick of making us attend to the one thing it cannot show.

When Lord Hertford's time as ambassador came to an end, Hume was initially set to accompany him on his next commission to Ireland. But Hume had no appetite for it. "It is like Stepping out of Light into Darkness to exchange Paris for Dublin." He seemed ready instead to return to a quiet life in Scotland, saying, "I believe a Fireside & a Book, the best things in World for my Age & Disposition."[136] He would return with a pension of £400 a year for life, free from all deduction, his cherished independence surely now secured.[137] Before he could enjoy that, however, he had one more bizarre, unexpected, and unwanted adventure left in him.

CHAPTER FIVE

Learning the Hard Way

No quality of human nature is more remarkable, both in itself and in its consequences, than that propensity we have to sympathize with others, and to receive by communication their inclinations and sentiments, however different from, or even contrary to our own.

In *My Own Life*, Hume wrote, "I have easily kept myself clear of all literary squabbles."[1] Either he had erased the episode that followed his stay in France from his memory, willfully ignored it, or did not judge his dispute with Jean-Jacques Rousseau to be sufficiently "literary" to qualify.

Rousseau was one of the most celebrated intellectuals in Europe, but one who seemed to make enemies easily. In 1762 he had fled France after the parliament had issued an arrest order against him, provoked by the heretical ideas in his book *Emile, or, On Education*. Although the book defended religious faith, it proposed that the right way to educate the young Emile is "to give him the means to choose for himself according to the right use of his own reason." In a notorious section that has come to be known as "The Profession of Faith of the Savoyard Vicar," the eponymous priest argued against the idea that "there were but one religion upon earth," saying that if this were so, "and if all beyond its pale were condemned to eternal punishment, and if there were in any corner of the world one single honest man who was not convinced by this evidence, the God of that religion would be the most unjust and cruel of tyrants."[2] Rousseau had gone to Bern in his native Switzerland, but the authorities there were just as unsympathetic and ordered him to leave. So he took sanctuary in Môtiers, fifteen miles from Neuchâtel, then under the control of Frederick the Great of Prussia. Soon unwelcome there, he went back to a tiny island, the Ile de St.-Pierre, within the Canton of Bern, with assurances that in his isolation he would not be persecuted.

These wanderings made him a cause célèbre among freethinkers, and several offered him a safe haven. The invitation he chose to accept was from David Hume. "Mr. Hume is the truest philosopher that I know and the only historian that has ever written with impartiality," he wrote. "He has measured and calculated the errors of men while remaining above their weaknesses."[3] The admiration was mutual. Hume's first letter to Rousseau in July 1762 declared "of all men of Letters in Europe, since the Death of President Montesquieu, you are the Person whom I most revere, both for the Force of your Genius and the Greatness of your Mind."[4] This was not mere flattery, as he expressed similar sentiments to Mme. de Boufflers, whom he told "there is no man in Europe of whom I have entertained a higher idea, and whom I would be prouder to serve."[5]

He also admired Rousseau as a writer. "All the writings of that author appear to me admirable, particularly on the head of eloquence; and if I be not much mistaken, he gives to the French tongue an energy, which it scarce seems to have reached in any other hands." However, from the very beginning he was less certain of Rousseau's philosophical talents. Hume observed

that Rousseau's "enemies" criticized the "degree of extrava-
gance" in his writing. What Hume was "apt to suspect" about
Rousseau could stand as a more general maxim, that *the worst
writer "chooses his topics less from persuasion, than from the
pleasure of showing his invention, and surprising the reader by
his paradoxes."*[6]

Where Hume always took pains to avoid causing unnecessary offense, Rousseau seemed to court it. Rousseau's difficul-
ties stemmed largely from the *Profession of Faith,* and when
Hume read it he found himself "not in the least surprised that
it gave offence. He has not had the precaution to throw any veil
over his sentiments; and as he scorns to dissemble his contempt
of established opinions, he could not wonder that all the zealots
were in arms against him."[7]

Hume's reservations, however, were not enough to prevent
him from taking on the task of Rousseau's protector, bringing
him back to England where Hume would secure him comfortable sanctuary. Before doing so, however, he sought assurances
of Rousseau's good character. Writing to Mme. Verdelin, he
said, *"I do not want to serve a man merely because he is celebrated.* If he is virtuous and persecuted, I would devote myself
to him. Are these stories true?" He was assured they were.[8]

So, with permission from the authorities, Rousseau arrived
in Paris on December 16, 1765, to meet up with the great Scot
and be taken back to Britain. In early 1766 they left Paris, knowing that the authorities were becoming impatient at Rousseau's
too-public defiance of the arrest warrant against him. On January 9 they embarked at Calais. Once again, the luckless-at-sea
Hume suffered a rough crossing, retiring to his cabin for the
whole trip. Rousseau, in contrast, stood on deck, battered by
wind and rain, belying his frequent protestations of his own
sickliness.[9]

FIGURE 20. Jean-Jacques Rousseau by Allan Ramsay
(1766).

On the thirteenth they arrived in London where crowds
turned out to catch sight of the famous M. Rousseau. He was
received with honor and sat for the celebrated portraitist Allan
Ramsay, who also painted Hume during this period.[10] Hume
soon arranged for Rousseau to stay at Wooton, a rural village in
Staffordshire, in the English Midlands. Before Rousseau left
London, they met for what was to be the last time at the lodgings Hume usually took in Lisle Street, off Leicester Square. By
this time, however, Rousseau was already becoming paranoid.
He would later claim that even Ramsay's portrait was part of a
plot to discredit him. "This terrible portrait," he said, "the face
of a frightful Cyclops" was painted to make him look bad and

FIGURE 21. Hume by Allan Ramsay (1766).

to make Hume look even better in contrast.[11] Looking at the portrait now in the Scottish National Gallery in Edinburgh, it is difficult to see what Rousseau was complaining about. Side by side with Hume's, Rousseau looks the more intelligent figure, his gaze fixing the viewer in a way Hume's more vacant stare does not. He is far more handsome than Hume and cuts an exotic figure in his Armenian coat and fur hat.

At first, Rousseau simply broke off his correspondence with Hume. His grievances only came to light when the *St. James Chronicle* published a satirical letter that had been circulating in Paris "from the King of Prussia" that mocked Rousseau. In it, the king offers Rousseau safe haven, as he in fact did. But he adds, "You have made yourself often talked about because of eccentricities inappropriate to a truly great man," saying "if you persist in rejecting my assistance I will tell no one of this. If you persist in seeking out ways to find new misfortunes then choose the ones you would like." The last line says, "I will cease to persecute you when you will cease to glory in being so."[12]

The mockery was hardly savage but Rousseau took great offense. He wrote an open letter to the journal saying "that this letter was fabricated at Paris, and, what rends and afflicts my heart, that the impostor hath his accomplices in England." Everyone saw this as a clear reference to Hume, thus accusing him of betraying their friendship. In fact, the letter had been written by Horace Walpole, an aristocrat, art historian, and Whig politician who had been in Paris around the time of Rousseau's fleeting visit.

At first, Hume seemed to be fairly sanguine, more bemused than stung. "Was ever any thing in the world so unaccountable?" he wrote to Mme. de Boufflers. *"For the purpose of life and conduct and society, a little good sense is surely better than all the genius, and a little good humour than this extreme sensibility."*[13]

Rousseau was testing his benefactor's patience in other ways too. Hume had arranged for Rousseau to receive a pension from the King of England of £100 a year. The Swiss man's pride made him resist, but eventually he agreed, as long as Hume collected it for him. However, by May 1766 Hume was reporting to Richard Davenport that "he has refused the king's bounty, though he allowed me to collect it, had allowed Mr. Conway to apply for it, had wrote to Lord Mareschal to obtain his consent for accepting it, and had given me authority to notify this consent to Mr. Conway; and though in all this affair he may seem to have used the king ill, and Mr. Conway and Lord Mareschal, and me, above all, he makes no apology for this conduct, and never writes me a word about it." Despite his evident exasperation,

Hume still concludes by noting that however "singular and odd" Rousseau is "in all his caprices," still "we must allow him to have his own way."[14]

Seven weeks later, Hume's charity seems to be exhausted. Writing to Davenport again he says he has still not heard a word from Rousseau and sees now "that this whole affair is a Complication of Wickedness and Madness; and you may believe, I repent heartily, that I ever had any connexions with so pernicious and dangerous a Man." He asks Davenport to tell Rousseau that he is "impatient to have an Answer."[15]

Hume may soon have been reminded of the old maxim to be careful what you wish for. Rousseau eventually wrote directly to him to air his grievances and make his accusations plain. He recalled how he had placed his trust in Hume. "You know I embraced you with tears in my eyes, and told you, if you were not the best of men, you must be the blackest of mankind." Having once believed the best, Rousseau now was convinced of the worst. "I threw myself into your arms; you brought me to England, apparently to procure me an asylum, but in fact to bring me to dishonour. You applied to this noble work, with a zeal worthy of your heart, and a success worthy of your abilities. You needed not have taken so much pains: you live and converse with the world; I with myself in solitude. The public love to be deceived, and you were formed to deceive them. I know one man, however, whom you can not deceive; I mean yourself."[16]

Hume responded incredulously but calmly: "Such violent accusations, confined altogether to generals, it is as impossible to answer, as it is impossible to comprehend them. But affairs cannot, must not remain on that footing. I shall charitably suppose, that some infamous calumniator has belied me to you."[17]

Rousseau responded with a mad eighteen-page rant, including the line "If you are guilty, I am the most unfortunate of mankind; if you are innocent, I am the most culpable."[18] Rousseau, always ready to believe he was the most unfortunate and equally unwilling to accept blame, had pronounced Hume guilty already.

History's verdict is that Hume was the innocent party. However, for some time Hume reacted to the injustice of the accusations with more pity than rage. He wrote that Rousseau was "desperately resolv'd to rush into this Solitude" and that Hume tried to dissuade him. But Hume had come to the conclusion that a happy ending was never on the cards. "I forsee, that he will be unhappy in that Situation, as he has indeed been always, in all Situations." Rousseau's problem, thought Hume, was that "he has only *felt*, during the whole Course of his Life." This gave him the most acute emotional sensibility Hume had ever seen, but one which "gives him a more acute Feeling of Pain than of Pleasure."[19] Hume accepted Rousseau's emotional sincerity but believed it clouded rather than sharpened his judgment. "I believe that he intends seriously to draw his own picture in its true colours," he wrote, "but I believe at the same time that nobody knows himself less."[20]

When Hume later heard an account from Turgot about the circumstances of Rousseau's departure from England, uttering paranoid and inconsistent stories, Hume was again charitable. "This poor Man is absolutely lunatic and consequently cannot be the Object of any Laws or civil Punishment," he wrote.[21] Writing to Davenport he said, "I am really sorry for him," even though in the same letter he says, "I would not, however, have you imagine that he has such an extreme Sensibility as he pretends," and that he "lies like the Devil." Still, he holds out for peace, once more asking Davenport to encourage Rousseau to write a "penitential Letter."[22] At these moments, Hume was surely the best version of himself, true to his own remark that

*"to a Philosopher & Historian the Madness and Imbecility &
Wickedness of Mankind ought to appear ordinary Events."*[23]

However, Hume did not manage to hold himself entirely
above the fray. In one letter to Baron d'Holbach, Hume lost his
cool, calling Rousseau "the blackest and most atrocious villain
that ever disgraced human nature."[24] He feared that Rousseau
intended to publish his version of the story and that some might
believe it.[25] In July 1766, he wrote to his French translator, Mme.
Belot, now Mme. la Présidente de Meinières, telling her that
since he was worried there would be "no-one to vindicate my
Memory," he "entertained Thoughts of giving the whole in-
stantly to the public." However, "mature reflection made me
depart from the Resolution."[26] But not for long. That same
month, d'Alembert wrote to Hume to say that he and his Parisian colleagues, who had previously counseled against going
public, now believed "the public is now too much concerned
with your quarrel, and things have advanced too far for you not
to give them the plain unvarnished facts."[27] So in October,
Hume's *Exposé succinct de la contestation qui s'est élevée entre M.
Hume et M. Rousseau*, edited by d'Alembert and Jean Baptiste
Suard, was published in Paris. The following month, it appeared
in Britain under the cumbersome title *A concise and genuine account of the dispute between Mr. Hume and Mr. Rousseau: with the
letters that passed between them during their controversy, also, the
letters of the Hon. Mr. Walpole, and Mr. D'Alambert, . . . Translated
from the French.*

It was uncharacteristic of Hume to allow himself to be
dragged into a public feud, and many have judged him harshly
for it. Baier regards it as his "least creditable publication,"[28] and
Greig says, "Hume behaved ill. He denounced Jean-Jacques in
violent terms. Just as, before, he had shown himself ridiculously
blind of Jean-Jacques's faults, despite the warnings he received

not to trust the fellow on the smallest point, so, now, he showed himself completely blind in his antipathy."[29] Hume certainly pulled no punches. Summing up the case against Rousseau, he concludes, "He imagines himself the sole important being in the universe: he fancies all mankind to be in a combination against him: his greatest benefactor, as hurting him most, is the chief object of his animosity: and though he supports all his whimsies by lies and fictions, this is so frequent a case with wicked men, who are in that middle state between sober reason and total frenzy, that it needs give no surprize to any body."[30]

Mossner is more understanding. "As a philosopher he might conceivably have been expected to hold himself above merely worldly opinion," he argues, "but as a man he recognised that there are limits to benevolence."[31] Hume certainly professed to go into print under great reluctance. His account ends with the assurance that "I am, and always have been, such a lover of peace, that nothing but necessity, or very forcible reasons, could have obliged me to give it to the public."[32] As soon after publication as December 1766, he wrote to John Crawford to say, "I am not supriz'd, that you are displeased with what I have done with regard to Jean-Jacques: I am not pleas'd with it myself."[33] However, he justifies the publication as something he allowed his friends to go ahead with, on their advice, rather than as something he actively chose himself, which seems to be something of an abrogation of responsibility.

Whether or not he eventually regretted publication, in retrospect he regarded "this whole adventure . . . as a Misfortune in my Life."[34] He did, at least, recover some composure and compassion. In May 1767, in two letters updating Davenport on Rousseau's paranoiac state of mind, Hume said that he had written to some friends in France to protect him, even though—or perhaps because—Hume also said "he is plainly and thoroughly mad."[35] Hume's final judgment on Rousseau is summed up in a letter to Adam Smith in which he described him as a "composition of Whim, Affectation, Wickedness, Vanity, Inquietude, Ingratitude, Feocity, Lying, Eloquence and Invention."[36]

The feud is of more than just biographical interest. It is an apt case study for Hume's moral philosophy and how it differs from Rousseau's. Rousseau was critical of the way in which the *philosophes* put rationality on a pedestal. He trusted emotions much more. The ways in which he allowed his emotions to entirely cloud his reason in the Hume affair show how questionable this view is.

But isn't one of Hume's most quoted lines "Reason is, and ought only to be, the slave of the passions"? On the face of it, his mistreatment at the hands of Rousseau would look like a strong challenge to that view too. However, the catchy slogan does not mean quite what it would seem to mean at first glance, in isolation.

Hume was certainly critical of the idea that morality could be grounded in pure reason. In an especially poetic passage in the essay "The Sceptic" he writes, "The reflections of philosophy are too subtle and distant to take place in common life, or eradicate any affection. The air is too fine to breathe in, where it is above the winds and clouds of the atmosphere."[37] Hume's belief that all philosophy must be grounded in a proper understanding of human nature led him to the conclusion that any moral philosophy that doesn't fully accommodate our emotions—or "passions" as they were then termed—is fundamentally unsound. Human behavior is largely governed by emotion, and to try to overwrite that and ask people to follow only reason is both futile and counterproductive. *"Those refined reflections, which philosophy suggests to us . . . cannot diminish or extinguish our vicious passions, without diminishing or extinguishing such as are virtuous, and rendering the mind totally indifferent and unactive.*"[38]

One corollary of this is that philosophies which advocate the governing of human life by reason alone are not, as they would maintain, compassionate but actually profoundly misanthropic. Ventriloquizing the Stoics, he says, "*Let not the injuries or violence of men ever discompose you by anger or hatred. Would you be angry at the ape for its malice, or the tyger for its ferocity?*" But this apparently understanding and forgiving stance in reality "leads us into a bad opinion of human nature, and must extinguish the social affections." It can even make people less inclined to judge themselves for their misdemeanors, as they are effectively being told "that vice is as natural to mankind, as the particular instincts to brute-creatures."[39]

The main reason, however, why we should not try to rid morality of emotion is that fellow-feeling is actually its very basis. For Hume, the root of morality is not reason but sympathy. "No quality of human nature is more remarkable, both in itself and in its consequences, than that propensity we have to sympathize with others, and to receive by communication their inclinations and sentiments, however different from, or even contrary to our own." Despite his remark about difference here, it is our essential similarity with each other that makes this possible. "Nature has preserv'd a great resemblance among all human creatures, and that we never remark any passion or principle in others, of which, in some degree or other, we may not find a parallel in ourselves."[40] Hence, *ethics without empathy is a contradiction in terms.*

Feeling is also the basis of our judgments about virtue and vice. Hume invites us to "take any action allow'd to be vicious: Wilful murder, for instance. Examine it in all lights, and see if

you can find that matter of fact, or real existence, which you call
vice." His wager is that "you never can find it, till you turn your
reflection into your own breast, and find a sentiment of disapprobation, which arises in you, towards this action. Here is a
matter of fact; but 'tis the object of feeling, not of reason. It lies
in yourself, not in the object."[41]

Right and wrong are not found in acts or in objects but in our
feelings toward them. "Every passion, habit, or turn of character . . .
which has a tendency to our advantage or prejudice, gives a
delight or uneasiness and 'tis from thence the approbation or
dis-approbation arises."[42] Cowardice, injustice, and pride in
others all tend to disadvantage us, and so we feel hostile to those
who display them, thinking them vicious. Courage, justice, and
humility in others serve us and others well, and so we feel well-
disposed toward people who display these, thinking them
virtuous.

It is important to note here that our judgments of right and
wrong are responding to real characteristics of the things we are
judging. Hume compares our moral sense with our five senses.
"Vice and virtue," he says, "may be compar'd to sounds, colours,
heat and cold, which, according to modern philosophy, are not
qualities in objects, but perceptions in the mind." But of course
whether we perceive something as hot or cold, red or blue, does
depend on the nature of the objects themselves. In a similar
way, virtue and vice are not properties of things in the world, but
it is not arbitrary which things we judge to be good, which bad.
It all depends on whether the thing in question is genuinely
useful or agreeable, to ourselves or others.

We also turn our moral judgments on ourselves, feeling a
good kind of pride when we judge that our own actions have
been noble, and appropriate humility or shame when we see we
have acted badly. Indeed, our judgments of virtue or vice in

others and pride or shame in ourselves are intimately linked. *"No person is ever prais'd by another for any quality, which wou'd not, if real, produce, of itself, a pride in the person possest of it."*[43]

We can now begin to understand the real meaning of "Reason is, and ought only to be, the slave of the passions." Reason helps us to work out the consequences of our actions and the means of achieving certain goals. This is what Aristotle called practical reason and is sometimes called instrumental reason: using our intellects to work out the best way of achieving a goal. But reason alone cannot tell us what goals are worth striving for. Hence in another striking sentence, Hume writes, "'Tis not contrary to reason to prefer the destruction of the whole world to the scratching of my finger."[44] Reason tells us what is logically possible or impossible, consistent or contradictory. But it cannot tell us what is good, what we ought to do. To wish the destruction of the world is not illogical, because there is nothing impossible or contradictory about the desire. What makes it wrong is that it shows an unfeeling disregard for the welfare of living creatures. *A person who wishes gratuitous harm is not irrational but callous.*

Similarly, a person who acts against their own interest is self-defeating but not irrational. The economist's idea that "rational choice" is self-interested choice links rationality and egoism in a way that is not justified. To take a simple example, most of us assume that it is rational to want to be happy. But rationality has nothing to do with it. The person who wants to be unhappy is not irrational but strange, perhaps emotionally troubled. The only reason to value happiness is that we find it pleasing, and being happy tends not to have any negative consequences that cancel that out. "Happiness is good" is not a truth established by logic but a principle we agree with on the basis of our experience of happiness and its alternatives.

A motivating passion can only be said to be unreasonable if it is "accompany'd with some false judgment" and "even then 'tis not the passion, properly speaking, which is unreasonable, but the judgment." There are only two forms of such unreasonableness. The first is "when a passion, such as hope or fear, grief or joy, despair or security, is founded on the supposition of the existence of objects, which really do not exist." For example, it is unreasonable to hope for a life to come if there is none, or to celebrate a victory that never occurred. The second case of a motivating passion being unreasonable is "when in exerting any passion in action, we chuse means insufficient for the design'd end, and deceive ourselves in our judgment of causes and effects."[45] In other words, we need reason to tell us whether our goals are coherent and the best way of achieving them.

Hume gives a neat example of this in the *Enquiry concerning the Principles of Morals* when he says that "giving alms to common beggars is naturally praised; because it seems to carry relief to the distressed and indigent." Sympathy motivates us to act. However, reason can make us change our mind: "when we observe the encouragement thence arising to idleness and debauchery, we regard that species of charity rather as a weakness than a virtue."[46]

The way in which reason and feeling work together in cases like these suggests that Hume's rhetoric of reason as passion's mere slave is hyperbolic and misleading. Hume's own account shows that **emotion and reason are not entirely separate and many of our emotions contain rational judgments.** "Passion," he observes, "in pronouncing its verdict, considers not the object simply, as it is in itself, but surveys it with all the circumstances, which attend it." For example, "A man transported with joy, on account of his possessing a diamond, confines not his view to the glistering stone before him: He also considers its rarity, and thence chiefly arises his pleasure and exultation. Here therefore a philosopher may step in, and suggest particular views, and considerations, and circumstances, which otherwise would have escaped us; and, by that means, he may either moderate or excite any particular passion."[47]

Hume's point is that the pleasure we take in certain things often rests upon views we take about it that might be incorrect. We can delight in a painting, believing it to be an original, when it is really a fake. Reason's role is to enable us to take a correct view of things, so that any delight or disgust is not based on error. That is why reason is so important for overcoming prejudice, because *prejudice is often no more than a negative emotional reaction based on false ideas.*

Hume was not the first to argue that human rationality is the slave of our emotions. But, James Harris argues, Hume understood the primacy of emotion in a very different way. "Hume's point was not that reason is bound always to lose out to passions that have all the advantages when it comes to strength and persistence," he says. "Instead, it was that no such conflict between reason and passion ever actually takes place. Reason by its very nature is unable to enter into a contest with passion for control over human life."[48] As Hume put it, "We speak not strictly and philosophically when we talk of the combat of passion and of reason." Reason is *motivationally inert.* "*Reason alone can never produce any action, or give rise to volition.*"[49] It doesn't lose out in a battle with emotion; it doesn't even show up for the fight.

The impotence of reason is explained in terms of what has come to be known as the "is/ought" gap. Hume observed that when reading any system of moral philosophy, he finds that people start discussing what *is* and *is not*, and then suddenly, "I meet with no proposition that is not connected with an *ought*, or an *ought not*." This shift passes unremarked, but it is of critical importance because statements of "is" and "is not" are purely *descriptive*, while those of "ought" and "ought not" are *prescriptive*. If a writer shifts from the former to the latter, "a reason should be given, for what seems altogether inconceivable, how this new relation can be a deduction from others, which are entirely different from it."[50] An important corollary of this is that what is natural is not the same as what is good, since nature is simply what is. *"Nothing can be more unphilosophical than those systems, which assert, that virtue is the same with what is natural, and vice with what is unnatural."*[51]

This is the sense in which Hume meant reason is the slave of the passions. His metaphor is, however, misleading. Whereas a slave merely does its master's bidding, reason has a role in questioning its master. If it did not, it would not have any function or anything to distinguish it from passion. That was Rousseau's problem. Passion was for him a tyrannical master that would not hear what reason had to say back to him. For Hume, *passion is a wise master only when it has reason as a loyal servant that can see things that by itself it cannot.*

We have to understand, however, that reason's ability to keep us in check and reform us is extremely limited. *If you want to get someone to do something, it is quicker to work on their passions than their intellect,* and the more violent the passion, the better.[52] It is not for nothing that most corruption scandals involve sex or money. As we have already seen, for Hume, the best means of changing our own behavior for the better is not simply to convince ourselves rationally that we ought to do so but to change our habits so that the behavior we desire becomes automatic. "Habit is another powerful means of reforming the mind, and implanting in it good dispositions and inclinations." Get used to eating healthily and junk food will start to appeal less. Force yourself to socialize more and you will become in time more sociable. *"Where one is thoroughly convinced that the virtuous course of life is preferable; if he have but resolution enough, for some time, to impose a violence on himself; his reformation needs not be despaired of."*[53]

Even this, however, has limits. Hume recognized that since virtue has its roots in our sympathy for others, neither habit nor reason is powerful enough to change an irredeemably unsympathetic person into a good one. "The misfortune is," he wrote, "that this conviction and this resolution never can have place, unless a man be, before-hand, tolerably virtuous." Perhaps this is why Rousseau could not, ultimately, become better. His character flaws were so deeply rooted that he was unable to even see clearly the shortcomings he needed to overcome.

In "The Sceptic" Hume describes clearly and eloquently how impotent rationality is in the face of an ill will. "Where one is born of so perverse a frame of mind, of so callous and insensible a disposition, as to have no relish for virtue and humanity, no sympathy with his fellow-creatures, no desire of esteem and applause; such a one must be allowed entirely incurable, nor is there any remedy in philosophy. . . . I know not how I should address myself to such a one, or by what arguments I should endeavour to reform him."[54] It's important to note that to deny reason such sovereignty in morality was profoundly radical. As Hume himself noted, "Nothing is more usual in philosophy, and even in common life, than to talk of the combat of passion and reason, to give the preference to reason, and assert that men are only so far virtuous as they conform themselves to its dictates."[55]

The sympathetic attitude Hume tried, without complete success, to show toward Rousseau reflects his view that we ought to have neither too bleak nor too rosy a view of human nature. Hume saw that the danger of "a delicate sense of morals," especially if accompanied by a "splenetic temper," is that it can give us "a disgust of the world" and a sense of indignation. Put simply, to anyone with high moral standards, the world seems a sorry and immoral place. This, however, ultimately undermines the sympathy toward our fellow human beings which morality depends upon. So *"the sentiments of those, who are inclined to think favourably of mankind, are more advantageous to virtue, than the contrary principles, which give us a mean opinion of our nature."*[56]

Does this mean we should pretend that human nature is better than it really is? No. Harris argues that Hume's idea is a "compromise position between a purely sceptical view of human beings as blind and selfish and an overly optimistic view of them as able to transcend their limitations by means of rational self-discipline."[57]

Hume's view was that very negative assessments of human nature are based on three mistakes. The first is to attend too much only of humanity's bad side and to neglect the good. This is very natural. Think of how, when watching the news, we hear stories of murder and corruption, forgetting that the vast majority of people have spent their day engaged in neither.

The second mistake is the widespread view that human beings are only motivated by selfishness. The source of this is simple. People observe that "every act of virtue or friendship was attended with a secret pleasure" and so conclude that we are only motivated to do what appears good *because* it gives us pleasure. Hume claims that "the fallacy of this is obvious. The virtuous sentiment or passion produces the pleasure, and does not arise from it. *I feel a pleasure in doing good to my friend, because I love him; but do not love him for the sake of that pleasure.*"[58] It would be a very odd world if people took no pleasure in doing what they believed to be good.

The third mistake is to compare humans with imaginary, perfect beings. This inevitably makes us look bad. For Hume, both wisdom and virtue are of their nature comparative terms: "To say, there are few wise men in the world, is really to say nothing; since it is only by their scarcity, that they merit that appellation. Were the lowest of our species as wise as Tully, or lord Bacon, we should still have reason to say, that there are few wise men."[59] *Perfectibility is a chimera, human weakness unavoidable. All human beings can do is "endeavour to palliate what they cannot cure."*[60]

All these mistakes are described in an essay called "The Sceptic." This might seem odd, since they all appear to be refutations of moral skepticism. Hume is very clear that he believes he is describing and advocating morality, not debunking it. "Those who have denied the reality of moral distinctions, may be ranked among the disingenuous disputants," he says. "Let a man's insensibility be ever so great, he must often be touched with the images of *right* and *wrong*; and let his prejudices be ever so obstinate, he must observe, that others are susceptible of like impressions."[61]

What Hume is skeptical about, argues Harris, is "the very idea of there being one proper means whereby human beings might make themselves happy. His view is that we are too different in our passions and pleasures for this to be plausible."[62] This skepticism extends to denying the possibility of one ideal political system that would work for all nations. To make this point, in "Of Some Remarkable Customs" he points to many of the strange ways in which cultures vary. *"All general maxims in*

politics ought to be established with great caution; and that ir-
regular and extraordinary appearances are frequently discov-
ered in the moral, as well as in the physical world."[63]

This talk of irregularity in morality and customs raises the
specter of moral relativism: the idea that there are no objective
standards of right and wrong and that all moral values are cultural constructs. Hume deals with this worry directly in a little-
known dialogue that was first published as a free-standing piece
at the end of the *Enquiry concerning the Principles of Morals*. A
well-traveled character called Palamedes tells of a nation called
Fourli where their moral principles are the opposite of all those
we recognize. This is actually a fictionalized version of ancient
Greece, where moral values were indeed often quite different,
especially concerning sexuality. The way Palamedes initially
describes Fourli does indeed make its morality seem perverse.
People are praised for infidelity, patricide, and suicide.

Anyone familiar with Hume's other works would know to
treat such stories with suspicion. "Mankind are so much the
same, in all times and places, that history informs us of nothing
new or strange in this particular," he says in *An Enquiry concern-*
ing Human Understanding.[64] *"If ever there was any thing, which*
cou'd be call'd natural," he wrote in the *Treatise*, *"the sentiments*
of morality certainly may; since there never was any nation of
the world, nor any single person in any nation, who was utterly
depriv'd of them."[65] In accordance with this, the narrator goes
on to explain how it is that the apparently very different moral
standards of the Fourlians are rooted in the same basic moral
principles as our own. For example, their motive for infanticide
is the same as ours for not killing our newborn: love. The difference is simply that in Fourli, a poor parent would say they
"regard the poverty which it must inherit from me, as a greater
evil than death, which it is not capable of dreading, feeling, or

resenting."[66] Hume argues that *"the principles upon which men reason in morals are always the same; though the conclusions which they draw are often very different."*[67]

Sometimes this is simply because circumstances differ and so what is most important changes. "It is not surprising," says Hume, "that, during a period of war and disorder, the military virtues should be more celebrated than the pacific, and attract more the admiration and attention of mankind."[68] This follows from the idea that the good is what is agreeable or useful: in different times and places, different things are agreeable or useful.

Sometimes differences in practice and custom are somewhat arbitrary. For example, "A Spaniard goes out of his own house before his guest, to signify that he leaves him master of all. In other countries, the landlord walks out last, as a common mark of deference and regard."[69] An even more interesting example comes when Hume says he finds it difficult to justify French or Greek "gallantry," by which he makes clear in a footnote means looser sexual moralities not "complaisance" (a desire to please). When he tries, he sees that they "have resolved to sacrifice some of the domestic to the sociable pleasures; and to prefer ease, freedom, and an open commerce, to a strict fidelity and constancy. These ends are both good, and are somewhat difficult to reconcile."[70] Hume is here expressing an idea that has come to be known as moral pluralism. This is not an anything-goes relativism but a recognition that *there are many things that make for a good life and it is not possible for any one life or any one society to have them all in full.* Choices have to be made. Hume was remarkably ahead of his time in advocating this view. When Isaiah Berlin first gave a name to the position in the 1960s, it was thought to be a new idea. But there it is, tucked away in the back of an old Hume volume, almost as an afterthought.

Hume's ideas about pluralism in ethics are reflected and enriched in his discussion of aesthetics. In his essay "Of the Standard of Taste" he confronts the paradox that, on the one hand, it is widely believed that "beauty is no quality in things themselves: It exists merely in the mind which contemplates them; and each mind perceives a different beauty." However, "though this axiom, by passing into a proverb, seems to have attained the sanction of common sense; there is certainly a species of common sense which opposes it, at least serves to modify and restrain it." That is to say, were someone to say Salieri was as great a composer as Mozart, or that their own photographs were as good as those of Cartier-Bresson, we would "pronounce without scruple the sentiment of these pretended critics to be absurd and ridiculous."[71]

Hume's solution to this paradox is subtle. It starts by acknowledging that *beauty may be in the eye of the beholder, but there must be something genuinely beautiful for the eye to behold.* Hume makes an analogy with the sense of taste: "Though it be certain, that beauty and deformity, more than sweet and bitter, are not qualities in objects, but belong entirely to the sentiment, internal or external; it must be allowed, that there are certain qualities in objects, which are fitted by nature to produce those particular feelings."[72]

There is, then, an objective side to taste. Some people have refined their aesthetic sensibilities more than others and so are better placed to observe them and judge their merits. Ask what qualifies someone to be such a qualified judge, however, and Hume concedes, "These questions are embarrassing; and seem to throw us back into the same uncertainty."[73] But we know such people when we see them. Although there are no strict criteria for determining who may join their ranks, "they are easily to be distinguished in society, by the soundness of their understanding and the superiority of their faculties above the rest of mankind."[74]

That does not put an end to all dispute, however. Many differences of opinion can be explained away by prejudice or ignorance. But even the most culturally refined people differ in their preferences, because everyone has a different character, different dispositions, a different personal history. Therefore "a certain degree of diversity in judgment is unavoidable, and we seek in vain for a standard, by which we can reconcile the contrary sentiments."[75] So *it's not that anything goes, simply that more than one thing goes.*

This principle applies as much to ethics as it does to aesthetics. Hume allows for human variability without allowing for everything. It's another example of how Hume's moral philosophy is deeply humanistic. Without recourse to a transcendental source of morality it gives us a means to "renounce the theory, which accounts for every moral sentiment by the principle of self-love." He is right to ask rhetorically, "What need we seek for abstruse and remote systems, when there occurs one so obvious and natural?" In place of pure selfishness or even enlightened self-interest, we put "a more public affection, and allow, that the interests of society are not, even on their own account, entirely indifferent to us."[76] It needs no divine source for morality but bases all judgments of right and wrong on what is "*useful* or *agreeable* to the *person himself* or to *others*."[77]

Hume's most persuasive portrait of the virtues of his own theory comes in the conclusion to the *Enquiry concerning the Principles of Morals*, in which he talks of virtue as a personified female:

The dismal dress falls off, with which many divines, and some philosophers have covered her; and nothing appears but gentleness, humanity, beneficence, affability; nay even, at proper intervals, play, frolic, and gaiety. She talks not of useless austerities and rigours, suffering and self-denial. She declares, that her sole purpose is, to make her votaries and all mankind, during every instant of their existence, if possible, cheerful and happy; nor does she ever willingly part with any pleasure but in hopes of ample compensation in some other period of their lives. The sole trouble, which she demands, is that of just calculation, and a steady preference of the greater happiness.[78]

Hume leaves readers in no doubt that the problem with philosophy, and ethics in particular, is that by his time it had "been more closely united with theology than ever they were observed to be among the Heathens." However, *"theology . . . admits of no terms of composition, but bends every branch of knowledge to its own purpose, without much regard to the phænomena of nature,* or to the unbiassed sentiments of the mind, hence reasoning, and even language, have been warped from their natural course."[79]

Little wonder the radically secular nature of his system made some of his moral views controversial, no more so than his views on suicide, which were considered so heretical that his essay on the subject remained unpublished in his lifetime. It is telling that the first paragraph concerns not suicide at all but argues that "superstition, being founded on false opinion, must immediately vanish, when true philosophy has inspired juster sentiments of superior powers." Hume is alerting the reader that it is superstition, not reason, that stands between them and accepting the arguments that follow.

Hume sets up his argument with this premise: "If Suicide be criminal, it must be a transgression of our duty, either to God, our neighbour, or ourselves." The rest of the essay shows why suicide transgresses none of these. The idea that suicide offends against God rests on the assumption that in taking our own lives we usurp a right only God has. But Hume persuasively argues that since God has evidently left us to act for ourselves, there is no reason why "the disposal of human life" should be uniquely "reserved as the peculiar province of the almighty." Everything we do, even "turning aside a stone, which is falling upon my head," disturbs "the course of nature." Everything is equally under the control of God, which means "when I fall upon my own sword, therefore, I receive my death equally from the hands of the deity, as if it had proceeded from a lion, a precipice, or a fever."[80]

There may be times when suicide transgresses our duties to our neighbors, such as when a parent orphans a child, or when someone has an important duty to carry out and avoids doing so by taking their own life. But there are also cases when "it is no longer in my power to promote the interest of the public," when "I am a burthen to it" or "my life hinders some person from being much more useful to the public." In such cases, "my resignation of life must not only be innocent but laudable." The duty to ourselves is even more easily dismissed. "Age, sickness, or misfortune may render life a burthen, and make it worse even than annihilation."[81]

Hume's one false note in this radical essay is his belief that "no man ever threw away life, while it was worth keeping" and that anyone who has had recourse to suicide "was curst with such an incurable depravity or gloominess of temper, as must poison all enjoyment, and render him equally miserable as if he had been loaded with the most grievous misfortunes." Sadly, we now have good evidence that this is not the case. Studies have shown that 90 percent of people who survive a suicide attempt do not go on to die by suicide. Most suicide attempts are impulsive: a study in the *New England Journal of Medicine* showed that "24% took less than 5 minutes between the decision to kill themselves and the actual attempt, and 70% took less than 1 hour."[82] Hume's argument is a strong defense of the morality of people choosing to take their own lives when they have a stable and settled wish to do so, but it should not be interpreted as meaning we should always stand by and let people attempt suicide.

Hume's suspicion of rational systems of morality and his emphasis on human sympathy mean he places greater importance on kindness than on following strict rules. "Am I a liar, because I order my servant to say, I am not at home, when I do not desire to see company?" he asks?[83] Well, yes, but the point is that it would be foolish to condemn him for the lie when its only intention is kindness. For example, more than once, Hume hid the truth from Rousseau in order to try to help him, since it was well known Rousseau refused to accept charity. On one occasion, he schemed to have Rousseau's *Dictionary of Music* published in London, inflating the publisher's advance with cash from friends.[84]

Truth is not always more important than courtesy, or even sometimes entertainment. "There is a sort of harmless liar, frequently to be met with in company, who deal much in the marvellous." He thought this to be entirely reasonable, commending "some indulgence" to invention in humorous stories "because it is there really agreeable and entertaining; and truth is not of any importance."[85] (Knowing this we should perhaps take some of Hume's own witty tales with a pinch of salt.) As is often the case, Hume sounds so sensible that his genius comes disguised almost as common sense. But it actually took a very uncommon mind to find the right path between the destructive emotionalism of Rousseau and the impersonal, cold morality of those who, in following reason, leave feeling behind.

In *My Own Life*, Hume said the *Enquiry concerning the Principles of Morals* was "of all my writings, historical, philosophical, or literary, incomparably the best."[86] This confirms an opinion he expressed many years earlier in 1753 when he told the lawyer David Dalrymple, "I must confess, that I have a partiality for that work, & esteem it the most tolerable of anything I have compos'd."[87] His moral philosophy has certainly stood the test as time, proof that *a morality based in nothing more than human nature is not only possible but much more humane than the religious or rationalist alternatives.*

Justice

Hume was interested in not only personal morality but the question of what makes for a just society. He set about answering this from the same basis as he did the question of morality: human nature.

Hume utterly rejected the idea that justice was some kind of abstract universal virtue that existed independently of human life and society and could be discovered by pure reason alone.[88] Justice only exists because we needed to invent it in order to manage harmonious societies. *Justice is made to fit human beings, not the other way around.* Had human nature or the human condition been different, we would have no need of it. Hume argued for this by imagining three possible worlds, different from our own.

In the first, "nature has bestowed on the human race such profuse abundance of all external conveniencies, that, without any uncertainty in the event, without any care or industry on our part, every individual finds himself fully provided with whatever his most voracious appetites can want, or luxurious imagination wish or desire."[89] In such a world there would be no need to establish any rules governing who should have what because there would be plenty for everyone.

In the second, "though the necessities of human race continue the same as at present, yet the mind is so enlarged, and so replete with friendship and generosity, that every man has the utmost tenderness for every man, and feels no more concern for his own interest than for that of his fellows."[90] Again, if we were as altruistic and benevolent as this, we would need to establish no rules for the fair distribution or ownership of any goods.

In the third, "Suppose a society to fall into such want of all common necessaries, that the utmost frugality and industry cannot preserve the greater number from perishing, and the whole from extreme misery." In this world there would be no possible way of giving everyone their fair due. "The strict laws of justice are suspended, in such a pressing emergence, and give place to the stronger motives of necessity and self-preservation."[91]

Hume therefore concludes "*that 'tis only from the selfishness and confin'd generosity of men, along with the scanty provision nature has made for his wants, that justice derives its origin.*"[92] Therefore, "the rules of equity or justice depend entirely on the particular state and condition, in which men are placed, and owe their origin and existence to that *utility*, which results to the public from their strict and regular observance."[93] Once again, Hume takes a traditionally highfalutin idea, in this case justice, and brings it right down to earth, making it nothing more or less than a practical principle for ordering the relations of human affairs.

Our ability to form societies governed by principles of justice grants us three advantages. First, by pooling our resources we collectively have more power than we do individually. Second, by the division of labor we can specialize and thus increase our abilities. When we don't have to divide up our own time baking, sewing, and building, but allow experts in each to do them for us, we eat better bread, wear better clothes, and live in better houses. Third, society allows us to provide mutual aid so that at any given time, the poor and sick can be helped by those who are affluent and well, who will have the favor returned should fortune change.[94]

In order for this pragmatic form of justice to work it has to be transparent, consistent, and predictable. *"Justice, in her decisions, never regards the fitness or unfitness of objects to particular persons, but conducts herself by more extensive views."* So we live under the principle that has come to be known as the rule of law, where the same laws apply to all equally, even if from a more objective standpoint that results in some unfairness. "Whether a man be generous, or a miser, he is equally well receiv'd by [justice], and obtains with the same facility a decision in his favours, even for what is entirely useless to him."[95]

Such is the need for some kind of shared concept of justice that even wicked communities have some version of it. "Robbers and pirates, it has often been remarked, could not maintain their pernicious confederacy, did they not establish a new distributive justice among themselves, and recal those laws of equity, which they have violated with the rest of mankind."[96]

Hume's emphasis on the need for an orderly society echoes the Confucian emphasis on harmony. Even philosophy requires a stable society to flourish. "From law arises security: From security, curiosity: And from curiosity, knowledge." It is even better when a number of different states all enjoy this stability and trade between themselves. "Nothing is more favourable to the rise of politeness and learning, than a number of neighbouring and independent states, connected together by commerce and policy."[97] That's a message many nativist, protectionist, populist political leaders should heed today.

Like Confucius, Hume thinks that it is sometimes necessary to sacrifice other values in order to maintain social harmony, even when those values are good. This is most evident in Hume when he discusses equality. He leaves the reader in no doubt that equality is a fine ideal. "Every person, if possible, ought to enjoy the fruits of his labour, in a full possession of all the necessaries, and many of the conveniencies of life," he writes. "No one can doubt, but such an equality is most suitable to human nature, and diminishes much less from the happiness of the rich than it adds to that of the poor."[98]

One passage in the *Enquiry concerning the Principles of Morals* is especially worth noting:

> It must, indeed, be confessed, that nature is so liberal to mankind, that, were all her presents equally divided among the species, and improved by art and industry, every individual would enjoy all the necessaries, and even most of the comforts of life; nor would ever be liable to any ills, but such as might accidentally arise from the sickly frame and constitution of his body. It must also be confessed, that, *wherever we depart from this equality, we rob the poor of more satisfaction than we add to the rich, and that the slight gratification of a frivolous vanity, in one individual, frequently costs more than bread to many families, and even provinces.*[99]

Here Hume sounds almost socialist in his ideals. However, as usual, his conservative impulse reins him back in. In order to create this utopian, equal society, "the most rigorous inquisition too is requisite to watch every inequality on its first appearance; and the most severe jurisdiction, to punish and redress it." This would require granting so much power to the authority charged with enforcing it that it "must soon degenerate into tyranny."[100] The experience of communist states in the twentieth century suggests that this was more than just a reactionary fear.

More questionable is Hume's concern that "perfect equality of possessions, destroying all subordination, weakens extremely the authority of magistracy, and must reduce all power nearly to a level."[101] The suggestion here is that we need hierarchies of power in order to have stable societies. There may be some truth in that, but Hume's fear of greater equality and less hierarchy seems excessive. He seems to be neglecting an important principle that *sometimes more is better but most is worst*. Perfect equality might be bad, but more equality would be wonderful. Less hierarchy might be good even if abolishing hierarchy altogether would not be. *You should judge an ideal by its best version, not its most extreme one.*

Much of Hume's work on justice concerns property. It overlaps with several of his essays on political economy. Hume's ideas were very influential on Adam Smith. Dennis Rasmussen says that "it is striking that both the most important arguments of *The Wealth of Nations* (regarding the way commerce helped to promote liberty and security) and the most celebrated argument of the book (regarding the benefits of free trade) are also found in earlier works by Hume."[102] Many of these ideas continue to be relevant today. One passage on taxation is worth quoting in full. It could come straight from a think tank report today:

> The best taxes are such as are levied upon consumptions, especially those of luxury; because such taxes are least felt by

the people. They seem, in some measure, voluntary; since a man may chuse how far he will use the commodity which is taxed: They are paid gradually and insensibly: They naturally produce sobriety and frugality, if judiciously imposed: And being confounded with the natural price of the commodity, they are scarcely perceived by the consumers. Their only disadvantage is, that they are expensive in the levying.[103]

Hume was perhaps never more insightful about the importance of the economy than when he related it to religion. Hume argued that religion thrives on fear and is absent when people are happy, and that nothing facilitates this more than prosperity, which "begets cheerfulness and activity and alacrity and a lively enjoyment of every social and sensual pleasure." When people are in this state of mind, they "have little leisure or inclination to think of the unknown invisible regions." It is only when disaster strikes or "apprehensions spring up with regard to futurity" that the mind sinks into "diffidence, terror, and melancholy" and "has recourse to every method of appeasing those secret intelligent powers, on whom our fortune is supposed entirely to depend." That is why religion needs to make people feel fearful, so "subduing their confidence and sensuality, which, in times of prosperity, make them forgetful of a divine providence."[104] That is also why "every kind of barbarity is ascribed to the supreme Being" since "the more tremendous the divinity is represented, the more tame and submissive do men become to his ministers."[105]

The evidence today is that Hume was spot-on about the link between religious belief and material prosperity. Generally speaking, the wealthier a country is, the less religious it is. For some time people have objected that the United States is the exception to this rule: it is one of the richest nations in the world and also one of the most religious. There are two reasons why this is not in fact a counterexample to Hume. First, religious belief is now declining in America too. More importantly, there is a lot of evidence that religious belief is greater in countries where people face "existential insecurity." Although this is usually correlated to material wealth, in the United States the relationship breaks down. The United States is wealthy, but it does not have a European-style welfare state. Many people are a paycheck away from poverty. True prosperity requires financial security. When people have that, they are less inclined to seek divine salvation. *When life on earth is good, we have no need to gaze longingly to imaginary heavens.*

Hume chose as the epigram for Book III of the *Treatise* on morals some lines from *Pharsalia*, Lucan's account of the Roman Civil War: "*Durae semper virtutis amator, Quaere quid est virtus, et posce exemplar honesti*" ("Lover of virtue, you should ask what Virtue is and demand to see Goodness in her visible shape"). In *Pharsalia*, the words are spoken to Cato, who is invited to channel the divine oracle in order to see what the future will hold, to ask "will the people be allowed to enjoy their laws and liberties, or has the civil war been fought in vain?" But Cato was not interested in divination. He simply wanted to do what was right. "Men who doubt and are ever uncertain of future events—let them cry out for prophets," he said. "I draw my assurance from no oracle but from the sureness of death."[106]

Hume's choice of epigram was very clever. On the one hand, it allows for a fig leaf of piety since Cato also says, "We men are all inseparable from the gods." But the real message is that we have no need of the Gods because, in a sense, we are Gods. "Why seek further for deities? All that we see is God; every motion we make is God also." Morality needs no transcendent source. It is rooted in a proper understanding of our human nature—from "the sureness of death." To "demand to see Goodness in her visible shape" is not to ask the divine to be made flesh. It is to see that goodness only exists in visible shape, in the conduct of physical, worldly human beings. Far from undermining morality, it actually puts it on a more secure footing, making "the rules of justice steadfast and immutable; at least, as immutable as human nature."[107]

CHAPTER SIX

Facing the End

Never think . . . that as long as you are master of your own
fireside and your own time, you can be unhappy, or that any
other circumstance can make an addition to your enjoyment.

Epicurus's Hog

On his return to Britain, Hume stayed a while in London before
heading back home to Scotland for what would be the last time
in August 1769. At first, he returned to the home in a tenement
block in James Court that he had first moved into in 1762,
shortly before going to Paris. He lived there with his sister
Katherine and his "little Pomeranian dog, Foxey." He was, at
last, both acclaimed and well-off, one of the first "men of letters"
to earn his living primarily by writing. Mossner says he "shared
his late affluence," financing and supervising the education of
his nephews and giving his sister an allowance.[1]

But although he described James Court as "very chearful, and
even elegant," it was "too small to display my great Talent for
Cookery, the Science to which I intend to addict the remaining
Years of my Life." Hume was not joking. Many historical records
attest to his gourmandism. In one letter to Gilbert Elliott he

wrote, "I have just now lying on the Table before me a Receipt for making *soupe a la Reine*, copy'd with my own hand. For Beef and Cabbage (a charming Dish), and old Mutton and old Claret, no body excels me. I also make Sheep head Broth in a manner that Mr [ambassador] Keith speaks of it for eight days after."[2] Boswell referred to his "northern Epicurus style."[3]

But did Hume actually cook himself? Mossner says his *scritoire* was filled with French recipes, his cellar the best French wines, and he "patiently instructed his 'lass', the faithful old housekeeper Peggy Irvine, in the art of sophisticated cookery."[4] Irvine managed the new house too with a small staff of servants. However, his and others' phraseology suggests that Hume did roll up his sleeves in the kitchen at least sometimes.

We can get some sense of what kind of fare earned Hume his reputation from a book of recipes called *A New and Easy Method of Cookery* by Elizabeth Cleland. The book was "chiefly intended for the young ladies who attend her school," which was very close to where Hume lived. There is no recipe for sheep's head broth in the book but we could perhaps devise one by combining two others.

A Calf's Head Soup

TAKE a Calf's Head, stew it tender; then strain off the Liquor, and put in a Bunch of sweet Herbs, Onions, Salt, Pepper, Mace, and some fine Barley, boil it till the Barley and Head is done; then serve it with the Head in the Middle.

To make Mutton Broth

TAKE about six Pounds of Mutton, boil it in three Scots Pints of Water, with sweet Herbs, Onions, two or three Turnips, a Quarter of a Pound of fine Barley or Rice, Salt and

Pepper; a little before you take it up, put in it a Handful of chopped Parsley.

If you dined chez Hume, you could expect to be well fed, quantitively as well as qualitatively. "I dined with the philosopher," wrote Colonel Edmonstoune, "and got myself tipsy."[5] Lord Kellie thought the Edinburgh *literati* would be better called the *Eaterati*. An English poet William Mason was, says Mossner, not being unkind when he wrote:

D**d, who there supinely deigns to lye,
The fattest Hog of Epicurus' sty

The phrase seems to have stuck. Gibbon wrote to a friend visiting Edinburgh, "You will not fail to visit the Stye of the fattest of Epicurus's Hogs."[6] Hume even mocked himself for his perhaps excessive love of food. "Ye ken I'm no epicure, only a glutton," he reassured a friend at whose house he had arrived unexpectedly to dine.[7]

Many are surprised to learn how much Hume enjoyed his food. With its Platonic-Christian history of denigrating the flesh, most Westerners do not associate culinary discrimination with intellectual acuity. Hume is a clear counterexample to the prejudice that good dining and good philosophy are incompatible. "An elegant Table has not spoilt my Relish for Sobriety," he wrote, "Nor Gaiety for Study."[8]

Hume's ability to enjoy good food without apology reflects a recurring theme in his writing. Whereas Christendom had historically asserted a clear divide between humanity and the animal kingdom, Hume argued that humans were in essence no different from animals. Pre-Darwin, this was quite extraordinary. Most remarkably, he claimed that "no truth appears to me more evident, than that beasts are endow'd with thought and reason as well as men."[9]

If it seems much less than obvious, that is probably because we are pretty sure that animals don't construct logical arguments. This misses the point. By saying animals reason, Hume is not so much raising them to the level of the highest philosophy but lowering the level of most human reasoning. *Animals are more intelligent than we tend to think because humans are not as intelligent as we would like to think.* For Hume, we have to remember that most of our "reasoning" is little more than making assumptions based on past experience without any logical inference at all. Animals do the same. "Animals, as well as men learn many things from experience, and infer, that the same events will always follow from the same causes."[10] Hume fully accepts that animals "are not guided in these inferences by reasoning" but "Neither are children: Neither are the generality of mankind, in their ordinary actions and conclusions: Neither are philosophers themselves, who, in all the active parts of life, are, in the main, the same with the vulgar, and are governed by the same maxims."[11]

Humans may have more brain power, but that does not mean they reason in a completely different way. So, for example, chains of cause and effect can be complicated, which means that "one mind may be much larger than another, and better able to comprehend the whole system of objects, and to infer justly their consequences." Similarly, "One man is able to carry on a chain of consequences to a greater length than another."[12]

Another way in which people like to distinguish humans from animals is to claim animals act on pure "instinct" whereas humans do not. But as we have seen, for Hume "reason is nothing but a wonderful and unintelligible instinct in our souls, which carries us along a certain train of ideas, and endows them with particular qualities, according to their particular situations and relations."[13]

Hume also attributes emotions to animals, saying "love and hatred are common to the whole sensitive creation."[14] As with humans, these are transmitted from animal to animal. "Fear, anger, courage and other affections are frequently communicated from one animal to another, without their knowledge of that cause, which produc'd the original passion."[15] Given that this sympathy is the basis of morality, Hume is suggesting that animals too have some kind of primitive moral sense. This can be seen in some of the moral emotions, which are rooted in implicit judgments that something is agreeable or useful, to the animal or others. We find some of these in animals. "'Tis plain, that almost in every species of creatures, but especially of the nobler kind, there are many evident marks of pride and humility. The very port and gait of a swan, or turkey, or peacock show the high idea he has entertain'd of himself, and his contempt of all others."[16] It's unclear whether Hume's examples are good ones, but anyone who lives with a dog, or perhaps even a cat, will agree that some kind of pride and humility can be seen in their behavior.

Hume's argument, however, is not fundamentally based on any claim to be able to spot thinking or feeling in animals. His most basic proposition is simply that "where the structure of parts in brutes is the same as in men, and the operation of these parts also the same, the causes of that operation cannot be different, and that whatever we discover to be true of the one species, may be concluded without hesitation to be certain of the other." Animals are so like humans in their basic physical structure that we must conclude that they function according to the same basic principles that we do. And since the "springs and principles" that govern action are hidden even from us, there is no reason to think they are "peculiar to man, or any one species of animals."[17]

Hume was remarkably ahead of his time in questioning the human-animal divide. That only makes it more disappointing, and less understandable, that he did not go further in attributing equal capacities to women and non-whites. Sadly, *when a person demonstrates freedom from some prejudices, that does not mean they are free from prejudice in all.*

Hume's Last Home

A chef and host such as Hume needed a larger home in which to cook and entertain. For a while he lodged in one of Allan Ramsay's houses in the vicinity of the castle while his more permanent solution was being constructed. He built a new house in the New Town which he described as "a small House," meaning "a large House for an author." It stood on the southwest corner of the new St. Andrew Square, one block north of Princes Street, the other side of the loch from the Old Town.

The short street linking the square and Princes Street was originally unnamed, as early maps show. Now it is St. David Street and that is no coincidence. Nancy Ord was a daughter of the Lord Chief Baron of the Court of the Scottish Exchequer, described by Mossner as "a lovely and charming English woman and a favourite of David's." One day she chalked on the side of his house "St David's Street." The jest took hold.[18]

There was some talk of Hume marrying Ord. In 1770 he had said that building a house "is the second great Operation of human Life, For the taking a Wife is the first, which I hope will

FIGURE 22. St. David's Street, jokingly named after the great infidel.

come in time."[19] Henry Mackenzie, a friend of Hume, wrote, "He certainly at one time meant to pay his addresses to [court] Miss Nancy Ord, at that time one of the most agreeable and accomplished women I ever knew."[20] Mossner reports that Hume even entrusted her to choose the wallpaper for his new home, a task more suited to a fiancée than a friend. But nothing happened.

A letter to Ord from Bath in June 1776 leaves us in no doubt of the genuine affection Hume felt for her. He wrote to tell her that the spa waters had failed to provide any cure for his illness and that "you are likely to lose, at no great distance of time, one of the Persons in the World, who has the greatest Regard and Affection for you." What follows makes it clear that this affection is romantic in nature:

I know what egregious Folly it is for a Man of my Years to attach himself too strongly to one of Yours; but I saw in you so much other Merit, beside that which is the common Object of Affection, that I easily excused to myself the Imprudence; and your obliging Behaviour always kept me from being sensible of it. It is the best placed Attachment of my Life; and will surely be the last. I know, that the Tear will be in your Eye when you read this; as it is in mine when I write it.[21]

Hume's lifelong bachelorship might seem puzzling. Ord is clearly not the only woman who piqued his interest. There was clearly some kind of chemistry with Mme. de Boufflers. There is also some suggestion of an aborted courtship in his youth. In an essay he wrote, "I remember I was once desired by a young beauty, for whom I had some passion, to send her some novels and romances for her amusement in the country." The relationship did not end well, according to this account, because he sent her *Plutarch's Lives*, assuring her "that there was not a word of truth in them from beginning to end." Once she came to Alexander and Caesar, however, whose names she recognized, she "returned me the book, with many reproaches for deceiving her."[22]

Despite his lack of any evident physical handsomeness, Hume seemed to be attractive to women. The German-born man of letters Friedrich Melchior Grimm wrote, "What is still more pleasant is that all the pretty women had a great run on him, and that the fat Scottish philosopher was pleased with their society. This David Hume is an excellent man; he is naturally placid; he listens attentively, he sometimes speaks with wit, although he speaks little; but he is clumsy, he has neither warmth, nor grace, nor charm of humour, nor anything that properly appertains to the chirping of those charming little mechanisms known as pretty women."[23]

Hume in return liked the company of women, whom he never described in the condescending and belittling language used by Grimm. He found that "mixt companies, without the fair-sex, are the most insipid entertainment in the world, and destitute of gaiety and politeness, as much as sense or reason. Nothing can keep them from excessive dulness but hard drinking; a remedy worse than the disease."[24]

It is of course possible that Hume was homosexual at a time when it would have been impossible to even hint at it. But we have no positive reason to think he was, and it is not in fact difficult to imagine why as a heterosexual Hume always ended up choosing singledom. He valued his independence and for most of his life was not wealthy enough to simply throw money at the problem of having to look after a family. It is interesting that Ord herself never married. Perhaps the very reason why they felt like kindred spirits was the independence of mind that meant they could never cement this bond in marriage.

Hume's New Town home was demolished years ago. Until the early part of this century, the modern block that stood in its place on what is now 21 South St. David Street hosted a simple stone plaque saying "In a house on this site David Hume lived 1771–1776." However, the whole site was recently completely redeveloped, and the new building does not see fit to commemorate its most important and famous former inhabitant. If they do not appreciate his philosophical legacy they should at least value his aesthetic one. The fact that today there are no buildings on the south side of Princes Street, preserving the stunning views of the Castle and the Old Town, is owed to Hume and others protesting a decision by the Town Council to overturn their previous commitment to leave this undeveloped.[25]

Everything was set for Hume to enjoy a comfortable retirement. But in 1772, not long after moving into his new home, his health started to decline. At first it was gradual but in spring 1775, he "was struck with a disorder in my bowels" which he soon realized was "mortal and incurable." Within a year he lost seven pounds. By the beginning of 1776, he told Smith he had lost "five compleat stone."[26] We cannot know exactly what the illness was. The bloody stools reported as symptoms suggest colon cancer but Mossner says that "modern medicine might agree that, although cancer of the bowel cannot be ruled out, Hume probably died of chronic ulcerative colitis, following an acute bacillary dysentery."[27]

And yet throughout his illness he remained remarkably good spirited and active. He kept reading, writing to both Edward Gibbon and Adam Smith to praise *The History of the Decline and Fall of the Roman Empire* and *The Wealth of Nations*, respectively.[28] On the way to London in April, he crossed dramatist John Home and Adam Smith heading the other way to Edinburgh to visit him. Home accompanied him and found him "never more cheerful, or in more possession of all his faculties, his memory, his understanding, his wit."[29]

Hume had never aspired to live as long as possible. "Extreme old age is certain misery," he wrote in a late letter. *Life can be too long as well as too short.* "May it be my fate for my own sake & for that of all my friends, to stop short at the threshold of old age, and not to enter too far into that dismal region."[30] In his autobiography, written as he knew he was dying, he declared, "I have suffered very little pain from my disorder; and what is more strange, have, notwithstanding the great decline of my person, never suffered a moment's abatement of my spirits; insomuch, that were I to name the period of my life, which I should most choose to pass over again, I might be tempted to point to this later period. I possess the same ardour as ever in study, and the same gaiety in company. I consider, besides, that a man of sixty-five, by dying, cuts off only a few years of infirmities; and though I see many symptoms of my literary reputation's breaking out at last with additional lustre, I knew that I could have but few years to enjoy it. It is difficult to be more detached from life than I am at present."[31]

Hume looked his impending death in the face with admirable clarity. Adam Smith recalled how Hume's doctor told him, "I shall tell your friend, Colonel Edmondstone that I left you much better, and in a fair way of recovery." Hume saw through the fake reassurance. "Doctor," he said, "as I believe you would not choose to tell any thing but the truth, you had better tell him, that I am dying as fast as my enemies, if I have any, could wish, and as easily and cheerfully as my best friends could desire."[32]

On Thursday, July 4, he had what was in effect a farewell dinner at St. David's Street. Most of his friends were there. They did not know it at the time, since transatlantic news moved slowly, but this was the day of the Declaration of Independence in the United States, a cause most of them supported.

A few days later on July 7, Hume received a visitor with less benign motives. James Boswell had come to the dying Hume out of a morbid curiosity about how an atheist would face death. Hume was kind to even receive him. Back in 1763 he had fallen out with him in another literary dispute his autobiography glossed over. Boswell and two coauthors had published a remark that Hume not only made to him in private but which Hume also denies he ever said at all, insulting a certain Mr. Malloch. Hume wrote to Boswell, "How the Devil came it into your Heads or rather your Noddles (for if there had been a Head among you, the thing would not have happened) . . . to publish in a Book to all the World what you pretend I told you in private Conversation?" Hume said he would not reply to any of his letters until he gave him "some satisfaction for this offence," saying that "among us, Gentlemen of the Quill, there is nothing of which we are so jealous, not even our wives, if we have any, as the Honour of our Productions."[33]

We can assume Boswell made his apologies, for Hume received him at his deathbed. What transpired gives us a remarkable insight into just how incredible many at the time found it that a non-believer could be preparing for the grave so calmly. Boswell describes Hume as "lean, ghastly, and quite of an earthy appearance" but "placid and even cheerful." But what Hume told him was shocking. "He then said flatly that the morality of every religion was bad, and, I really thought, was not jocular when he said that when he heard a man was religious, he concluded he was a rascal, though he had known some instances of very good men being religious. This was just an extravagant reverse of the common remark as to infidels."

Boswell had "a strong curiosity to be satisfied if he persisted in disbelieving a future state even when he had death before his eyes. I was persuaded from what he now said, and from his manner of saying it, that he did persist. I asked him if it was not possible that there might be a future state. Hume answered it was possible that a piece of coal put upon the fire would not burn; and he added that it was a most unreasonable fancy that we should exist for ever."

The conversation made Boswell feel "a degree of horror, mixed with a sort of wild, strange, hurrying recollection of my excellent mother's pious instructions, of Dr. Johnson's noble lessons, and of my religious sentiments and affections during the course of my life. I was like a man in sudden danger eagerly seeking his defensive arms; and I could not but be assailed by momentary doubts while I had actually before me a man of such strong abilities and extensive inquiry dying in the persuasion of being annihilated." Although Boswell steadfastly says "I maintained my faith," he also reports that "I left him with impressions which disturbed me for some time."

Boswell at least seemed to respect Hume's fortitude. "Mr. Hume's pleasantry was such that there was no solemnity in the scene; and death for the time did not seem dismal," he says. "It surprised me to find him talking of different matters with a tranquility of mind and a clearness of head which few men possess at any time." Other believers took Boswell's reports in a very different spirit. William Johnstone Temple said callously, "If he continue obstinate [he] will die the death of a Dog. . . . Let him die then & be thrown into the ditch."[34]

One of the most moving accounts of Hume's last days comes in a letter from Adam Smith to William Strahan, Hume's publisher in London. This again reiterates Hume's good spirits and sanguineness in the face of death. The letter includes an extended account of Hume's reaction to reading Lucian's *Dialogues of the Dead*, in which those unwilling to accept their death offer excuses to Charon, who carries the souls of the recently deceased across the Styx to Hades. Hume was struck by how he could not offer any such excuses, since "he had no house to finish, he had no daughter to provide for, he had no enemies upon whom he wished to revenge himself." He concluded that "I therefore have all reason to die contented." But then Hume amused himself imagining what other reasons he could offer Charon for letting him remain in the land of the living. Smith takes up the story:

"Good Charon, I have been correcting my works for a new edition. Allow me a little time, that I may see how the public receives the alterations." But Charon would answer, "When you have seen the effect of these, you will be for making other alterations. There will be no end of such excuses; so, honest friend, please step into the boat." But I might still urge, "Have a little patience, good Charon; I have been endeavoring to open the eyes of the public. If I live a few years longer, I may have the satisfaction of seeing the downfall of some of the prevailing systems of superstition." But Charon would then lose all temper and decency. "You loitering rogue, that will not happen these many hundred years. Do you fancy I will grant you a lease for so long a term? Get into the boat this instant, you lazy loitering rogue."[35]

On August 13 Hume wrote to his brother to say, "Dr Black tells me plainly, like a man of sense, that I shall die soon, which was no disagreeable news to me."[36] His last letter, to Smith, dated August 23, said, "I go very fast to decline, and last night had a small fever, which I hoped might put a quicker period to this tedious illness, but unluckily it has, in a great measure, gone off."[37]

The manner in which Hume approached his death has been taken by many as exemplary, a model for others to emulate. If we are to do so, however, it is important that we are not misled by its superficial resemblance to Stoicism. As we have seen, Hume was no Stoic. In fact he had explicitly rejected that philosophy, having suffered as a youth for trying too hard to follow its maxims.

Stoics attempt to be equanimous before death by convincing themselves that life is of little value. Life is a "preferred indifferent," meaning that we can enjoy it if we happen to have it but we should desire neither to have it nor not have it. "We too are extinguished; we too are lighted," wrote Seneca. "Betweentimes there is something that we feel; on either side is complete lack of concern."[38] Marcus Aurelius expresses a similar indifference toward life in sentences such as "Altogether the interval is small between birth and death; and consider with how much trouble, and in company with what sort of people and in what a feeble body, this interval is laboriously passed."[39] Hume never wrote, or would have written, anything like this. Hume evidently loved life, with all its intellectual and bodily pursuits. For Hume, like the Stoics, there is nothing before or after death, but talking of these times as ones of "peace" is nonsense. *Without life, there is neither peace nor disturbance, only nothing.*

Hume's ability to face death sanguinely was therefore nothing to do with any disdain for life. It came simply from an acceptance that death is inevitable and the most any of us can ask for is to lead a good life for the few years we are granted. There are many oft-quoted Stoic aphorisms that capture this thought, such as Marcus Aurelius's "No man can escape his destiny, the next inquiry being how he may best live the time that he has to live,"[40] or Epictetus's blunt "death is an inevitable thing. For what can I do? Where shall I go to escape it."[41] But these are not distinctively Stoic perspectives. They are shared by anyone who is prepared to confront the fundamental fact of our mortality. Stoicism adds to this an indifference to whether we live or die. That, they argue, is what enables us to escape the fear of death. Hume's life and work is a rebuttal of this. He showed that you can love life and even the pleasures of the flesh and still face death without fear or regret—or at least with not enough regret to be able to accept Charon's instance that your time is up with a shrug. *Accepting death is not the same as welcoming it; loving life does not mean clinging to it.*

Another respect in which Hume differed from the Stoics is that he attributed his ability to face death well as much to good fortune as to any morally praiseworthy effort. For the Stoics, all life is a preparation for death, and we are only able to face it well if we have cultivated the right attitudes of detachment to life. For Hume, however, his ability to face death well is in part due to his natural disposition—"a man of mild disposition, of command of temper, of an open, social, and cheerful humour"—and the good fortune not to have suffered any great calamities. For instance, he also wrote in *My Own Life*, "though most men, any wise eminent, have found reason to complain of calumny, I never was touched, or even attacked by her baleful tooth."[42]

Much as we might admire his philosophical life and death, his own words suggest to us that we should not overestimate the extent to which philosophy, rather than fortune and temperament, was responsible for it. I find this a helpful corrective to the idea that philosophy can and should make us able to come to terms with death, a sentiment often expressed with the help of Socrates's saying that "philosophy is a preparation for death." Although I agree that philosophy can help us to accept our mortality at the intellectual level, I have seen that for many people this does not translate to any kind of sanguinity. *Knowing that something is inevitable does not necessarily make you happy to take it when it comes.* People who "rage against the dying of the light," as Dylan Thomas put it, are not necessarily making a philosophical mistake.

Hume died Sunday, August 25, at around 4:00 p.m. The funeral was on the twenty-ninth. Mossner reports that "a large crowd had gathered in St David Street to watch the coffin being carried out. One of the crowd was overheard to remark, 'Ah, he was an Atheist.' To which a companion returned: 'No matter, he was an *honest* man.'"[43] Not all were so respectful. Hume's family had to guard the grave in the days after the funeral to prevent it from being desecrated.[44]

More refined attacks followed. John Wesley, the founder of Methodism, preached a sermon after Hume's death titled "The Deceitfulness of the Human Heart" in which he said, "Did Mr. David Hume . . . know the heart of man? No more than a worm or a beetle does. After 'playing so idly with the darts of death,' do you now find it a laughing matter? What think you now of Charon? Has he ferried you over Styx? At length he has taught you to know a little of your own heart! At length you know it is a fearful thing to fall into the hands of the living God!"[45]

I thought about this when I attended a concert at the New Room in Bristol, the world's first Methodist chapel, where Wesley often preached. It struck me that it could have been in this very room that Wesley denounced Hume. In fact, the sermon in question was given in Halifax, West Yorkshire. Still, a connection had been made which got me thinking. Methodism these days is often a very liberal faith and Wesley is considered a good Christian man. Yet there was a meanness of spirit in his attack on Hume that illustrates better than any argument how religion and higher morality are not necessarily connected. The secular sympathy Hume advocated seems much more appealing to me than the righteous antipathy generated by much religion. Where Hume's morality is gentle, that of the early Methodists was as hard as the pews built in the chapel, designed to make sinners uncomfortable rather than to comfort them. *Better a humane sympathy than a harsh, divine morality.*

Hume's will contained a playful codicil that ensured his good humor outlived him. He left to John Home of Kilduff "ten dozen of my old Claret at his Choice; and one single Bottle of that other Liquor called Port. I also leave to him six dozen of Port, provided that he attests under his hand signed *John Hume*, that he himself alone finishd that bottle at two sittings. By this

Concession, he will at one terminate the only two Differences, that ever arose between us, concerning temporal Matters."[46] The first difference presumably concerns Hume's decision to reject the historical spelling of their family's name as a concession to English pronunciation. The second surely reflects differing opinions about how much it is appropriate to drink at one time. Home must have been more abstemious than Hume, who used his will as a way of trying to force his friend to loosen his self-restraint, at least temporarily.

More seriously, his will decreed "a Monument be built over my Body at an Expence not exceeding a hundred pounds, with an Inscription containing only my Name and the Year of my Birth and Death, leaving it to Posterity to add the Rest." This was designed by the architect Robert Adams, a friend of Hume's.[47] Smith said, "I don't like that monument; it is the greatest piece of vanity I ever saw in my friend Hume."[48]

The mausoleum still stands and it is easy to see why Smith didn't like it. It is in Old Calton Burial Ground, a small cemetery at the foot of Calton Hill, which overlooks the city of Edinburgh, where we started our journey with Hume. Hume is by far and away the biggest of the "celebrities interred" there, listed on a wooden plaque at its entrance, including the philosopher Thomas Reid and the mathematician John Playfair.

The mausoleum itself is a gray stone cylinder in an ancient Roman style, simply decorated, with the floral frieze around the top the most elaborate adornment. Inside it is completely plain, with an open roof looking up to the sky. After many years of neglect, which saw vegetation growing within it, the monument has been recently restored and is now in good condition. Although not gaudy, its size gives it an air of self-importance and grandeur that does not sit well with Hume's professed modesty.

FIGURE 23. The Hume Mausoleum in in Old Calton Burial Ground.

To visit it, however, is a moving experience. I've been more than once, and it has never been overrun by visitors, even during the Edinburgh Festival when the city is packed with people. The fact that the main physical memorial of arguably the greatest philosopher in history sits quietly and obscurely in a forgotten corner of a major city, without attracting many visitors, is testimony to the modesty all philosophers should have about their importance to humanity.

The mausoleum also has some interesting additions. In a niche above the entrance is an urn in the memory of Hume's nephew's wife, with the touching tribute in Latin which translates as "To Jane Alder, a wife of great kindness, most delightful. This urn was placed in her memory by her fortunate husband."[49]

Another Design of a Monument for the late David Hume Esq.

B.

FIGURE 24. Robert Adams's design for the Hume Mausoleum.

Beneath it is a biblical inscription, combining two New Testament verses from the Book of Revelation and Paul's First Letter to the Corinthians: "Behold I come quickly. Thanks be to God which giveth us the victory through our lord Jesus Christ."[50] That is not, however, the only Christian addendum to the monument. Inside, now remounted on the wall is a small stone tablet, but which as recently as 2008 I found simply resting on the ground. This is headed with a quote from John's Gospel: "I am the resurrection and the life." This is dedicated to the memory of the Hon. David Hume of Ninewells, the philosopher's nephew, and his sons John, David, and Joseph, who were buried there, and also their sister Elizabeth.

The fact that David's nephew was willing to add not one but two biblical inscriptions to his non-believing uncle's mausoleum is curious, but perhaps not disrespectful. Hume was not a believer but nor was he a zealous atheist. He showed little interest in trying to take away faith from those who had it. Were Hume to know what his nephew would do, it is just as likely he would have been wryly amused as irritated.

Adam Smith's distaste for Hume's monument was not, however, the greatest of the trials he suffered for his late friend. The letter he wrote to Strahan after Hume's death was published together with Hume's autobiography, *My Own Life*, in 1777. Although Smith thought it was "a very harmless Sheet of paper" he found it brought him "ten times more abuse than the very violent attack I had made upon the whole commercial system of Great Britain."[51] The reason for this is simply that Smith dared to not only present Hume as an unrepentant unbeliever but expressed the view that he considered this infidel "both in his lifetime and since his death, as approaching as nearly to the idea of a perfectly wise and virtuous man, as perhaps the nature of human frailty will permit."[52]

We know that Smith took care to tone down Hume's more controversial opinions because of the differences between this letter and a private one he sent to Wedderburn. In that letter Hume is reported to have desired to see "the churches shut up, and the Clergy sent about their business."[53] In the letter to Strahan this becomes the much less provocative wish to see "the downfall of some of the prevailing systems of superstition." In the Wedderburn letter Smith also said Hume was dying "with more real resignation to the necessary course of things, than any whining Christian ever dyed with a pretended resignation to the will of God."

But despite his detractors, Hume died, according to Harris, "one of the most famous and widely respected men of letters of his day." As a friend testified in a letter in 1767, "it is not flattery when I assure you that you are more universally loved by all ranks of people than any man I ever knew." A letter to the *London Chronicle* said, "No modern has been more read, or has commanded a larger share of the public approbation than the late Mr Hume."[54]

Capturing Character

It took a very long time for the significance of Hume's achievements to be truly recognized. Mossner laments that Hume's "science of human nature" was "either ignored or misunderstood by his own generation" and that "only in the twentieth century has it met with sympathy and understanding."[55] This might be an overstatement but it is unhappily close to the truth. Consider that apart from the private mausoleum Hume himself left money to build, there was no monument to Edinburgh's greatest philosopher in that city until 1997, when a one and a half times life-size statue was unveiled on the Royal Mile.

This neo-classical sculpture by the Edinburgh-born artist Sandy Stoddart is even more controversial than the mausoleum. It depicts Hume seated in the robes of an ancient Greek philosopher, the draped cloth leaving his right arm and chest bare. On his right knee he is holding a blank tablet, representing the contrast between his skepticism and the religious certainties he rejected, such as the ten commandments. Stoddart makes Hume look serious and handsome, but in reality he looked neither. For most of his life he was far too chubby for his bare torso to look attractive. Diderot confided in a letter to Hume that he would have mistaken him for a fat well-fed

FIGURE 25. Sandy Stoddart's 1997 statue of Hume on Edinburgh's Royal Mile.

Bernardine monk. "Mme Diderot will kiss your two large Bernardine cheeks," adding "I salute you—I love you—I revere you" to make it clear he only meant friendly teasing.[56] Hume would surely not have taken offense since he was often the first to mock his own ample girth. In one letter, he made himself the butt of a joke that "taxes on Luxury are almost always most approv'd of: and no one will say, that the carrying of a portly Belly is of any use or Necessity."[57]

James Caulfield, later Lord Charlemont, said that "Nature, I believe, never yet formed any Man more unlike his real Character than David Hume. . . . His face was broad and fat, his Mouth wide, and without other Expression than that of Imbecility. His eyes vacant and spiritless, and the Corpulence of his whole Person was far better fitted to communicate the Idea of a Turtle-eating Alderman than of a refined Philosopher."[58] Mme. du Deffand called him le *paysan du Danube* (the peasant of the Danube), after the eponymous protagonist of a Jean de La Fontaine *Fable*, which opens with the line "You shouldn't judge people by their appearance."[59]

Another of Hume's less attractive features was his voice. Caulfield wrote, "His Speech in English was rendered ridiculous by the broadest and the most vulgar Scottish Accent, and his French was, if possible, still more laughable."[60] Caulfield wasn't the only person to comment on Hume's accent. One of his relatives observed that "he retained the accent, expression and vulgarity of his paternal stile on the Banks of the White Water and Tweed, in such a degree that you would have imagined he had never conversed with any person but the commonest farmer in the Merse, or ever sett foot out of the parish of Chirnside."[61] At the same time, in his written English he was keen to eradicate "Scotticisms," often pointing them out in comments on others' drafts and drawing up a list of them to be avoided.[62] This short document, unpublished in his lifetime, contains some gems for logophiles. "To be difficulted" is a lovely Scotticism for "to be puzzled," Scots "cry" rather than "call" a person, while the Scotch usage of "learn" to mean "teach" is the same as many English regional argots.

Mossner also notes, "More philosophic observers, however, than this Academy student were thrown into confusion by the phenomenon of David Hume's vacant stare." D'Alembert even wrote to Hume, confiding, "I remember when you were once talking to me and at the same time staring fixedly at me that I advised you in a friendly manner to break off as much as possible that habit because it might play you a nasty trick. . . . It is not necessary to gaze intently at the people you are speaking to."[63]

Contemporary portraits certainly don't show a handsome man. An engraving by A. B. Duhamel portrays a dignified, serious demeanor but doesn't disguise flabby jowls, also evident in Tassie's medallion. A very realistic miniature in watercolor on ivory by Archibald Skirving shows a flat countenance, not exactly vacant but not exuding a penetrating gaze. John Donaldson's much copied line engraving (sometimes reversed) is most unflattering and gives a sense of the slightly imbecilic face described with his fat, almost boyish cheeks. The famous Ramsay portrait gives him a certain dignity and grandeur due to his pose and gold-hemmed red jacket/cape, believed to be the uniform of the Embassy Secretary. But his double chin is prominent and his eyes are again far from penetrating, "staring directly at, but not apparently seeing, the viewer" in Nigel Warburton's description.[64]

If Stoddart's statue impressionistically captured the inner Hume, its lack of physical resemblance would not matter. However, from what I can tell, it doesn't do this either. Hume was neither imperious nor superior, as the statue suggests. Caulfield, for instance, while mocking his appearance, said Hume was endowed with "real benevolence ... His Love to mankind was universal and vehement; and there was no Service He wou'd not cheerfully have done to his Fellow Creatures. . . . He was tender hearted, friendly, and charitable in the extreme."[65]

One anecdote shows him to be especially soft-hearted. The young Hume attended an evening dinner party given by Lady Dalrymple in Edinburgh. She had a dog called Pod who stank terribly, and many guests clamored to "kick him down stairs." Hume said, "Oh do not hurt the beast. It is not Pod, it is Me!" As Lady Anne Lindsay remarked in a letter, "How very few people would take the evil odour of a stinking Conduct from a guiltless Pod to wear it on their own rightful Shoulders."[66]

Perhaps this incident is better understood as an example of Hume's silly side. "Deep in the nature of David Hume ran a streak of frivolity," judges Mossner, who thought Hume shared with many intellectuals a love of banter and practical jokes. According to Hume's contemporary Dr. Robertson, Hume's jollity often bordered on the infantile, but he had observed the same disposition so often in his friends that he "was almost disposed to consider it as characteristic of genius."[67]

Hume was wildly admired as a man of virtue. But was he modest? In his letters he often seems to try to come across as modest, but as we have seen he also appears to have a degree of pride. Few would go so far as the Chevalier Ramsay, who wrote in 1742 that Hume was "too full of himself, to humble his pregnant, active, protuberant Genius to drudge at translation."[68] But there does seem to be a tension in him between pride and modesty, as reflected in his leaving the large sum of £100 to build a memorial to himself, while at the same time insisting on a plain inscription.

Hume often made passing reference to his character in letters, often mocking his own vanity. In one early letter he wrote, "You'll excuse the natural Frailty of an Author in writing so long a Letter about nothing but his own Performances. Authors have this Privilege in common with Lovers, & founded on the same Reason, that they are both besotted with a blind Fondness of their Object."[69] At least twice, however, he attempted a more systematic description of himself. In *My Own Life*, written as he knew he was dying, he offered this generous summary:

I am, or rather was (for that is the style I must now use in speaking of myself, which emboldens me the more to speak my sentiments); I was, I say, a man of mild dispositions, of command of temper, of an open, social, and cheerful humour, capable of attachment, but little susceptible of enmity, and of great moderation in all my passions. Even my love of literary fame, my ruling passion, never soured my temper, notwithstanding my frequent disappointments. My company was not unacceptable to the young and careless, as well as to the studious and literary; and as I took a particular pleasure in the company of modest women, I had no reason to be displeased with the reception I met with from them. In a word, though most men any wise eminent, have found reason to complain of calumny, I never was touched, or even attacked by her baleful tooth: and though I wantonly exposed myself to the rage of both civil and religious factions, they seemed to be disarmed in my behalf of their wonted fury. My friends never had occasion to vindicate any one circumstance of my character and conduct: not but that the zealots, we may well suppose, would have been glad to invent and propagate any story to my disadvantage, but they could never find any which they thought would wear the face of probability. I cannot say there is no vanity in making this funeral oration of myself, but I hope it is not a misplaced one; and this is a matter of fact which is easily cleared and ascertained.[70]

A more critical account is given in a paper held by the Royal Society of Edinburgh called "Character of⸺⸺, written by himself." This is not in Hume's hand, but it is corrected in his handwriting and is assumed by scholars to be by him and about him. This lists sixteen of his defining characteristics, the first ten of which are:

1. A very good man, the constant purpose of whose life is to do mischief.
2. Fancies he is disinterested, because he substitutes vanity in place of all other passions.
3. Very industrious, without serving either himself or others.
4. Licentious in his pen, cautious in his words, still more so in his actions.
5. Would have had no enemies, had he not courted them; seems desirous of being hated by the public, but has only attained the being railed at.
6. Has never been hurt by his enemies, because he never hated any one of them.
7. Exempt from vulgar prejudices, full of his own.
8. Very bashful, somewhat modest, no way humble.
9. A fool, capable of performances which few wise men can execute.
10. A wise man, guilty of indiscretions which the greatest simpletons can perceive.

This is a self-consciously paradoxical portrait, with each characteristic being contradicted by its opposite. Because of this ironical spirit, it is difficult to know the extent to which each trait described is genuine or an exaggeration for comic effect. Overall, however, it reveals a high degree of self-awareness and self-knowledge. It shows a man who has noble aspirations to be reasonable; wise; cool and calm; without petty, negative emotions. But this is also a man who knows he falls short, that he is also proud, prejudiced, self-indulgent in pursuing what interests him rather than what necessarily serves others. This provides a model for how we should assess our characters and those of others. *Do not ask yourself whether you are brave or cowardly, generous or selfish, calm or volatile, but to what extent and in what ways you exhibit all of these traits.*

The last six items, however, become less ironical and more sincere:

11. Sociable, though he lives in solitude.
12. An enthusiast, without religion.
13. A philosopher, who despairs to attain truth.
14. A moralist, who prefers instinct to reason.
15. A gallant, who gives no offence to husbands and mothers.
16. A scholar, without the ostentation of learning.[71]

The first of these pairs is the defining tension of his life: between the desire to be alone, as he was in Flèche, and his love of company, which he enjoyed in Paris. Hume seemed to accept this contradiction as natural and would surely have approved of the lines in Walt Whitman's *Song of Myself*:

Do I contradict myself?
Very well then I contradict myself,
(I am large, I contain multitudes.)

Hume wrote about his own self-contradictions a hundred years before Whitman and went one better by explaining just why a person contains multitudes. His "bundle" theory of the self makes it almost inevitable that the mass of desires, beliefs, thoughts, and memories that make up a person is going to lack anything close to perfect coherence.

The last five items on the list, however, appear to be a more serious attempt to pinpoint Hume's strengths. They also serve as a kind of summation of his philosophical views. First, he is "An enthusiast, without religion." As we have seen, Hume was opposed to "enthusiasm" where that meant an excessive zeal. As Samuel Johnson's dictionary shows, "enthusiasm" was a generally negative word at the time. An enthusiast was a person who "vainly imagines a private revelation," "has a vain confidence of his intercourse with God," is "of a hot imagination, or violent passions" or "elevated fancy, or exalted ideas." Here, Hume is simply acknowledging with honesty that he is not entirely free of the vices he sees in the religious. He does not pretend to know the mind of God, but he has nonetheless had the chutzpah to set out a complete theory of human nature, making him a prime candidate for a person of "elevated fancy, or exalted ideas." Hume's willingness to accept this helps us to see why he was so tolerant of religious belief, unlike the French *philosophes*. For Hume, *if you forget that we are all somewhat silly, fallible creatures, you become just the kind of dogmatist it is essential not to be.*

Second, he is "a philosopher, who despairs to attain truth." This is a concise, poetic statement of the condition of the true philosopher. Hume accepted that in matters of fact, certainty is always beyond us and that therefore the kind of truth traditionally sought by philosophers—pure, certain, and clear—is something we should despair of attaining. But one can still be a philosopher, one who tried to understand things better, to get closer to truth, to see more of it. *To despair of attaining ultimate truth is not to despair of being a philosopher—it is actually necessary to be a good and honest one.*

Third, Hume is "a moralist, who prefers instinct to reason." If this strikes anyone as a contradiction, that simply shows they have a mistaken view of what morality is. Like the previous comment about philosophers, the point is that to abandon a belief that reason can provide the foundations of morality is not the end of being a moralist but the start of being the right kind of one. Moral philosophy has to be based on an understanding of human nature and sentiment.

Fourth, Hume says he is "a gallant, who gives no offence to husbands and mothers." The word "gallant" is archaic now and survives only in the sense of gallantry, meaning polite, charming, brave, or heroic. In Hume's day a gallant was a more ambiguous figure. Johnson gives its primary meaning as "a gay, sprightly, airy, splendid man" but also notes it can mean "a whore master," who intends to "debauch" women, or more acceptably "a wooer; one who courts a woman for marriage." Hume's self-description is not therefore so much a contradiction as a clarification: he was a jolly man who enjoyed the company of women and although he enjoyed "seducing" them with his charm was always perfectly chaste and modest in his behavior. He is "gallant" only in the right way.

Finally, he is "a scholar, without the ostentation of learning." This closing observation is the closest Hume gets to unambiguous self-praise, but even here the message is not straightforward. As Johnson's dictionary shows, although ostentation could refer to boasting, it could also mean the plainer "outward show" or "appearance." Hume is saying that he made no attempt to show off his learning but also that it simply didn't show, which could be a failing as well as a virtue. Whatever his precise intent, the fact that Hume mentions it last, but not least, is significant. For Hume, it was always important that we do not let our intellectual reflections obscure our humanity. His lack of ostentation in learning was therefore not just a matter of modesty, it was about putting learning in its rightful place. *Learning should be part of a life well-lived, not something we do as though we were mere learning machines.*

That is not to say, however, that learning must always have some practical end result. Hume observed that "many philosophers have consum'd their time, have destroy'd their health, and neglected their fortune, in the search of such truths, as they esteem'd important and useful to the world, tho' it appear'd from their whole conduct and behaviour, that they were not endow'd with any share of public spirit, nor had any concern for the interests of mankind." This might seem to be little more than teasing and mockery of the kind of head-in-the-clouds philosopher Hume often criticized. In fact, his assessment is much more sympathetic than this, perhaps because he was in part describing himself. "The pleasure of study consists chiefly in the action of the mind, and the exercise of the genius and understanding in the discovery or comprehension of any truth." In other words, *study and learning is rewarding in itself and therefore worth doing for its own sake.* However, if you undertake an activity that has some kind of end result that can be judged a success or a failure, "by the natural course of the affections, we acquire a concern for the end itself, and are uneasy under any disappointment we meet with in the pursuit of it." That's why philosophers care about being right even if nothing in the world depends upon it. And that's also why Hume says, "there cannot be two passions more nearly resembling each other, than those of hunting and philosophy." Both have their quarry, but it's the thrill of the chase that draws people to them.[72]

Another reason why we should be tolerant of philosophers who don't seem to be doing much practical good is that the good ones, at least, display skills and talents that the world would be poorer without. "If refined sense and exalted sense be not so useful as common sense, their rarity, their novelty, and the nobleness of their objects make some compensation, and render them the admiration of mankind: As gold, though less serviceable than iron, acquires, from its scarcity, a value, which is much superior."[73]

Hume needs no such special pleading. His philosophy helps us to live well, and better. It seems unbelievably apt that the Home clan's motto is "True to the end." These words are on the family coat of arms that Hume used for his own bookplates, labels that were stuck to the opening pages of a book to indicate it belonged to your library. I was lucky enough to see one in a volume owned by a private collector, bearing the name David Hume, Esq. Hume stayed true to the end, standing by his skeptical beliefs and facing death with the same honesty with which he faced life. So much of what he wrote also remains true today and I expect will continue to do so, at least until we fallible humans come to our own collective end.

Perhaps my favorite summation of the attitude to life Hume both described and exemplified comes in the essay "The Sceptic." Hume is presenting a philosophy that he does not necessarily entirely endorse, but I think in this paragraph, what Hume really *feels* as well as thinks shines through:

> In a word, human life is more governed by fortune than by reason; is to be regarded more as a dull pastime than as a serious occupation; and is more influenced by particular humour, than by general principles. Shall we engage ourselves in it with passion and anxiety? It is not worthy of so much concern. Shall we be indifferent about what happens? We lose all the pleasure of the game by our phlegm and

carelessness. While we are reasoning concerning life, life is gone; and death, though perhaps they receive him differently, yet treats alike the fool and the philosopher. *To reduce life to exact rule and method, is commonly a painful, oft a fruitless occupation*: And is it not also a proof, that we overvalue the prize for which we contend? Even to reason so carefully concerning it, and to fix with accuracy its just idea, would be overvaluing it, were it not that, to some tempers, this occupation is one of the most amusing, in which life could possibly be employed.[74]

APPENDIX

Humean Maxims and Aphorisms

On Reason

"Understanding, when it acts alone, and according to its most general principles, entirely subverts itself, and leaves not the lowest degree of evidence in any proposition, either in philosophy or common life."

You cannot argue against reason without employing reason, since argument requires reason or it is nothing but ungrounded assertion.

We must be modest about and in our reasoning.

A rational argument should offer compelling reasons for belief.

"Rational" is not the same as "logical."

There is no algorithm for good reasoning.

Reason is the worst means of understanding except for all those other forms that have been tried from time to time.

Do not be fooled by the apparent ubiquity of rational thought: we use reason more than we are governed by it.

To understand how you should best think, you need to understand how you actually think.

"Reason alone can never produce any action, or give rise to volition."

Animals are more intelligent than we tend to think because humans are not as intelligent as we would like to think.

On Philosophy and Philosophers

Philosophy succeeds when it addresses human beings as they are and fails when it treats them only as philosophers imagine them to be.

"Nothing is more dangerous to reason than the flights of the imagination, and nothing has been the occasion of more mistakes among philosophers."

"Let us not pretend to doubt in philosophy what we do not doubt in our hearts." *Charles Sanders Peirce*

"To philosophise . . . is nothing essentially different from reasoning on common life; and we may only expect greater stability, if not greater truth, from our philosophy, on account of its exacter and more scrupulous method of proceeding."

Truly ambitious philosophers must also be modest and as willing to doubt and question themselves as they are to doubt and question others.

"Whatever has the air of a paradox, and is contrary to the first and most unprejudic'd notions of mankind is often greedily embrac'd by philosophers, as shewing the superiority of their science, which cou'd discover opinions so remote from vulgar conception."

What appears to be a fundamentally philosophical disagreement is often simply a matter of different people using the same terms differently (and also legitimately).

Philosophy is either continuous with other disciplines or it is sterile, lifeless, and alone.

"Happy, if we can unite the boundaries of the different species of philosophy, by reconciling profound enquiry with clearness, and truth with novelty!"

Be a philosopher; but, amidst all your philosophy, be still a human being.

He may be a philosopher, but amidst all his philosophy, he is usually still all too much a man.

If philosophy is indeed part of a good life, no philosophy should tell us to treat life as though it were not good.

To despair of attaining ultimate truth is not to despair of being a philosopher—it is actually necessary to be a good and honest one.

On Acquiring Knowledge of the World

"A weaker evidence can never destroy a stronger."

The wise proportion their beliefs to the evidence.

Do not waste time thinking about what may or may not happen in a possible world when you have no reason to believe it happens in the actual world.

Assume no more and no less than you have to assume.

"A correct *Judgment*, avoiding all distant and high enquiries, confines itself to common life, and to such subjects as fall under daily practice and experience; leaving the more sublime topics to the embellishment of poets and orators, or to the arts of priests and politicians."

Before you begin to reason and draw conclusions, attend carefully to whatever it is you are seeking to understand.

The world of experience and our representations of it is the only world we can know, and so that has to be the world we seek to understand better.

"Nothing in this world is perpetual, every thing however seemingly firm is in continual flux and change."

"When we infer any particular cause from an effect, we must proportion the one to the other, and can never be allowed to ascribe to the cause any qualities, but what are exactly sufficient to produce the effect."

On Politics and the Good Society

To understand how we should live—as individuals and as a society—learn from every source that offers something to teach you.

Inhuman perfection is the enemy of humanity's best.

"Public Spirit shou'd engage us to love the Public, and to bear an equal Affection to all our Country-Men; not to hate one Half of them, under Colour of loving the Whole."

"As government is a mere human invention for mutual advantage and security, it no longer imposes any obligation, either natural or moral, when once it ceases to have that tendency."

The certain harms of the status quo are sometimes more real than the uncertain dangers of reform.

Fine minds grow best in a rich intellectual culture.

A vibrant economy requires a society rich in intellectual as well as economic capital.

"All general maxims in politics ought to be established with great caution; . . . irregular and extraordinary appearances are frequently discovered in the moral, as well as in the physical world."

There are many things that make for a good life, and it is not possible for any one life or any one society to have them all in full.

"Wherever we depart from equality, we rob the poor of more satisfaction than we add to the rich, and that the slight gratification of a frivolous vanity, in one individual, frequently costs more than bread to many families, and even provinces."

On Skepticism and Doubt

A skeptical, open mind has nothing to fear and much to gain from seeking the company and opinions of those it seriously disagrees with.

"The best expedient to prevent this confusion, is to be modest in our pretensions; and even to discover the difficulty ourselves before it is objected to us."

Confidence should always be challenged, since if it is merited, it will withstand the challenge, and if it is not, it will justly crumble.

"The greater part of mankind may be divided into two classes; that of shallow thinkers, who fall short of the truth; and that of abstruse thinkers, who go beyond it."

"A scrupulous hesitation to receive any new hypothesis is so laudable a disposition in philosophers, and so necessary to the examination of truth, that it deserves to be comply'd with."

"All doctrines are to be suspected, which are favoured by our passions."

Accepting an astonishing mystery is better than believing an incredible explanation.

"Whereof one cannot speak, thereof one must be silent." *Ludwig Wittgenstein*

On Character

Practice doing the right thing in every situation, trivial or important, and you will build the kind of character that tends to act well in all situations.

"No quality is absolutely either blameable or praise-worthy. It is all according to its degree."

Our tendency to overrate our own virtues leads us to overlook our own vices.

Proper pride is taking satisfaction from having done what you judge to be right or of value, without the vanity of believing that makes you superior or special.

"No person is ever prais'd by another for any quality, which wou'd not, if real, produce, of itself, a pride in the person possest of it."

"Where one is thoroughly convinced that the virtuous course of life is preferable; if he have but resolution enough, for some time, to impose a violence on himself; his reformation needs not be despaired of."

Do not ask yourself whether you are brave or cowardly, generous or selfish, calm or volatile, but to what extent and in what ways you exhibit all of these traits.

Travel can only expand the mind if the mind is already expansive.

On Balance

"The mind requires some relaxation, and cannot always support its bent to care and industry."

It is admirable to refuse to look harsh reality in the eye, foolish and destructive never to avert our gaze from it.

The ability to form an accurate view of reality and human nature requires a willingness to attend to all of experience and how it fits together, not specialized scientific knowledge.

Moderation too must be moderated.

To never compromise is a mark of excessive rigidity, to always compromise an even surer sign of having no standards at all.

Sometimes more is better, but most is worst.

Being right shows the quality of your intellect; being wrong but able to acknowledge and learn from your mistakes shows the quality of your character.

"For the purpose of life and conduct and society, a little good sense is surely better than all the genius, and a little good humour than [an] extreme sensibility."

Truth is not worth dying for, but some things worth dying for demand that we uphold the truth, no matter what.

Life can be too long as well as too short.

On Human Nature

"Such is the nature of novelty, that, where any thing pleases, it becomes doubly agreeable, if new; but if it displeases, it is doubly displeasing, upon that very account."

We have only a fragile grip on reality, one we cling to by custom, habit, and instinct.

"Nature is always too strong for principle."

"Obscurity, indeed, is painful to the mind as well as to the eye; but to bring light from obscurity, by whatever labour, must needs be delightful and rejoicing."

"We can form no wish which has not a reference to society. A perfect solitude is, perhaps, the greatest punishment we can suffer."

"There is no quality in human nature, which causes more fatal errors in our conduct, than that which leads us to prefer whatever is present to the distant and remote, and makes us desire objects more according to their situation than their intrinsic value."

Imagination, not reason, reigns sovereign in the human mind and it can only be overthrown by great effort.

"The greatest part of mankind float betwixt vice and virtue."

"To a Philosopher & Historian the Madness and Imbecility & Wickedness of Mankind ought to appear ordinary Events."

Perfectibility is a chimera, human weakness unavoidable. All human beings can do is "endeavour to palliate what they cannot cure."

If you forget that we are all somewhat silly, fallible creatures, you become just the kind of dogmatist it is essential not to be.

On Religion

"Generally speaking, the errors in religion are dangerous; those in philosophy only ridiculous."

"The soul, . . . if immortal, existed before our birth: And if the former state of existence no wise concerned us, neither will the latter."

Belief in an eternal life is a lie we comfort ourselves with, knowing in our hearts it is a lie, but preferring the comfort to the truth.

"What so pure as some of the morals, included in some theological systems? What so corrupt as some of the practices, to which these systems give rise?"

"Theology . . . admits of no terms of composition, but bends every branch of knowledge to its own purpose, without much regard to the phænomena of nature."

When life on earth is good, we have no need to gaze longingly to imaginary heavens.

Better a humane sympathy than a harsh, divine morality.

On Prejudice

"There are great Advantages, in travelling, & nothing serves more to remove Prejudices."

"Prejudice is destructive of sound judgment, and perverts all operations of the intellectual faculties."

Never slavishly follow even the greatest minds, for they too have prejudices, weaknesses, and blind spots.

Many blind spots are remarkably local, leaving the general field of vision perfectly clear.

"When men act in a faction, they are apt, without shame or remorse, to neglect all the ties of honour and morality, in order to serve their party."

"I do not want to serve a man merely because he is celebrated."

Even the keenest eye has blind spots: no one's field of vision is entirely in focus.

To have reasons for suspicion is not to have reasons for pronouncing guilt.

Be as willing to share your friends' loves as you are reluctant to embrace their hatreds.

Prejudice is often no more than a negative emotional reaction based on false ideas.

When a person demonstrates freedom from some prejudices, that does not mean they are free from prejudice in all.

On Argument and Discussion

Refuse to meet intolerance with intolerance, religious extremism with secular extremism.

When people strongly disagree, try to find what they haven't noticed unites them, not what they already know divides them.

Analogy is only as strong as the similarity between the two cases being compared.

When reason has nothing to do with why people hold their beliefs, reason is powerless to change them.

We should never completely dismiss even those who are almost always wrong, as they are almost always sometimes right too.

"When any opinion leads us into absurdities, 'tis certainly false; but 'tis not certain an opinion is false, because 'tis of dangerous consequence."

You cannot judge a good argument by an absolute standard. The best argument is simply the one that has no better rival.

Beauty may be in the eye of the beholder, but there must be something genuinely beautiful for the eye to behold.

Avoid "that Vulgar error . . . of putting nothing but nonsense into the Mouth of the Adversary."

You should judge an ideal by its best version, not its most extreme one.

On Morality

Ethics without empathy is a contradiction in terms.

A person who wishes gratuitous harm is not irrational but callous.

"Nothing can be more unphilosophical than those systems, which assert, that virtue is the same with what is natural, and vice with what is unnatural."

"I feel a pleasure in doing good to my friend, because I love him; but do not love him for the sake of that pleasure."

"If ever there was any thing, which cou'd be call'd natural, the sentiments of morality certainly may; since there never was any nation of the world, nor any single person in any nation, who was utterly depriv'd of them."

"The principles upon which men reason in morals are always the same; though the conclusions which they draw are often very different."

It's not that anything goes, simply that more than one thing goes.

Truth is not always more important than courtesy, or even sometimes entertainment.

A morality based in nothing more than human nature is not only possible, but much more humane than most religious or rationalist alternatives.

Justice is made to fit human beings, not the other way around.

"Justice, in her decisions, never regards the fitness or unfitness of objects to particular persons, but conducts herself by more extensive views."

On the Necessity of Emotion

Passion is a wise master only when it has reason as a loyal servant that can see things that by itself it cannot.

If you want to get someone to do something, it is quicker to work on their passions than their intellect.

"The sentiments of those, who are inclined to think favourably of mankind, are more advantageous to virtue, than the contrary principles, which give us a mean opinion of our nature."

Emotion and reason are not entirely separate, and many of our emotions contain rational judgments.

"'Your sorrow is fruitless, and will not change the course of destiny.' Very true: And for that very reason I am sorry."

"'Tis not solely in poetry and music, we must follow our taste and sentiment, but likewise in philosophy."

Knowing that something is inevitable does not necessarily make you happy to take it when it comes.

"Those refined reflections, which philosophy suggests to us, is, that commonly they cannot diminish or extinguish our vicious passions, without diminishing or extinguishing such as are virtuous, and rendering the mind totally indifferent and unactive."

On Reading and Writing

"There is nothing to be learnt from a Professor, which is not to be met with in Books."

"The book carries us, in a manner, into company, and unites the two greatest and purest pleasures of human life, study and society."

The worst writers choose their topics "less from persuasion, than from the pleasure of showing their invention, and surprising the reader by their paradoxes."

Learning should be part of a life well-lived, not something we do as though we were mere learning machines.

Study and learning is rewarding in itself, and therefore worth doing for its own sake.

Never confuse a lightness of touch in the writing with a lightness of mind in the thinking.

The best writing combines rigor of thought with clarity of expression, difficulty of substance with ease of style.

On the Good Life

"To imagine, that the gratifying of any sense, or the indulging of any delicacy in meat, drink, or apparel, is of itself a vice, can never enter into a head, that is not disordered by the frenzies of enthusiasm."

"Philosophers have endeavoured to render happiness entirely independent of every thing external. That degree of perfection is impossible to be attained."

Do not depend on others or chance more than is necessary for attaining all the satisfaction that life has to offer.

You can only follow your dreams if you're completely awake.

Goodness is multifaceted, and so there is more than one way to live a good life.

Possession of a large fortune is largely dependent on fortune.

To believe that the universe is governed by laws, not chance, is to believe more strongly in the reality of luck in everyday life.

Although the worst is to be among the worst off, and it's better to be among the best off, it's best merely to be better off.

"Never think . . . that as long as you are master of your own fireside and your own time, you can be unhappy, or that any other circumstance can make an addition to your enjoyment."

Without life, there is neither peace nor disturbance, only nothing.

Accepting death is not the same as welcoming it; loving life does not mean clinging to it.

"To reduce life to exact rule and method, is commonly a painful, oft a fruitless occupation."

ACKNOWLEDGMENTS

This book grew out of a project for Book21 in South Korea. I am grateful to everyone I worked with there, including Sae-eun Lim, Eugene, Lee Yun-Kyung, Chang Soo-Yeon, Jungwoo Lim, Mihyun Jeong, and especially Jinny Park. Without the painstaking work of Lizzy Kremer and Maddalena Cavaciuti at David Higham, this much revised English iteration could not have happened. And without the copyediting of Jenn Backer it would have been rougher around the edges.

My research for the book was helped by Capitaine Olivier Frémont and Sylvie Tisserand of the Prytanée national militaire in La Flèche; Alfred van Lelyveld and Olivier Trebosc of Trebosc + van Lelyveld, Paris; Mme. Cherel of Yvandeau; Mungo Bovey QC and Sara Berry of the Advocates Library in Edinburgh; Jean-François Matacz and Sylviane Vatel of the Présidence de l'Assemblée nationale, Paris; Fabrice Gerschel and Jules Veyrat of Philonomist; Kevin Prior of the Chirnside Common Good Association; and Philipp Blom, Amy Cools, Dario Perinetti, Felix Waldmann, and William Zachs.

I have received tremendous support from the whole team at Princeton, including Amy Stewart, Maria Whelan, Eleanor Smith, Kimberley Williams, Dayna Hagewood, Maria Lindenfeldar, Jason Anscomb, and above all my wonderful editor, Matt Rohal.

NOTES

Introduction. Scotland's Hidden Gem

1. Charles Robert Cockerell and William Henry Playfair.

2. *Letters of David Hume, Volume 1*, ed. J.Y.T. Greig (Oxford University Press, 1932), Letter 135.

3. philpapers.org/surveys/demographics.pl.

4. "Of Essay-Writing," 4.

5. Einstein to Moritz Schlick, December 14, 1915, Papers, A, vol. 8A, Doc. 165.

6. Interview with Julian Baggini, *Philosophers' Magazine*, issue 42 (2008): 120–26.

7. *A Treatise of Human Nature*, 3.3.6.6.

8. *Letters of Eminent Persons, Addressed to David Hume*, ed. John Hill Burton (W. Blackwood and Sons, 1849), Letter 16, March 1766, p. 234.

9. Adam Smith to William Strachan, November 9, 1776, available at several online sources including www.ourcivilisation.com/smartboard/shop/smitha/humedead .htm.

10. *An Enquiry concerning the Principles of Morals*, 1.1.

11. "Of the Dignity or Meanness of Human Nature," 5.

12. *Essays, Moral, Political, and Literary*, Advertisement (1752), 2.

13. *Letters of David Hume, Volume 1*, Letter 64.

1. The Foundations of a Thinker

Note to epigraph: "Of the Rise and Progress of the Arts and Sciences," 8.

1. E. C. Mossner, *The Life of David Hume* (Oxford University Press, 1980), 6.

2. "Of the Rise and Progress of the Arts and Sciences," variant reading in *Essays, Moral, Political, and Literary*, ed. Eugene F. Miller (Liberty Fund, 1987), 626.

3. *A Treatise of Human Nature*, 1.4.7.12.

4. Carol Jefferson-Davies, "World's Scholars at Chirnside," *Berwickshire News*, Saturday, July 30, 2011, www.humesociety.org/about/ScholarsAtChirnside.asp.

5. Mossner, *The Life of David Hume*, 39.

6. Ibid., 44.

7. Ibid., 35.

8. *Letters of David Hume, Volume 1*, Letter 227.

9. Ibid., 240–42.

10. The Scottish Index of Multiple Deprivation (SIMD), www.gov.scot.

11. E. C. Mossner, "Hume at La Flèche, 1735: An Unpublished Letter," *Texas Studies in English* 37 (1958): 30–33.

12. Mossner, *The Life of David Hume*, 39.

13. Ibid., 48.

14. Ibid., 51.

15. Dennis C. Rasmussen, *The Infidel and the Professor* (Princeton University Press, 2017), 20.

16. *An Enquiry concerning the Principles of Morals*, 9.3.

17. "Of Refinement in the Arts," 1.

18. *Letters of David Hume, Volume 1*, Letter 72.

19. Mossner, *The Life of David Hume*, 64.

20. Mossner says Hume "may have left Edinburgh University in 1725 or perhaps not until 1726" (*The Life of David Hume*, 49). James A. Harris cites evidence it was the latter (*Hume: An Intellectual Biography* [Cambridge University Press, 2015], 41).

21. *Letters of David Hume, Volume 1*, Letter 3.

22. *An Enquiry concerning Human Understanding*, 1.6.

23. *A Treatise of Human Nature*, 3.3.6.6.

24. *Letters of David Hume, Volume 1*, Letter 3.

25. Epictetus, *Enchiridion* (Handbook), Chapter 3.

26. Epicurus, *The Extant Remains*, trans. Cyril Bailey (Clarendon Press, 1926), 111.

27. Seneca, *Letters on Ethics*, trans. Margaret Graver and A. A. Long (University of Chicago Press, 2015), Letter 119 to Lucilius, p. 477.

28. *Musonius Rufus*, trans. Cynthia King (CreateSpace, 2011), 34.

29. Epictetus, *Discourses*, trans. Thomas Wentworth Higginson, Book 3, Chapter 3, at Online Library of Liberty (oll.libertyfund.org).

30. *Letters of David Hume, Volume 1*, Letter 3.

31. *An Enquiry concerning the Principles of Morals*, 7.16–17.

32. Ibid., 6.21.

33. "The Sceptic," 43.

34. "Of the Delicacy of Taste and Passion," 3.

35. *Letters of David Hume, Volume 1*, Letter 3.

36. "Of Moral Prejudices," 3.

37. *Letters of David Hume, Volume 1*, Letter 3.

38. Ibid.

39. *My Own Life*, 4.

40. "Of National Characters," n6.1.

41. "Of the Standard of Taste," 22.

42. *A Treatise of Human Nature*, 1.3.13.7.

43. "Of National Characters," 20.

44. Ibid., 17.

45. Ibid., 14.

46. Ibid., 32.

47. John Immerwahr, "Hume's Revised Racism," *Journal of the History of Ideas* 53, no. 3 (July–September 1992): 481–86.

48. *The History of England*, 5.9.

49. "Of the Populousness of Ancient Nations," 6.

50. *Further Letters of David Hume*, ed. Felix Waldmann (Edinburgh Bibliographical Society, 2014), Letter 30.

51. James Beattie, *An Essay on the Nature and Immutability of Truth, in Opposition to Sophistry and Scepticism*, 2nd ed. (A. Kincaid & J. Bell, 1771), 508–10.

52. *Letters of David Hume, Volume 2*, ed. J.Y.T. Greig (Oxford University Press, 1932), Letter 509.

53. The following paragraphs draw on my essay "Why Sexist and Racist Philosophers Might Still Be Admirable," *Aeon* (aeon.co), November 7, 2018.

54. Edith Hall, *Aristotle's Way* (Bodley Head, 2018), 17–18.

55. *My Own Life*, 4.

56. Mossner, *The Life of David Hume*, 90.

2. Natural Wisdom

Note to epigraph: "Whether the British Government inclines more to Absolute Monarchy, or to a Republic," 4.

1. *My Own Life*, 4.

2. Mossner, "Hume at La Flèche, 1735: An Unpublished Letter."

3. Harris, *Hume: An Intellectual Biography*, 79.

4. Quoted in Dario Perinetti, "Hume at La Flèche: Skepticism and the French Connection," *Journal of the History of Philosophy* 56, no. 1 (January 2018): 49.

5. Ibid.

6. Mossner, "Hume at La Flèche, 1735: An Unpublished Letter."

7. Harris, *Hume: An Intellectual Biography*, 80.

8. Ibid., 83, citing Tadeusz Kozanecki, "Dawida Hume'a Nieznane Listy W Zbiorach Muzeum Czartoryskichp," *Archiwum Historii Filozofi Społecznej* 9 (1963): 127–41.

9. René Descartes, *Meditations on First Philosophy with Selections from the Objections and Replies*, trans. John Cottingham (Cambridge University Press, 1986), 7:481, CSM II 324, p. 63.

10. *An Enquiry concerning Human Understanding*, 12.3.

11. *An Enquiry concerning the Principles of Morals*, 1.10.

12. Descartes, *Meditations on First Philosophy with Selections from the Objections and Replies*, First Meditation, 17, p. 12.

13. *A Treatise of Human Nature*, 0.6.

14. A. J. Ayer, *The Problem of Knowledge* (Macmillan, 1956), 73.

15. Ludwig Wittgenstein, *On Certainty*, trans. Dennis Paul and G.E.M. Anscombe (Basil Blackwell, 1969), para. 248, p. 33.

16. *A Treatise of Human Nature*, 2.2.2.1.

17. Annette C. Baier, *The Pursuits of Philosophy* (Harvard University Press, 2011), 38.

18. Perinetti, "Hume at La Flèche," 54.

19. Ibid., 56.

20. Information for visitors from the Prytanée when I visited.

21. Mossner, *The Life of David Hume*, 545.

22. "On the First Principles of Government," 3.

23. "Of Parties in General," 2.

24. Advertisement to *Essays, Moral, Political, and Literary* (1741), 1.

25. *Letters of David Hume, Volume 1*, Letter 194.

26. *An Enquiry concerning Human Understanding*, 10.1.

27. Ibid., 10.12.

28. *Letters of David Hume, Volume 1*, Letter 188.

29. *An Enquiry concerning Human Understanding*, 10.15.

30. Ibid., 10.27.

31. Ibid., 10.4.

32. Ibid., 10.31.

33. Ibid., 10.16–17.

34. Ibid., 10.40.

35. Ibid., 10.20.

36. Ibid., 10.41.

37. Ibid., 10.24.

38. *Letters of David Hume, Volume 1*, Letter 6.

39. Ibid., Letter 194.

40. Mossner, *The Life of David Hume*, 100.

41. Mossner, "Hume at La Flèche, 1735: An Unpublished Letter."

42. "Of Civil Liberty," 6.

43. *Letters of David Hume, Volume 1*, Letter 4.

44. *An Enquiry concerning the Principles of Morals*, 8.9 and Appendix 4, 12. See also Aristotle, *Nichomachean Ethics*, 1125a.20.

45. *An Enquiry concerning the Principles of Morals*, 6.2.

46. Ibid., 6.12.

47. Ibid., Appendix 4, 22.

48. Ibid., Appendix 4, 20.

49. *A Treatise of Human Nature*, 3.3.4.3.

50. *An Enquiry concerning the Principles of Morals*, Appendix 4, 3.

51. Mossner, *The Life of David Hume*, 73–74.

52. Abstract of *A Treatise of Human Nature*, 27.

53. *An Enquiry concerning Human Understanding*, 1.12.

54. Ibid., 4.2.

55. Ibid., 12.34.

56. Abstract of *A Treatise of Human Nature*, 4.

57. Ibid., 14.

58. "That Politics may be reduced to a Science," 12.

59. *A Treatise of Human Nature*, 1.3.3.3.

60. Ibid., 1.3.3.5.

61. Ibid., 1.4.7.7.

62. *An Enquiry concerning Human Understanding*, 7.28.

63. *A Treatise of Human Nature*, 1.4.7.7.

64. Ibid., 1.4.7.9.

65. *An Enquiry concerning Human Understanding*, 5.6.

66. *A Treatise of Human Nature*, 1.4.4.1.

67. Mossner, *The Life of David Hume*, 123.

68. *Letters of David Hume, Volume 1*, Letter 91.

69. *A Treatise of Human Nature*, 1.3.15.

70. *An Enquiry concerning Human Understanding*, 4.21.

71. Ibid., 8.4.

72. Ibid., 7.29.

73. Isaac Newton, *Philosophiæ Naturalis Principia Mathematica*, 3rd ed. (Henry Pemberton, 1726), Part 3.

74. *An Enquiry concerning the Principles of Morals*, A Dialogue, 57.

75. *An Enquiry concerning Human Understanding*, 12.17.

76. Sextus Empiricus, *Outlines of Pyrrhonism*, trans. R. G. Bury (W. Heinemann, 1933), 10, available at sophia-project.org.

77. *An Enquiry concerning Human Understanding*, 12.23.

78. *A Treatise of Human Nature*, 1.4.1.12.

79. Ibid., 1.4.2.57.

80. *Dialogues concerning Natural Religion*, 1.9.

81. *An Enquiry concerning Human Understanding*, 12.24.

82. Ibid., 4.14.

83. Ibid., 12.25.

84. *Confucian Analects*, Book 17, Chapter 19.3, in James Legge, *The Chinese Classics*, vol. 1 (Oxford University Press, 1893), 326.

85. *An Enquiry concerning Human Understanding*, 1.10.

86. *A Treatise of Human Nature*, 1.3.8.12.

87. Ibid., 3.2.10.16.

88. "Of Eloquence," 21.

89. Annette Baier, *A Progress of Sentiments: Reflections on Hume's "Treatise"* (Harvard University Press, 1991), 280.

90. Hugo Mercier and Dan Sperber, *The Enigma of Reason: A New Theory of Human Understanding* (Allen Lane, 2017), 4, 183, 247.

91. *A Treatise of Human Nature*, 1.4.7.7.

92. Ibid., 1.4.7.14.

93. "Of Impudence and Modesty."

94. *A Treatise of Human Nature*, 1.4.7.13.

95. *An Enquiry concerning Human Understanding*, 2.1.

96. *A Treatise of Human Nature*, 3.3.2.3.

97. Ibid., 2.1.11.7.

98. Baier, *The Pursuits of Philosophy*, 32.

99. John Locke, *An Essay Concerning Human Understanding* (Herrnstein & Murray, 1994), 311.

100. Bertrand Russell, *The Problems of Philosophy* (Williams and Norgate, 1912), chap. 7.

101. *A Treatise of Human Nature*, 1.1.1.10.

102. *An Enquiry concerning Human Understanding*, 7.28.

103. Ibid., 5.8.

104. *A Treatise of Human Nature*, 1.3.16.9.

105. *An Enquiry concerning Human Understanding*, 9.6.

106. *Letters of David Hume, Volume 1*, Letter 3.

107. *A Treatise of Human Nature*, 1.2.1.1.

108. Harris, *Hume: An Intellectual Biography*, 1.

3. The Meaning of Success

Note to epigraph: *Letters of David Hume, Volume 1*, Letter 6.

1. Mossner, *The Life of David Hume*, 106.

2. Ibid., 133.

3. *New Letters of David Hume*, ed. Raymond Klibansky and Ernest C. Mossner (Oxford University Press, 1954), Letter 3.

4. Rasmussen, *The Infidel and the Professor*, 25.

5. Mossner, *The Life of David Hume*, 299–300.

6. Harris, *Hume: An Intellectual Biography*, 4.

7. *My Own Life*, 6.

8. Mossner, *The Life of David Hume*, 125.

9. *Letter from a Gentleman*, 21.

10. Mossner, *The Life of David Hume*, 162.

11. Rasmussen, *The Infidel and the Professor*, 24.

12. *Dialogues concerning Natural Religion*, 6.12.

13. Ibid., 9.3.

14. *A Treatise of Human Nature*, 1.3.12.1.

15. Ibid., 2.3.1.12.

16. Ibid., 3.2.4.1.

17. Ibid., 2.1.3.5.

18. "Of National Characters," 6n2.2, Mil 200.

19. "Of the Rise and Progress of the Arts and Sciences," 1.

20. *Letters of David Hume, Volume 1*, Letter 77.

21. *A Treatise of Human Nature*, 3.3.2.13.

22. "Of the Dignity or Meanness of Human Nature," 11.

23. *An Enquiry concerning the Principles of Morals*, 9.10.

24. *An Enquiry concerning Human Understanding*, 8.25.

25. Ibid., 8.16.

26. *A Treatise of Human Nature*, 2.3.1.17.

27. *An Enquiry concerning Human Understanding*, 8.15.

28. *A Treatise of Human Nature*, 2.3.1.

29. Ibid., 2.3.2.1.

30. *An Enquiry concerning Human Understanding*, 8.23.

31. *A Treatise of Human Nature*, 2.3.2.3.

32. *An Enquiry concerning Human Understanding*, 8.28.

33. Ibid., 8.18.

34. *A Treatise of Human Nature*, 2.3.1.13.

35. *An Enquiry concerning Human Understanding*, 8.29.

36. Ibid., 8.31.

37. *A Treatise of Human Nature*, 2.3.1.15.

38. *An Enquiry concerning Human Understanding*, 8.23.

39. "Of the Middle Station of Life," 3.

40. *A Treatise of Human Nature*, 2.2.5.1.

41. Harris, *Hume: An Intellectual Biography*, 143, 248.

42. *Letters of David Hume, Volume 1*, Letter 50.

43. David Hume, *Essays Moral, Political, and Literary: Volume 2*, ed. T. H. Green and T. H. Grose (Longmans, Green, and Company, 1898), 443–60. Now available in David Hume, *A Petty Statesman: Writings on War and International Affairs*, ed. Spartaco Pupo (Mimesis International, 2019).

44. Harris, *Hume: An Intellectual Biography*, 426–28.

45. *Letters of David Hume, Volume 2*, Letter 41.

46. *Letters of David Hume, Volume 1*, Letter 165.

47. "Of the Original Contract," 20.

48. "Idea of a Perfect Commonwealth," 50.

49. Harris, *Hume: An Intellectual Biography*, 429–30.

50. *Letters of David Hume, Volume 2*, Letter 512.

51. "Whether the British Government inclines more to Absolute Monarchy, or to a Republic," 8.

52. *A Treatise of Human Nature*, 3.3.2.11.

53. "Of Civil Liberty," 1.

54. "Idea of a Perfect Commonwealth," 1.

55. *Letters of David Hume, Volume 2*, Letter 417.

56. "Of Passive Obedience," 3.

57. *A Treatise of Human Nature*, 3.2.10.1.

58. "Of the Origin of Government," 7.

59. *A Treatise of Human Nature*, 1.3.9.1.

60. "Of the First Principles of Government," 8.

61. *Letters of David Hume, Volume 1*, Letter 64.

62. Letter to Harry Erskine, January 20, 1756, in J. C. Hilson and John Valdimir Price, "Hume and Friends, 1756 and 1766: Two New Letters," *Yearbook of English Studies* 7 (1977): 121–27.

63. *My Own Life*, 7.

64. *A Treatise of Human Nature*, 1.4.6.1.

65. Ibid., 1.1.6.1.

66. Ibid., 1.4.6.7.

67. Ibid., 1.4.6.8.

68. Ibid., 1.4.6.11.

69. Thomas Hobbes, *De Corpore* (1655), part 2, chapter 11.

70. *A Treatise of Human Nature*, 1.4.6.14.

71. Ibid., 3.3.4.13.

72. Ibid., 1.4.6.20.

73. Ibid., 1.4.6.21.

74. "Of the Dignity or Meanness of Human Nature," 4.

75. *A Treatise of Human Nature*, 1.4.6.3–4.

76. Ibid., 1.4.2.39.

77. Thomas Reid, *Essays on the Intellectual Power of Man* (1785), Essay 2, "Of the Powers we have by means of our External Senses," §12.

78. "The Sceptic," 1.

79. *A Treatise of Human Nature*, Appendix 21.

80. Mossner, *The Life of David Hume*, 223.

81. *Letters of David Hume, Volume 1*, Letter 156.

82. *My Own Life*, 10.

83. *A Treatise of Human Nature*, 2.2.5.15.

84. "Of the Delicacy of Taste and Passion," 7.

85. These two paragraphs are adapted from my essay "Hume the Humane," *Aeon*, August 15, 2018.

86. Mossner, *The Life of David Hume*, 240–43.

87. William Smellie, *Literary and Characteristical Lives of John Gregory, M.D., Henry Home, Lord Kames, David Hume, Esq., and Adam Smith, L.L.D* (Edinburgh, 1800), 161–62.

88. "Of Refinement in the Arts," 4.

89. *Letters of David Hume, Volume 1*, Letter 77.

90. Ibid.

91. Ibid., Letter 103.

92. Mossner, *The Life of David Hume*, 252–53.

93. Ibid., 281.

94. Rosalind Carr, *Gender and Enlightenment Culture in Eighteenth-Century Scotland* (Edinburgh University Press, 2014), 43. Thanks to Amy Cools for the pointer.

95. Cited by Amy Cools in "Enlightenment Scotland: Edinburgh's Select Society," ordinaryphilosophy.com, February 10, 2018.

96. Mossner, *The Life of David Hume*, 285.

97. Ibid., 245.

98. Ibid., 244.

99. www.royal-mile.com/history/history-canongate.html.

100. *Letters of David Hume, Volume 1*, Letter 79.

101. Rasmussen, *The Infidel and the Professor*, 71.

102. "Of the Standard of Taste," 29.

103. Mossner, *The Life of David Hume*, 318.

104. *My Own Life*, 11.

105. Mossner, *The Life of David Hume*, 305–6.

106. David Hume, *Essays, Moral, Political, and Literary*, ed. Eugene F. Miller (Liberty Fund, 1987), xv–xvii.

107. Mossner, *The Life of David Hume*, 223.

108. Harris, *Hume: An Intellectual Biography*, 250.

109. "History of the Editions," in *The Philosophical Works of David Hume*, ed. T. H. Green and T. H. Grose (Longmans, Green, and Co., 1889), cited in Hume, *Essays, Moral, Political, and Literary*, ed. Miller, xviii.

110. Harris, *Hume: An Intellectual Biography*, 2, 15.

111. *Letters of David Hume, Volume 1*, Letter 94.

112. Rasmussen, *The Infidel and the Professor*, 72.

113. "Of the Study of History," 3.

114. "Of Commerce," 1.

115. Ibid.

116. "Of Essay-Writing," 1.

117. *New Letters of David Hume*, ed. Klibansky and Mossner, Letter 6.

118. *An Enquiry concerning Human Understanding*, 1.17.

119. "Of Essay-Writing," 5.

120. *Letters of David Hume, Volume 2*, Letter 511.

121. Harris, *Hume: An Intellectual Biography*, 23.

122. *A Treatise of Human Nature*, Appendix, 1.

123. *Letters of David Hume, Volume 1*, Letter 169.

124. Mossner, *The Life of David Hume*, 556.

125. *Letters of David Hume, Volume 2*, Letter 432.

126. Edinburgh World Heritage, ewh.org.uk/iconic-buildings-and-monuments/james-court/.

127. Rasmussen, *The Infidel and the Professor*, 152.

128. Mossner, *The Life of David Hume*, 394.

129. *New Letters of David Hume*, ed. Klibansky and Mossner, Letter 33.

130. *Essays and Observations, Physical and Literary, read before the Philosophical Society of Edinburgh*, vol. 3, ed. G. Hamilton and J. Balfour (1771).

131. Mossner, *The Life of David Hume*, 403, 228.

132. *Letters of David Hume, Volume 1*, Letter 187.

133. *New Letters of David Hume*, ed. Klibansky and Mossner, Letter 32.

4. Retaining Our Humanity

Note to epigraph: *A Treatise of Human Nature*, 1.4.7.13.

1. *Letters of David Hume, Volume 1*, Letter 156.

2. Mossner, *The Life of David Hume*, 560.

3. Ibid., 441, 423.

4. Ibid., 242.

5. Ibid., 456.

6. Ibid., 425.

7. *Letters of David Hume, Volume 1*, Letter 184.

8. "Of Love and Marriage," 6.

9. "Of Essay-Writing," 7.

10. *A Treatise of Human Nature*, 2.2.7.4.

11. "Of the Rise and Progress of the Arts and Sciences," 40.

12. "Of the Immortality of the Soul," 17.

13. "Of Essay-Writing," 8.

14. "Of the Study of History," 1.

15. "On Women" (cf. "Sur les femmes"), cited in Philipp Blom, *A Wicked Company* (Basic Books, 2010), 227.

16. "Of Polygamy and Divorces," 182.

17. Ibid., 184.

18. Ibid., 16.

19. Ibid., 22.

20. *A Treatise of Human Nature*, 2.1.9.13.

21. *An Enquiry concerning Human Understanding*, 1.6.

22. Mossner, *The Life of David Hume*, 431–32.

23. *Letters of David Hume, Volume 1*, Letter 211.

24. Ibid., Letter 214.

25. Ibid., Letter 213.

26. Ibid., Letter 216.

27. Mossner, *The Life of David Hume*, 440.

28. *Letters of David Hume, Volume 1*, Letter 222.

29. Ibid., Letter 223.

30. Ibid., Letter 227.

31. Ibid., Letter 233.

32. Mossner, *The Life of David Hume*, 443, 447.

33. Ibid., 98.

34. *Letters of David Hume, Volume 1*, Letter 225.

35. Ibid., Letter 224.

36. Ibid., Letter 242.

37. Ibid., Letter 225.

38. Ibid., Letter 237.

39. *New Letters of David Hume*, ed. Klibansky and Mossner, Letter 65.

40. "Of Eloquence," variant reading in *Essays, Moral, Political, and Literary*, ed. Eugene F. Miller (Liberty Fund, 1987), 622.

41. *New Letters of David Hume*, ed. Klibansky and Mossner, Letter 101.

42. Ibid., Letter 110.

43. Ibid., Letter 43.

44. Mossner, *The Life of David Hume*, 448.

45. *Letters of David Hume, Volume 1*, Letter 233.

46. Mossner, *The Life of David Hume*, 476.

47. Ibid., 454.

48. Ibid., 456–57.

49. Ibid., 460.

50. *Letters of David Hume, Volume 1*, xxv.

51. Ibid., Letter 247.

52. Ibid., Letter 257.

53. Mossner, *The Life of David Hume*, 473–74.

54. Ibid., 453.

55. Ibid., 452–53.

56. Ibid., 459.

57. *A Treatise of Human Nature*, 1.3.13.2.

58. Ibid., 3.2.7.8.

59. Ibid., 3.2.7.2.

60. Ibid., 3.3.2.8.

61. *An Enquiry concerning Human Understanding*, 5.1.

62. *A Treatise of Human Nature*, 3.3.5.3.

63. *An Enquiry concerning the Principles of Morals*, 6.25.

64. *A Treatise of Human Nature*, 3.2.12.4.

65. Ibid., 3.2.12.7.

66. wikipedia.org/wiki/Café_de_la_Régence.

67. Mossner, *The Life of David Hume*, 476.

68. Diderot to Sophie Volland, October 6, 1765, fr.wikisource.org/wiki/Lettres _à_Sophie_Volland/94.

69. Mossner, *The Life of David Hume*, 483.

70. *Letters of David Hume, Volume 2*, Letter 484.

71. Blom, *A Wicked Company*, 170.

72. Mossner, *The Life of David Hume*, 485–86.

73. *Dialogues concerning Natural Religion*, 12.29.

74. *An Enquiry concerning Human Understanding*, 11.2.

75. *New Letters of David Hume*, ed. Klibansky and Mossner, Letter 25.

76. "Whether the British Government inclines more to Absolute Monarchy, or to a Republic," 5.

77. "Of Superstition and Enthusiasm," 3.

78. *Dialogues concerning Natural Religion*, 10.11; "Of Superstition and Enthusiasm," 8.

79. Bertrand Russell, "Am I an Atheist Or an Agnostic?" (1949), originally published as "Agnosticism v. Atheism," *Literary Guide and Rationalist Review* 64 (July 1949): 115–16.

80. Mossner, *The Life of David Hume*, 343–47.

81. *Letters of David Hume, Volume 1*, Letter 130.

82. Mossner, *The Life of David Hume*, 232.

83. Ibid., 354.

84. "Of the Immortality of the Soul," 3.

85. John Locke, "Of Identity and Diversity," Chapter XXVII of *An Essay Concerning Human Understanding*, 2nd ed. (1689), section 16.

86. "Of the Immortality of the Soul," 6.

87. Ibid., 13.

88. Ibid., 29.

89. Ibid., 34–38.

90. *A Treatise of Human Nature*, 1.3.9.13.

91. Aristotle, *Nichomachean Ethics*, Book III.1117b.

92. Mossner, *The Life of David Hume*, 563.

93. Ibid., 274.

94. *Letters of David Hume, Volume 1*, Letter 272.

95. Mossner, *The Life of David Hume*, 365.

96. David Edmonds and John Eidinow, *Rousseau's Dog* (Faber & Faber, 2006), 68.

97. *New Letters of David Hume*, ed. Klibansky and Mossner, Letter 12.

98. Mossner, *The Life of David Hume*, 502–3.

99. *The Natural History of Religion*, 14.1.

100. *Letters of David Hume, Volume 2*, Letter 525.

101. *New Letters of David Hume*, ed. Klibansky and Mossner, Letter 35.

102. Mossner, *The Life of David Hume*, 592–93.

103. *The Natural History of Religion*, 15.6.

104. Ibid., 12.4.

105. Mossner, *The Life of David Hume*, 332.

106. *The Natural History of Religion*, 15.11–12.

107. Rasmussen, *The Infidel and the Professor*, 193.

108. *Dialogues concerning Natural Religion*, 0.5.

109. Psalm 14:1; *Dialogues concerning Natural Religion*, 1.18.

110. *Dialogues concerning Natural Religion*, 12.22.

111. *Letters of David Hume, Volume 1*, Letter 72.

112. *Dialogues concerning Natural Religion*, 0.4.

113. Ibid., 12.7.

114. *New Letters of David Hume*, ed. Klibansky and Mossner, Letter 6.

115. *Dialogues concerning Natural Religion*, 2.4.

116. Ibid., 7.8.

117. Ibid., 2.14.

118. Ibid., 2.7.

119. Ibid., 2.24.

120. Ibid., 7.3.

121. Ibid., 9.7.

122. *An Enquiry concerning Human Understanding*, 11.12.

123. *Dialogues concerning Natural Religion*, 5.12.

124. Ibid., 4.2–3.

125. Ibid., 10.25.

126. Ibid., 11.14.

127. Ibid., 2.21.

128. Ibid., 2.22–23.

129. Ludwig Wittgenstein, *Tractatus Logico-Philosophicus*, trans. C. K. Ogden (Routledge & Kegan Paul, 1922), 7.

130. *The History of England*, 48.23n18.

131. Ibid., 29.5.

132. Harris, *Hume: An Intellectual Biography*, 409.

133. Mossner, *The Life of David Hume*, 504.

134. Ibid., 490.

135. The poem's concluding lines are:

> *Hume, souris à mes chansons,*
> *Enfants légers de mon délire:*
> *Ma main, parcourant tous les tons,*
> *Aime à s'égarer sur la lyre.*
> *J'oublois, pour déraisonner,*
> *La Philosophe respectable;*
> *Et ne voyois que l'homme aimable*
> *Qui voudra bien me pardonner*

> Hume, smile at my songs,
> Light children of my delirium:
> My hand, running through all the tones,
> Likes to get lost on the lyre.
> I forget, through unreason,
> The respectable philosopher;
> And see only the lovable man
> Who will forgive me

136. *Letters of David Hume, Volume 1*, Letter 282.

137. Mossner, *The Life of David Hume*, 494.

5. Learning the Hard Way

Note to epigraph: *A Treatise of Human Nature*, 2.1.11.2.

1. *My Own Life*, 9.

2. Rousseau, *Emile*, Book 4, "The Creed of a Savoyard Priest," trans. Barbara Foxley, available at Project Gutenberg, www.gutenberg.org.

3. Mossner, *The Life of David Hume*, 507.

4. *Letters of David Hume, Volume 1*, Letter 196.

5. Ibid., Letter 195.

6. Ibid., Letter 200.

7. Ibid.

8. Mossner, *The Life of David Hume*, 511.

9. Edmonds and Eidinow, *Rousseau's Dog*, 3.

10. Mossner, *The Life of David Hume*, 517.

11. Ibid., 536.

12. Reproduced in David Hume, *A concise and genuine account of the dispute between Mr. Hume and Mr. Rousseau* (1766), available at quod.lib.umich.edu.

13. *Letters of David Hume, Volume 2*, Letter 322.

14. *New Letters of David Hume*, ed. Klibansky and Mossner, Letter 67.

15. Ibid., Letter 68.

16. Mossner, *The Life of David Hume*, 526.

17. *Letters of David Hume, Volume 2*, Letter 333.

18. Mossner, *The Life of David Hume*, 528.

19. *Letters of David Hume, Volume 2*, Letter 314.

20. Ibid., Letter 298.

21. Ibid., Letter 385.

22. *New Letters of David Hume*, ed. Klibansky and Mossner, Letter 70.

23. Ibid., Letter 99.

24. *Letters of David Hume, Volume 2*, Letter 334.

25. *New Letters of David Hume*, ed. Klibansky and Mossner, Letter 70.

26. Ibid., Letter 72.

27. Mossner, *The Life of David Hume*, 529.

28. Baier, *The Pursuits of Philosophy*, 111.

29. *Letters of David Hume, Volume 1*, xxvi.

30. *A concise and genuine account of the dispute between Mr. Hume and Mr. Rousseau* (1766).

31. Mossner, *The Life of David Hume*, 532.

32. *A concise and genuine account of the dispute between Mr. Hume and Mr. Rousseau* (1766).

33. *New Letters of David Hume*, ed. Klibansky and Mossner, Letter 75.

34. *Letters of David Hume, Volume 2*, Letter 358.

35. *New Letters of David Hume*, ed. Klibansky and Mossner, Letters 84, 88.

36. Ibid., Letter 91.

37. "The Sceptic," 36.

38. Ibid., 37.

39. Ibid., 38.

40. *A Treatise of Human Nature*, 2.1.11.5.

41. Ibid., 3.1.1.26.
42. Ibid., 2.1.7.3.
43. Ibid., 2.1.11.9.
44. Ibid., 2.3.3.6.
45. Ibid.
46. *An Enquiry concerning the Principles of Morals*, 2.18.
47. "The Sceptic," 35.
48. Harris, *Hume: An Intellectual Biography*, 114.
49. *A Treatise of Human Nature*, 2.3.3.4.
50. Ibid., 3.1.1.27.
51. Ibid., 3.1.2.10.
52. Ibid., 2.3.4.1.
53. "The Sceptic," 32.
54. Ibid., 29.
55. *A Treatise of Human Nature*, 2.3.3.1.
56. "Of the Dignity or Meanness of Human Nature," 2.
57. Harris, *Hume: An Intellectual Biography*, 155.
58. "Of the Dignity or Meanness of Human Nature," 10.
59. Ibid., 7.
60. "Of the Origin of Government," 3.
61. *An Enquiry concerning the Principles of Morals*, 1.2.
62. Harris, *Hume: An Intellectual Biography*, 193–94.
63. "Of Some Remarkable Customs," 1.
64. *An Enquiry concerning Human Understanding*, 8.7.
65. *A Treatise of Human Nature*, 3.1.2.8.
66. *An Enquiry concerning the Principles of Morals*, A Dialogue, 30.
67. Ibid., 36.
68. Ibid., 39.
69. Ibid., 8.2.
70. Ibid., 32.
71. "Of the Standard of Taste," 8.
72. Ibid., 16.
73. Ibid., 24.
74. Ibid., 27.
75. Ibid., 28.
76. *An Enquiry concerning the Principles of Morals*, 5.17.
77. Ibid., 9.1.
78. Ibid., 9.15.
79. Ibid., Appendix 4, 21.
80. "Of Suicide," 14.
81. Ibid., 28.

82. Matthew Miller and David Hemenway, "Guns and Suicide in the United States," *New England Journal of Medicine* 359 (2008): 989–91, DOI: 10.1056/NEJMp0805923.

83. *Letters of David Hume, Volume 1*, Letter 238.

84. Edmonds and Eidinow, *Rousseau's Dog*, 104.

85. *An Enquiry concerning the Principles of Morals*, 8.6.

86. *My Own Life*, 10.

87. *Letters of David Hume, Volume 1*, Letter 82.

88. *A Treatise of Human Nature*, 3.2.2.20.

89. *An Enquiry concerning the Principles of Morals*, 3.2–3.

90. Ibid., 3.6.

91. Ibid., 3.8.

92. *A Treatise of Human Nature*, 3.2.2.18.

93. *An Enquiry concerning the Principles of Morals*, 3.12.

94. *A Treatise of Human Nature*, 3.2.2.3.

95. Ibid., 3.2.3.2.

96. *An Enquiry concerning the Principles of Morals*, 4.15.

97. "Of the Rise and Progress of the Arts and Sciences," 14–16.

98. "Of Commerce," 17.

99. *An Enquiry concerning the Principles of Morals*, 3.25.

100. Ibid., 3.26.

101. Ibid.

102. Rasmussen, *The Infidel and the Professor*, 168.

103. "Of Taxes," 5.

104. *The Natural History of Religion*, 3.4–5.

105. Ibid., 14.8.

106. Lucan, *The Civil War (Pharsalia)*, trans. J. D. Duff, Loeb Classical Library 220 (Harvard University Press, 1928), 560–85, 546–69.

107. *A Treatise of Human Nature*, 3.3.6.5.

6. Facing the End

Note to epigraph: *Letters of David Hume, Volume 1*, Letter 223.

1. Mossner, *The Life of David Hume*, 571–74.

2. *Letters of David Hume, Volume 2*, Letter 433.

3. James Boswell, *Letters of James Boswell, Volume 1*, ed. Chauncey Brewster Tinker (Clarendon Press, 1924), 233.

4. Mossner, *The Life of David Hume*, 560.

5. Ibid.

6. Ibid., 561.

7. *An Enquiry concerning the Principles of Morals*, 560–61.

8. *New Letters of David Hume*, ed. Klibansky and Mossner, Letter 9.

9. *A Treatise of Human Nature*, 1.3.16.1.

10. *An Enquiry concerning Human Understanding*, 9.2.

11. Ibid., 9.5.

12. Ibid., 9.n20.4–5.

13. *A Treatise of Human Nature*, 1.3.16.9.

14. Ibid., 2.2.12.1.

15. Ibid., 2.2.12.6.

16. Ibid., 2.1.12.4.

17. Ibid., 2.1.12.1–2.

18. Mossner, *The Life of David Hume*, 566.

19. *Letters of David Hume, Volume 2*, Letter 451.

20. Mossner, *The Life of David Hume*, 566.

21. Ibid., 643.

22. "Of the Study of History," 1.

23. Mossner, *The Life of David Hume*, 479.

24. "Of the Rise and Progress of the Arts and Sciences," variant reading in *Essays, Moral, Political, and Literary*, ed. Eugene F. Miller (Liberty Fund, 1987), 626.

25. Mossner, *The Life of David Hume*, 565.

26. *Letters of David Hume, Volume 2*, Letter 514.

27. Mossner, *The Life of David Hume*, 596.

28. Ibid., 589.

29. Ibid., 593.

30. *New Letters of David Hume*, ed. Klibansky and Mossner, 228.

31. *My Own Life*, 20.

32. Adam Smith to William Strachan, November 9, 1776, available at several online sources including www.ourcivilisation.com/smartboard/shop/smitha/humedead.htm.

33. *New Letters of David Hume*, ed. Klibansky and Mossner, Letter 34.

34. Rasmussen, *The Infidel and the Professor*, 207.

35. Adam Smith to William Strachan, November 9, 1776.

36. *Letters of David Hume, Volume 2*, Letter 535.

37. Ibid., Letter 540.

38. Seneca, *Letters on Ethics*, trans. Margaret Graver and A. A. Long (University of Chicago Press, 2015), Letter 119 to Lucilius, p. 156, Letter 54.

39. Marcus Aurelius, *Meditations*, trans. George Long, Book 4.50, available online at http://classics.mit.edu//Antoninus/meditations.html.

40. Ibid., Book 7.46.

41. Epictetus, *Discourses*, trans. George Long (D. Appleton & Co., 1904), Book I, Chapter 27.7, p. 76.

42. *My Own Life*, 21.

43. Mossner, *The Life of David Hume*, 603.

44. Rasmussen, *The Infidel and the Professor*, 215.

45. Sermon 123, Halifax, April 21, 1790, https://www.umcmission.org/Find -Resources/John-Wesley-Sermons/Sermon-123-The-Deceitfulness-of-the-Human -Heart.

46. Mossner, *The Life of David Hume*, 599.

47. Ibid., 591.

48. Rasmussen, *The Infidel and the Professor*, 215.

49. Thanks to Natalie Haynes for the translation.

50. Revelation 22:12–14; 1 Corinthians 15:57.

51. Rasmussen, *The Infidel and the Professor*, 223.

52. Adam Smith to William Strachan, November 9, 1776.

53. Ernest Campbell Mossner and Ian Simpson Ross, eds., *The Glasgow Edition of the Works and Correspondence of Adam Smith, Vol. 6: Correspondence*, 2nd ed. (Oxford University Press, 1987), Letter 163 to Alexander Wedderburn, August 14, 1776.

54. Harris, *Hume: An Intellectual Biography*, 472.

55. Mossner, *The Life of David Hume*, 5.

56. Ibid., 477–78.

57. *Letters of David Hume, Volumes 1*, Letter 74.

58. Mossner, *The Life of David Hume*, 213.

59. Edmonds and Eidinow, *Rousseau's Dog*, 90.

60. Mossner, *The Life of David Hume*, 213.

61. Ibid., 370.

62. David Hume, "A list of Scotticisms," published in the *Scots Magazine*, 1760 (first printed in 1752), available at National Library of Scotland online, digital.nls.uk.

63. Mossner, *The Life of David Hume*, 477.

64. Nigel Warburton, "Art and Allusion," *Philosophers' Magazine*, issue 19 (summer 2002): 40–42.

65. Mossner, *The Life of David Hume*, 213.

66. Ibid., 65.

67. Ibid., 233.

68. Ibid., 94.

69. *New Letters of David Hume*, ed. Klibansky and Mossner, Letter 2.

70. *My Own Life*, 21.

71. Mossner, *The Life of David Hume*, 569–79.

72. *A Treatise of Human Nature*, 2.3.10.7.

73. *An Enquiry concerning the Principles of Morals*, 6.18.

74. "The Sceptic," 55.

FURTHER READING

Hume's Writings

Almost all of Hume's writings, except his letters, are available free at Hume Texts Online (https://davidhume.org). Most are available in various print editions. His main works are:

A Treatise of Human Nature
    Book One: *Of the Understanding* (1739)
    Book Two: *Of the Passions* (1740)
    Book Three: *Of Morals* (1740)
Essays, Moral, Political, and Literary, Part 1 (1741)
Essays, Moral, Political, and Literary, Part 2 (1752)
Philosophical Essays concerning Human Understanding (1748), subsequently renamed
    An Enquiry concerning Human Understanding
An Enquiry concerning the Principles of Morals (1751)
Political discourses (1752)
The History of England, from the Invasion of Julius Cæsar to the Revolution in 1688
The history of Great Britain. Vol. I. Containing the reigns of James I. and Charles I (1754)
The history of Great Britain. Vol. II. Containing the Commonwealth, and the reigns of
    Charles II. and James II (1757)
The history of England, under the House of Tudor Comprehending the reigns of K. Henry
    VII. K. Henry VIII. K. Edward VI. Q. Mary, and Q. Elizabeth (1759)
The history of England, from the invasion of Julius Cæsar to the accession of Henry VII
    (1762)
Four Dissertations (1757)
The Life of David Hume, Esq. Written by Himself (1777)
Dialogues Concerning Natural religion (1779)
Letters of David Hume, Volumes 1 and 2, ed. J.Y.T. Greig (Oxford University Press, 1932)
New Letters of David Hume, ed. Raymond Klibansky and Ernest C. Mossner (Oxford
    University Press, 1954)

Further Letters of David Hume, ed. Felix Waldmann (Edinburgh Bibliographical Society, 2014)

Recommended Books about Hume

Baier, Annette C. *The Pursuits of Philosophy: An Introduction to the Life and Thought of David Hume*. Harvard University Press, 2011.

An excellent lucid and short introduction to Hume's life and thought.

Blom, Philipp. *A Wicked Company: The Forgotten Radicalism of the European Enlightenment*. Basic Books, 2010.

An account of Paris salon life that is both vivacious and scholarly.

Edmonds, David, and John Eidinow. *Rousseau's Dog: Two Great Thinkers at War in the Age of Enlightenment*. Faber & Faber, 2006.

A painstakingly researched and entertaining account of the Hume-Rousseau affair.

Harris, James A. *Hume: An Intellectual Biography*. Cambridge University Press, 2015.

For those more interested in Hume's ideas than his life, this displaces Mossner as the go-to biography.

Mossner, E. C. *The Life of David Hume*. Oxford University Press, 1980.

Since its first edition in 1954, this has been considered the definitive biography.

Rasmussen, Dennis C. *The Infidel and the Professor: David Hume, Adam Smith, and the Friendship That Shaped Modern Thought*. Princeton University Press, 2017.

A fascinating and illuminating book about the friendship between Hume and Adam Smith, and their exchange of ideas.

Selected Bibliography

Ainslie, D. C. *Hume's True Scepticism*. Oxford University Press, 2015.

Ainslie, D. C., and Annemarie Butler, eds. *The Cambridge Companion to Hume's Treatise*. Cambridge University Press, 2015.

Allison, H. E. *Custom and Reason in Hume*. Oxford University Press, 2008.

Baier, A. C. *Death and Character: Further Reflections on Hume*. Harvard University Press, 2008.

———. *A Progress of Sentiments: Reflections on Hume's "Treatise."* Harvard University Press, 1991.

Beauchamp, T. L., and A. Rosenberg. *Hume and the Problem of Causation*. Oxford University Press, 1981.

Cohon, R. *Hume's Morality*. Oxford University Press, 2008.

Fodor, J. A. *Hume Variations*. Clarendon Press, 2003.

Fogelin, R. J. *Hume's Skeptical Crisis*. Oxford University Press, 2009.

Garrett, D. *Hume*. Routledge, 2015.

Millican, P., ed. *Reading Hume on Human Understanding*. Clarendon Press, 2002.

Noonan, H. W. *Hume on Knowledge*. Routledge, 1999.

Norton, D. F. *David Hume: Common-Sense Moralist, Sceptical Metaphysician*. Princeton University Press, 1982.

Norton, D. F., and J. Taylor, eds. *The Cambridge Companion to Hume*. 2nd ed. Cambridge University Press, 2009.

Noxon, J. *Hume's Philosophical Development*. Oxford University Press, 1973.

Pears, D. *Hume's System*. Oxford University Press, 1990.

Penelhum, T. *Themes in Hume: The Will, the Self, Religion*. Clarendon Press, 2000.

Radcliffe, E. S., ed. *A Companion to Hume*. Blackwell, 2008.

———. *Hume, Passion, and Action*. Oxford University Press, 2018.

Read, R., and K. A. Richman, eds. *The New Hume Debate*. Routledge, 2000.

Russell, P. *The Oxford Handbook of Hume*. Oxford University Press, 2016.

Strawson, G. *The Secret Connexion: Causation, Realism and David Hume*. Oxford University Press, 1989.

Taylor, J. *Reflecting Subjects: Passion, Sympathy, and Society in Hume's Philosophy*. Oxford University Press, 2015.

INDEX